# RODALE'S
## SUCCESSFUL ORGANIC GARDENING®
# FRUITS AND BERRIES

TEXT BY SUSAN McCLURE

"UNCOMMON FRUITS, BERRIES, AND NUTS" BY LEE REICH

Rodale Press, Emmaus, Pennsylvania

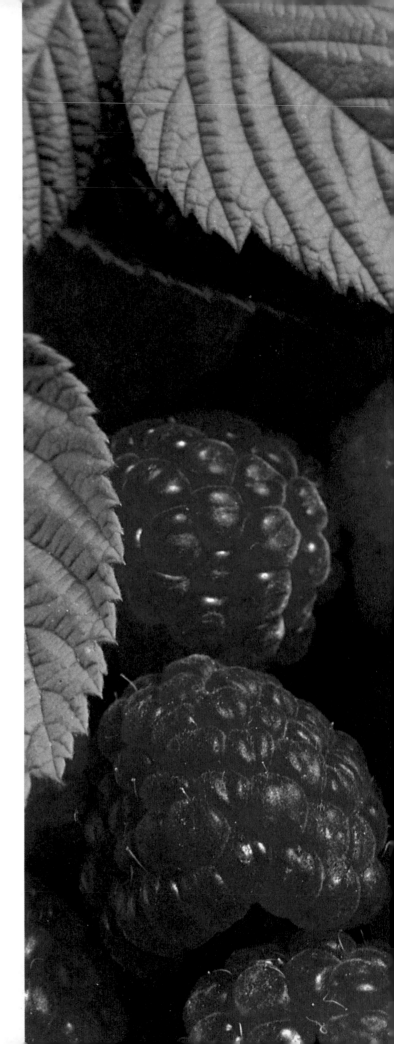

Rodale Press
Book Readers' Service
33 East Minor Street
Emmaus, PA 18098

Library of Congress Cataloging-in-Publication Data
McClure, Susan, date.
    Fruits and berries / text by Susan McClure. "Uncommon
fruits, berries, and nuts" / by Lee Reich.
        p.   cm. — (Rodale's successful organic gardening)
    Includes index.
    ISBN 0–87596–671–3 (hardcover : alk. paper). —
    ISBN 0–87596–672–1 (paperback : alk. paper)
    1. Fruit–culture. 2. Berries. 3. Organic gardening. 4. Landscape
gardening.   I. Reich, Lee. Uncommon fruits, berries, and nuts.
II. Title.  III. Title: Uncommon fruits, berries, and nuts.  IV. Series.
SB357.24.M38  1995
634—dc20                      95–4857
                             CIP

Rodale Press Staff:
    Editorial Director, Home and Garden Books: Margaret Lydic Balitas
    Editor: Nancy J. Ondra
    Copy Editor: Carolyn R. Mandarano
    Editor-in-Chief: William Gottlieb

Produced for Rodale Press by Weldon Russell Pty Ltd
107 Union Street, North Sydney NSW 2060, Australia
a member of the Weldon International Group of Companies

    Chief Executive: Elaine Russell
    General Manager: Karen Hammial
    Managing Editor: Ariana Klepac
    Editor: Libby Frederico
    Editorial Assistant: Cassandra Sheridan
    Horticultural Consultant: Cheryl Maddocks
    Copy Editor: Yani Silvana
    Designer: Honor Morton
    Picture Researcher: Elizabeth Connolly
    Illustrators: Tony Britt-Lewis, Barbara Rodanska, Jan Smith,
       Kathie Smith
    Indexer: Michael Wyatt
    Production Manager: Dianne Leddy

A KEVIN WELDON PRODUCTION

**Distributed in the book trade by St. Martin's Press**

2  4  6  8  10  9  7  5  3      hardcover
2  4  6  8  10  9  7  5  3  1  paperback

Opposite: Raspberries
Half title: Apples
Opposite title page: Figs
Title page: Currants and Berries
Opposite contents: Plums

# CONTENTS

INTRODUCTION 8

HOW TO USE THIS BOOK 10

LANDSCAPING WITH
FRUITS AND BERRIES 12
*Fruits and Berries for Your Backyard •
Fruits for Walls and Fences •
Fruits for Hedges •
Fruits for Small Gardens •
Fruits for Containers • Home Orchards*

PLANNING YOUR PLANTINGS 26
*Understanding Your Site •
Deciding What to Grow •
Favorite Fruits and Nuts at a Glance •
Planning for Season-long Harvests*

BUYING AND PLANTING
FRUITS AND BERRIES 38
*Buying the Best Plants •
Preparing the Planting Site •
Planting Fruit Trees, Shrubs, and Vines*

FRUIT CARE BASICS 48
*Mulching Basics •
Fertilizing for Fruitful Growth •
Watering Wisely • Pruning Primer •
Easing into Espalier •
Harvesting and Storing Fruit •
Making More Plants*

DEALING WITH FRUIT
PESTS AND DISEASES 66
*Preventing Pests and Diseases •
Managing Minor Problems •
Handling Serious Problems •
Coping with Animal Pests*

FRUIT TREES 78
*Apples • Apricots • Cherries • Citrus • Figs •
Peaches and Nectarines • Pears • Plums*

FRUITING VINES AND
BUSHES 100
*Blackberries • Blueberries •
Currants and Gooseberries • Grapes •
Kiwis • Raspberries • Strawberries*

NUT-BEARING PLANTS 116
*Almonds • Chestnuts • Hazelnuts •
Hickories • Pecans • Walnuts*

UNCOMMMON FRUITS,
BERRIES, AND NUTS 124

USDA PLANT HARDINESS
ZONE MAP 154

INDEX 156

ACKNOWLEDGMENTS 160

# INTRODUCTION

Few things can be more rewarding than having a season-long supply of fresh fruit right in your own backyard. When you grow your own fruit, you get to enjoy the sweet, juicy taste of just-picked produce at its peak of freshness. And when you grow it organically, you get the added bonus of knowing that it's safe to eat, free of any traces of synthetic pesticides.

With so many great reasons to grow fruit at home, it's hard to understand why everyone doesn't do it. Maybe it's because people think you need lots of space. Actually, though, fruiting plants come in all shapes and sizes to fit into any home landscape. Many are also quite attractive, so you can appreciate their beauty as landscape plants and harvest their fruit, too. Strawberries, for instance, can make a great groundcover, while blueberries can fit perfectly into foundation plantings.

Sometimes people associate fruit growing with using lots of chemical sprays. While some fruiting plants do have their share of pest and disease problems, there are also many kinds that are practically problem-free. If you do decide to grow a crop that can be prone to problems, such as apples or peaches, you can use organic techniques and materials to greatly reduce the pests and diseases you have to deal with.

Afraid that the maintenance will be overwhelming? It doesn't have to be. Many fruiting plants can produce generous harvests with little more care than a regular landscape plant; a yearly pruning may be all it needs. To make picking and pruning easier, you can choose dwarf or semidwarf trees that produce generous yields without taking up a lot of space or maintenance time. And by growing a selection of different cultivars, you can spread your harvest out over a longer season, so you aren't stuck with loads of produce that you need to pick and preserve immediately.

This book will guide you through all of the steps you need to know to find the perfect fruit, berry, and nut-producing plants for your needs. You'll learn how to figure out what growing conditions your site has available and how to choose fruiting plants that are naturally well adapted to those conditions. You'll find tips for choosing the best plants, preparing the ideal planting site, and getting your plants well established for good future growth. From watering and mulching through pruning and pest control, all of the basics of good fruit care are at your fingertips in this handy volume. Whether you plan to stick with old favorites like apples and cherries or unusual crops like pawpaws and pine nuts, you'll find everything you need to enjoy successful fruit growing.

Fruit trees may need a little more care than ordinary landscape plants, but they give something back, too. Once you savor your first harvest, you'll realize that the careful planning and care was all worth it.

# HOW TO USE THIS BOOK

If you're thinking about planting a few fruit trees, you probably have some questions: What should I grow? How much room do I need? How much work will it take? Once you choose your plants and get them established, you'll likely to come up with *more* questions. When should I prune? What should I use to control pest problems? How can I tell when the fruit is at the peak of ripeness? Well, wonder no longer— *Rodale's Successful Organic Gardening: Fruits and Berries* has the answers you need to get your fruit crops off to a good start and keep them healthy for years of bountiful harvests.

When you're looking for new ideas on how to add fruiting plants to your yard, turn to "Landscaping with Fruits and Berries," starting on page 12. Here you'll find lots of intriguing ideas, such as including fruiting plants in foundation plantings, using them as hedges and groundcovers, training them to grow over walls and fences, or growing them in containers. If you prefer to grow all of your fruit crops in one spot for easy maintenance and harvesting, you'll find plenty of planning pointers for home orchards, too.

Once you know where you want them to go, it's time to start choosing your crops. Begin by taking a good look at your site, so you know what growing conditions your yard has to offer. Then try matching the needs of the crops you're interested in with the growing conditions and space you have available. Round out your crop choices by including different species and cultivars to extend your harvests over the longest possible season. Sound like a big job? Not with the pointers you'll find in "Planning Your Plantings," starting on page 26.

Now you're ready to get your garden started. Turn to "Buying and Planting Fruits and Berries," starting on page 38, to learn the secrets of buying the best possible plants and creating a great planting site. You'll also find step-by-step guidelines for planting both bareroot and container-grown fruit trees.

Give your established fruit crops good care, and they'll reward you with generous harvests. "Fruit Care Basics," starting on page 48, covers what you need to know, from mulching, watering, fertilizing, and pruning to harvesting and storing your bounty. You'll even learn how to make new plants from existing ones by sowing seed, layering, cuttings, dividing, and grafting.

As you watch the fruits of your labor ripen through the season, remember that you're not the only one that would like to enjoy your crop. "Dealing with Fruit Pests and Diseases," starting on page 66, covers the basics of preventing pests and diseases from attacking and offers pointers on dealing with minor problems before they get out of hand. You'll also find tactics for dealing with serious insect or disease outbreaks, as well as tips for outwitting birds, deer, and other animal pests.

Want to know the scoop on growing apples, apricots, cherries, citrus, figs, peaches, pears, or plums? "Fruit Trees," starting on page 78, covers these popular crops in detail, with information on each crop's preferred climate and site, best cultivars, planting and care, pruning and training, harvesting, and problem prevention and control.

"Fruiting Vines and Bushes," starting on page 100, also offers complete growing and harvesting information. Here is where you'll find care guidelines for blackberries, blueberries, currants and gooseberries, grapes, kiwis, raspberries, and strawberries.

Interested in trying some nut crops? Check out "Nut-bearing Plants," starting on page 116, for details on growing almonds, chestnuts, hazelnuts, hickories, pecans, and walnuts.

## Plant-by-Plant Guide

Deciding which crops you want to grow is one of the most fun parts of growing fruits and berries. But before you settle for just the common favorites, check out "Uncommon Fruits, Berries, and Nuts," starting on page 124. Plants in this section are arranged in alphabetical order by their common name. When you're interested in a particular plant, you can look it up directly in the guide. Or you could just skim through the guide and look at the pictures, then read about the plants that interest you.

Each entry gives you all the basics you need to grow these fascinating and worthwhile crops successfully. You'll find a description and height and spread information in every entry, so you'll know what kind of fruit or nut the crop produces, where it grows best, and how big you can expect the plant to get. You'll also find growing guidelines, pruning and propagation tips, pest and disease control advice, and harvesting and storage suggestions. The diagram below is a sample of one of these practical pages.

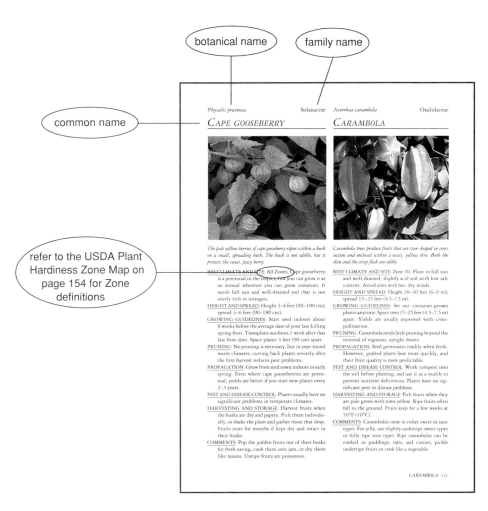

Sample page from "Uncommon Fruits, Berries, and Nuts."

# LANDSCAPING WITH
# FRUITS AND BERRIES

There's nothing quite like the taste of just-picked, sun-warmed, homegrown fruit. And it's even better when you know that the fruit has been grown organically, so you're free to enjoy it right off the plant without worrying about residues from synthetic pesticides. But what's best of all is harvesting these juicy, flavor-packed fruits right from your own yard. In this chapter, you'll learn about all the different ways you can work fruit- and nut-bearing plants into your landscape to create a yard that's productive as well as beautiful.

"Fruits and Berries for Your Backyard" on page 14 is a good place to start if you're new to the idea of "edible landscaping." In this section, you'll find an overview of your options for adding edibles to existing plantings. You'll discover exciting and inspiring ideas for growing fruits, berries, fruiting vines, and nut trees for shade, screening, and seasonal interest as well as for their useful harvest.

One place you may decide to grow fruits and berries is along a wall or boundary fence, as explained in "Fruits for Walls and Fences" on page 18. Training apples, pears, or other dwarf trees to grow against a flat surface is a good way to use space that might otherwise be wasted. Fruiting vines are also a natural choice for training to climb walls, fences, and arbors.

If you don't already have a fence around your yard, consider planting a fruiting hedge. "Fruits for Hedges" on page 19 offers ideas of suitable plants, as well as ideas on arranging them for formal or informal effects.

Fruiting plants come in all shapes and sizes, so you can find some to grow even if you have a small yard. "Fruits for Small Gardens" on page 20 suggests a number of compact, easy-to-grow fruits that will provide a good harvest from a small space.

If your garden is especially tiny or if you'd like to grow fruit right on your deck or patio, check out "Fruits for Containers" on page 22. You'll find tips on selecting, planting, and caring for container-grown fruits and berries for surefire success.

When space is not a problem, a home orchard is another way to include fruits and nuts in your landscape. Even a half-dozen trees can provide an ample supply of fresh produce for your whole family, and you'll probably have lots left over for preserving as well. "Home Orchards" on page 24 covers the factors you need to consider before making the time and space commitment. It also includes tips on planning the orchard layout and spacing plants properly for healthy growth and easy harvesting.

You don't necessarily need a big property to grow fruits. Some, like blackberries, do need plenty of room to roam. But if your yard is small, you can choose dwarf or compact crops that fit well into flower and shrub borders.

# Fruits and Berries for Your Backyard

It's surprising that fruiting plants have been neglected so long for landscape use. After all, most of them have at least two outstanding features: attractive flowers and edible fruits. Many have other special features as well, such as showy fall color or interesting bark. Compare that to a traditional but limited-interest ornamental, such as a forsythia or a lilac, and you too may wonder why you never thought of growing fruiting plants instead.

## Options for Edible Landscaping

The options for including edibles in your yard are as extensive as your imagination. Here are some suggestions of ways you can add these beautiful and productive plants to your landscape plans.

**Shade Trees** If you're starting a new landscape or renovating an old one, consider growing an edible plant as a shade tree. Walnuts, hickories, beeches, oaks, pines, and other full-sized fruit and nut trees provide height and shade just like a maple or oak tree; plus, they produce a useful crop.

Many fruiting plants have showy flowers, making them valuable as ornamentals as well as productive crops.

**Flowering Trees** Short fruit trees, such as peaches, semidwarf apples, almonds, and sour cherries, make excellent small trees as handsome as any dogwood or crab apple. Use them alone as special specimens, or include them as accents in a large foundation planting, mixed border, or shrub bed. For even more excitement, try an extra-showy type like weeping 'Santa

## Making the Transition

Unless you have the freedom to start your new landscape from scratch, you'll probably want to phase in your edible plantings over a period of time. Basically, you'll use the same techniques as you would for renovating an older ornamental landscape. But instead of replacing your old flowering shrubs with new ones, for example, you'll replace them with attractive fruiting shrubs instead.

It's helpful to start with a long-term (perhaps 5-year) planting plan. Measure your existing yard layout and make a rough sketch of where the plants are growing now. Then review the ideas in "Options for Edible Landscaping" to figure out different ways you could add fruiting plants to your yard.

In the first year or two, you may choose to plant in previously unused (probably lawn) areas. All you'll need to do is remove any existing turf, prepare the soil, and plant.

Container plantings are also easy projects you can do right away for fast results.

As you make your plans, include notes of bigger renovation projects you want to tackle in the future. These might involve replacing old or unwanted trees and shrubs with fruiting plants. Or perhaps you'd like to link individual ornamental shrubs and trees with beds of low-growing fruit bushes and fruiting groundcovers. Each winter, review your planting progress and pick one or two new projects to concentrate on each year.

While it may be hard to resist doing everything at once, following this gradual plan will help you create a successful landscape with a realistic investment of time and labor. It also allows you to use the knowledge you've gained from previous projects to fine-tune your plant choices and planting plans, so your chances of success will improve with each season.

Currants grow on bushy plants that are useful for hedges and shrub borders. The fruit is beautiful, too.

Use dwarf and semidwarf fruit trees in place of small flowering trees for seasonal interest.

Rosa' plums, double-flowered 'Double Delight' and 'Double Jewel' peach trees, or curly stemmed 'Flying Dragon' citrus trees.

**Shrubs and Hedges**  Instead of a boring evergreen hedge or another single-season flowering shrub, why not add some fruiting shrubs to your landscape? Fruit- and nut-bearing bushes, such as European filberts, Manchurian bush apricots, elderberries, currants, and highbush blueberries, form large shrubs substantial enough to edge the boundary of your property, mass into an informal hedge, or naturalize. Prickly shrubs such as raspberries, blackberries, citrons, and goose-berries make a barrier that neighborhood children, dogs, and deer won't be quick to push through.

**Flower Borders and Foundation Plantings**  Low-growing fruit bushes, such as compact half-high blueberries, make great shrubs for foundation plantings or mixed flower borders. Creeping fruit-bearing plants—including lowbush blueberries and strawberries—fit easily in the foreground of a flower or shrub border. They also make interesting ground-covers, just as long as they get their fair share of

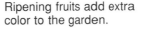

Ripening fruits add extra color to the garden.

Cover arbors, trellises, and other structures with carefully trained fruiting trees or fruit-bearing vines.

With their prickly stems and bushy habit, brambles are excellent as barrier plants. You'll enjoy the fruit, too.

sunshine and a little help from you to beat the weeds.

**Walls, Fences, and Trellises** Vining fruits such as grapes and kiwis can cover arbors or trellises, shading sitting areas, highlighting special views, or screening off utility areas. Espaliered trees (those trained to grow flat against a wall or trellis) can form a living fence that's both unique and productive.

**Containers** Decks, patios, and even balconies can be fruitful when you grow suitable edibles in containers. Dwarf citrus, apple, and peach trees are all good candidates for container culture. Strawberries also look super cascading out of hanging baskets or strawberry pots.

### Factors to Consider

With so many exciting edible plants to choose from, it can be tempting to start filling your yard with them right away. But there are factors you need to consider in order to have success with fruits and berries. Before you start digging holes and buying plants to fill them, review the points below, and keep them in mind as you plan and plant your new landscape.

**Think about maintenance.** Just like any other landscape plant, fruiting plants need care to keep them healthy and productive. While some have lower maintenance needs than others, all will require some

Training fruit trees and vines to grow along walls will give you a harvest from a previously useless space.

of your time. If you don't have a lot of time to devote to yard care, stick with some of the less complicated crops, such as strawberries, blueberries, gooseberries, currants, blackberries, and raspberries. For ideas on making maintenance easier, see "Pointers for an Easy-care Edible Landscape."

**Choose adapted crops.** It's possible to grow just about any fruiting plant in any climate, but it isn't always easy. To have healthy, high-yielding plants, it's best to stick with crops and cultivars that are naturally well adapted to the growing conditions in your area. These conditions include the amount of sunlight, the fertility and drainage of the soil, the amount and distribution of rainfall, and the high and low yearly temperatures.

---

### Pointers for an Easy-care Edible Landscape

Don't wait until your fruit trees are delivered to your doorstep to decide what to do with them. An attractive, easy-care landscape requires planning in advance, starting with careful plant and site selection. Here are a few points to consider as you choose the crops you want to grow and decide where you're going to put them.

- **Pick problem-resistant plants.** For easiest maintenance, look for cultivars that are naturally resistant to the pests and diseases that are common in your area. (Local fruit growers and your Cooperative Extension Service can tell you which problems to watch out for; catalog descriptions will list the problems a particular cultivar can resist or tolerate.)

- **Plan for plant size.** Think carefully about how large a tree you can handle. Trees over 6 feet (1.8 m) high will require you to climb on a ladder to harvest or prune; that will slow you down and be more strenuous.

- **Consider the water supply.** When picking a planting spot, try to find one near a water supply that you can tap into without much trouble. Otherwise, you may be spending lots of time hauling buckets of water or lugging long hoses around. If dry spells are common in your area, you may want to install permanent irrigation systems before you plant. This can save you hours of labor and provide super results.

Oranges and other citrus fruits are best suited to warm climates; they will be damaged in frost-prone areas.

Grapevines grow quickly and can be quite heavy, so make sure you can provide a sturdy structure for them to climb.

If you've been gardening for a while, you're probably familiar with the growing conditions that your yard and your climate have to offer. If you're just starting out or if you need a review, check out "Understanding Your Site" on page 28. Then you can compare the needs of the plants you're interested in with the conditions you can offer. The individual entries in "Fruit Trees," starting on page 78, "Fruiting Vines and Bushes," starting on page 100, and "Nut-bearing Plants," starting on page 116, will give you guidelines on the best climate and site for each crop. You can also talk with your local Cooperative Extension Service, fruit tree nurseries, and nearby gardening organizations or publications to find out which fruits do well in your area and which don't.

**Allow ample space.** Fruiting plants come in a range of sizes, from tall trees to compact container plants, so there's at least one kind for any size garden. Before you buy, however, make sure you have enough space to allow each plant to grow up and out without crowding. You'll also need to consider whether you have to grow more than one plant of each kind for cross-pollination. Sweet cherries, apples, pears, blueberries, and most nuts, for example, need at least one other plant with compatible pollen, so you need to have enough space for at least two plants. The individual entries later in this book will tell you whether a particular crop needs a pollination partner or not.

**Pick a good planting place.** Put fruiting plants where they can grow easily, without a lot of competition from other woody plants and turf when they are young. It's also best to keep them away from the road, so they won't be doused by exhaust fumes. If you grow fruiting plants that need spraying, put them where the spray won't drift to other crops, garden furniture, or house siding.

**Consider plant habits.** As you're deciding where to put a particular plant, also think about the kind of fruit it produces and how the fruit falls. Tall hickory trees, for example, let large nuts drop fast, which could be very unpleasant if you're lounging on the patio below. The hulls of black walnuts contain a black dye that can discolor pavement and garden furniture (as well as your hands). Cherries and mulberries can stain clothes and walkways. Soft fruits can be slippery if they drop on a walk or driveway. Fallen fruit can attract yellow jackets, so keep fruit trees away from children's play areas. Rodents may also feed on dropped fruit, so you'll need to be careful about cleanup with plants next to the house.

Carefully trained fruit trees can produce a unique and effective fence that's both beautiful and productive.

Growing fruiting plants on walls is an excellent way to liven up an otherwise unused space.

# Fruits for Walls and Fences

Some fruits can go where no plant has gone before—squeezing in next to walls, along fences, and in narrow areas where an ordinary bush would be crushed. That's because many fruiting plants are incredibly versatile. You can train them into a variety of shapes to fit almost any space. Keep this in mind as you plan planting schemes to enliven small side yards, cramped courtyards, tight property lines, and landscape sites with walls and fences.

Of course, you'll need to identify the growing conditions the site has to offer (as explained in "Understanding Your Site" on page 28), then make your plant choices accordingly. Keep in mind that walls can block or reflect sunlight, making the site brighter or darker than you might otherwise expect; consider watching the site through one growing season to see how the conditions change before you choose any plants to grow there. Also be aware that narrow or sheltered spaces tend to have poor air circulation, so it's especially smart to look for disease-resistant fruit species and cultivars.

In the meantime, here are some ideas on how you can turn these tough planting sites into beautiful, productive areas.

### Experiment with Espalier

Train dwarf fruit trees into an espalier that will grow flat along a trellis or wall,

stretching horizontally and upward. You can give espaliered plants many fanciful shapes. (See "Easing into Espalier" on page 61 for complete details.) Espaliered plants paint a beautiful scene with greenery, flowers, and fruits and appear especially prominent against the quiet backdrop of the wall. In addition, your espalier will soften the hard lines of a wall, blending it into the landscape. If you have a solid wood, stone, or brick wall, plant the espalier on the sunny side, where it will get at least 6 hours of sun a day.

### Include Some Climbers

Vines have an almost fluid flexibility when they're young, so you can manipulate them as you wish. Grow fruiting vines like grapes and hardy kiwis on vertical trellises; or, if you have enough space and a vigorous growing vine, use broader V- or T-shaped wire trellises. (For more information on training systems, see "Grapes" on page 107.) A strongly growing grapevine can fill out a trellis to form a solid wall of foliage, making a handy summer screen for privacy. A less aggressive grower will still produce an abundance of greenery but will leave some sunny openings.

For more fun with flexible plants, allow grapes, kiwi, or thornless blackberries to climb on arbors, arching trellises, or pergolas. Situate them at the garden entrance, over a sitting area, or anywhere you want shade, beauty, and abundant fruit.

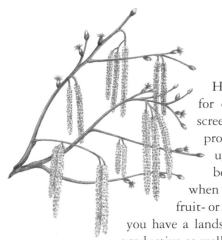

# Fruits for Hedges

Hedges are handy for creating attractive screens and barriers to provide privacy, block ugly views, or mark boundary lines. And when you have a hedge of fruit- or nut-bearing plants, you have a landscape feature that's productive as well as pretty.

## Freestanding Hedges

Fruit- and nut-bearing shrubs work best as informal hedges, since the shearing needed to keep formal hedges neat will drastically reduce fruit production. Few fruiting shrubs are evergreen, so fruiting hedges will be most attractive and effective during the growing season. Good choices for edible hedges include red and white currants, American filberts, Nanking cherries, blueberries, blackberries, dwarf citrus trees, raspberries, wineberries, elderberries, dwarf figs, Manchurian bush apricots, gooseberries, and currants.

For an informal hedge, plant bush fruits close enough together that their branch tips will intermingle when they mature. If you need to prune them, thin out crowded stems instead of shearing off the stem tips. This lets light penetrate into the interior of the hedge so the plants can continue producing new growth and fruit. (For more information on pruning, see the "Pruning Primer" on page 58.)

Brambles are good for marking boundaries. Their thorny stems discourage all but the most determined visitors.

## Trellised "Hedges"

You also can train some dwarf or compact-growing fruit trees into a highly productive trellised hedge. Commercial fruit growers developed this technique to make mechanical harvesting easy. But in the process, they discovered that trellis-trained hedges produce three times more fruit per acre than individually planted trees. Dwarf apples, dwarf pears, dwarf peaches, and European plums are all good candidates for this simple training system.

To train a trellised hedge, set up a 5-foot (1.5 m) tall post-and-wire trellis where you want the hedge to be. Plant dwarf trees along it, spaced 4 to 6 feet (1.2 to 1.8 m) apart. Prune them to develop three or four main branches that fan out along the trellis. Hold the main branches in place as they grow to the top of the trellis by tying them loosely to the wires. Cut back side branches to about 12 inches (30 cm) long in summer, encouraging them to form a wall of greenery. Limit nitrogen fertilizers to minimize new growth.

Freestanding espaliered fruit trees provide attractive screens and make effective boundary markers. They require careful trimming to stay neat, though.

# Fruits for Small Gardens

Fruiting plants can pack a lot of pizzazz into small gardens, letting you make the most of limited space. But you'll need to choose pint-sized plants that won't overwhelm your yard or require extensive pruning to stay small. Fortunately, you can choose from a wide array of compact edibles that let you grow two or three plants in the space you'd otherwise devote to one full-sized tree. Adding a few more fruit crops in containers (as discussed in "Fruits for Containers" on page 22) will further expand your planting options.

Fruit-bearing bushes and groundcovers are natural choices for spots where space is limited. Fruit trees are also an option, since they come in an assortment of sizes. The smallest are normal trees grafted on dwarfing rootstocks or natural dwarfs growing on their own roots.

## Grafted Dwarf Trees

When fruit trees are grafted, the top of the graft is called the scion, and the bottom part of the graft is called the rootstock. The scion grows into the trunk and branches and produces the fruit. The rootstock forms the base of the tree and the roots.

Fruit trees are sometimes grafted onto particular rootstocks to take advantage of the rootstocks' special characteristics, such as dwarfing. Dwarfing rootstocks can keep a normally full-sized tree from growing out

Sweet cherries usually grow as full-sized trees; sour and Nanking cherries are better suited to small yards.

of your reach, which is convenient when tending the tree and nearly essential in a small garden. Although the plant is dwarf, the fruit is full-sized. Compared with full-sized trees of the same cultivar, dwarfs bear fewer fruit per tree, but you can plant more dwarf trees in a given space and end up with a larger harvest.

Many dwarfing rootstocks have been developed for apples. These different rootstocks are best for different soil conditions and climates; some are even resistant to common soilborne diseases. If none of the dozens of dwarfing apple rootstocks is perfect for your situation, you can buy a tree grafted on more vigorous roots with a dwarfing interstem (a short piece of trunk from a

Cold-tender kumquats usually grow as shrubs or small trees—just right if you have limited growing space.

If space is really at a premium, consider trying one of the single-stemmed apple cultivars that are now available.

Containers allow you to grow fruit in areas that you normally can't plant, such as patios and decks.

Plum trees grafted onto dwarfing rootstocks stay small enough to fit easily into a medium-sized to small yard.

compact tree) that will keep its height down. For more information on choosing apple rootstocks, see "Apples" on page 80.

Dwarfing rootstocks are not as well developed for other fruit trees. Most pears can be dwarfed with reasonable success by grafting them onto quince rootstocks. Cherries will grow a little smaller if grafted on roots of *Prunus mahaleb*. Plums can grow on over 50 other species of plant roots, including some good dwarfing forms. Peaches and nectarines also have a wide variety of root compatibility. To date, there are no truly dwarfing rootstocks for apricots, sweet cherries, or nut trees. But work is continuing on dwarfing rootstocks, so keep an eye on the nursery catalogs for new developments.

While dwarfing rootstocks are very useful, they are

not without drawbacks. They do, for instance, tend to shorten the life span of peach and nectarine trees. Most dwarfing apple roots are brittle, so you'll need to stake dwarf apple trees to keep them from falling over when laden with fruit or tossed in a strong wind. 'Bartlett' pears tend to bond weakly with quince roots, so the resulting trees may break off at the graft. And 'Anjou' pears grafted onto *Pyrus betulifolia* roots will develop dark, corky spots inside the fruit. Differences caused by rootstocks are less common in cherry, peach, and nut trees than in apple, pear, and plum types.

When growers mix up tree parts in an attempt to build a better plant, they can end up with some unexpected results. The same rootstock, for instance, can produce very different-sized trees when grafted to scions of different cultivars. Reputable nurseries should be able to tell you what characteristics to expect from the different grafts they sell.

## Genetic Dwarf Trees

You can avoid rootstocks entirely by planting genetic dwarfs, which grow on their own roots. These plants naturally stay small and bushy, and they grow well in containers. Unfortunately, genetic dwarfs often lack good fruit flavor and disease resistance. But now that they have the size down, fruit breeders are working on developing great flavor, so keep an eye out for improved types when new nursery catalogs arrive.

---

### Great Fruits and Nuts for Small Gardens

Even if your growing space is limited, your choices aren't! Here are some suggestions for compact fruiting plants that can enhance any small yard.

- **Trees:** Dwarf and spur forms of apples, dwarf peaches and nectarines, dwarf pears, dwarf plums, sour cherries, Nanking cherries, compact citrus, dwarf almonds, and dwarf figs
- **Shrubs:** Blueberries, elderberries, blackberries, raspberries, currants, and gooseberries
- **Perennials:** Strawberries

## Fruits for Containers

Container gardens give you tremendous flexibility to experiment with fruit growing. If your soil is so poor or hard that you have to dig it with a pick, containers give your crops better conditions for good root growth. Containers also allow you to grow fruit on a deck, patio, or balcony and to move plants around to take advantage of the available sunlight in a mostly shaded garden. In cold climates, containers let you grow tender plants—such as citrus and figs—indoors in a greenhouse or sunroom.

### Choosing a Container

The ideal containers for fruit growing have thick walls that slow moisture loss and insulate the roots from extreme air temperature swings. Clay pots are attractive and work fine for strawberries, but they tend to dry out quickly, and they chip or crumble if left outdoors during a cold winter. For fruit trees, look for durable, thick-walled plastic pots that resemble clay but retain more moisture. You also can plant fruit trees in wooden half-barrels and planters.

Whatever container you choose, check that it has drainage holes so the roots won't get waterlogged. Also make sure it has a wide, stable base so it won't tip over when the plant gets tall and heavy with fruit. The best size of the container varies, depending on

Containers give you the freedom to move plants around to find where they look and grow the best.

what you want to grow. Here are some suitable pot sizes for different crops:

- Dwarf apples, apricots, cherries, peaches, pears, citrus, plums: Thick wooden or plastic tubs or barrels at least 2 feet (60 cm) wide and 3 feet (90 cm) deep.
- Blueberries: Large plastic, wooden, or ceramic pots at least 2 feet (60 cm) wide and deep.
- Strawberries: Plastic or clay pots, strawberry pots, hanging baskets, or strawberry towers at least 8 inches (20 cm) deep and 12 inches (30 cm) wide.

### Caring for Containers

Growing fruiting plants in containers isn't hard, but it does take some care to keep them in peak production. Regular watering is one of the most important aspects of care, since containers can dry out quickly, especially in hot, dry weather. Here

Wooden half-barrels are ideal for dwarf trees.

are some other care considerations to keep in mind.

**Provide the right rooting conditions.** The roots of container plants are much more limited than those growing in the ground. Roots in containers can't stretch in search of moisture and nutrients, so you'll have to water and fertilize much more often than you would for a garden plant.

You'll also need to provide a growing medium that

---

### Combining Plants in Containers

If you have a roomy container, you can blend fruiting plants with ornamentals and herbs for extra interest. Look for companions that don't spread aggressively; otherwise, they'll compete with your fruiting plant for moisture and nutrients. They also should be low-growing, so they won't block the free air movement or sunshine your fruiting plant needs.

Edibles such as leaf lettuces, basil, and parsley make especially pretty and practical edgings for container fruits. For a particularly attractive combination, use companions with blooms or leaves that match the fruiting plant's flowers or fruit. Purple bush basil looks stunning under dark red apples, for example, while yellow-variegated sage complements yellow apples.

Strawberries are super for containers. Try them in pots or hanging baskets, or grow them in special "strawberry jars."

Dwarf peach trees adapt well to life in planters at least 2 feet (60 cm) wide and 3 feet (90 cm) deep.

will nourish and support plant roots (and thus the rest of the tree) while still providing plenty of air and moisture. Not just any soil will do. This kind of challenge calls for specially blended mixes that can be either soil-less or soil based.

Make your own soil-based mix by blending 2 parts of good garden soil with 1 part each of compost, peat moss, vermiculite, and perlite. If you don't have garden soil to spare, you can also use soil-less, peat-based mixes that contain a combination of peat moss, perlite, vermiculite, and compost—a light and airy yet moisture-retentive blend. You can buy commercial soil-less mixes, such as Jiffy Mix, and add 1 part of compost for each 3 parts of mix. Or make your own soil-less mix of equal parts of compost, perlite, and peat moss.

**Fertilize for good growth.** Even compost-rich potting soil won't have enough nutrients to keep fruit plants growing for long. It helps to blend some fertilizers into the growing mix before planting. To every bushel-basket of mix, add a sprinkle of bloodmeal and a handful each of greensand, rock or colloidal phosphate, and bonemeal.

After the first year, keep plants growing strong by fertilizing with a liquid material, such as fish emulsion. Dilute and apply the fertilizer according to the label directions for container plants. If there are no specific guidelines for containers, dilute the fertilizer to half the normal strength and use it twice as often. You can also use dry organic fertilizers for potted plants; just follow the label directions.

**Check the pH.** Since your plants may grow in the same container for several seasons, it pays to check the pH at least once a year. Peat-based mixes tend to become acidic over time. To check the pH, use litmus paper (usually available from garden centers and garden-supply catalogs). Unless you're growing acid-loving plants, such as blueberries, you'll want to raise the pH if it is below 6.0. Scatter a heaping tablespoon of limestone over the soil of a 5-gallon (23 l) pot; use a smidge less than 1/8 cup for a half-barrel.

**Protect containers in cold weather.** Even thick-walled containers can expose roots to damaging temperature extremes, especially in the cold of winter. To protect the roots of potted plants, surround the container with leaf-filled garbage bags. If you can move the container, you could instead sink it in well-drained soil amid your foundation plants and mulch over the top of the roots. Dormant hardy trees will also survive well in a cool garage over winter. Bring cold-tender plants indoors to a greenhouse or sunroom until warm weather returns. The containers will be easier to move if you set them on a wheeled platform.

**Rejuvenate overgrown container plants.** After a few years, fruit trees and bushes will outgrow their pots and begin to decline. When roots form a solid mass in the pot, repot the plant in a larger container with some fresh potting soil. Or prune the larger roots and branches back so you can replant in the original pot with some fresh soil.

# Home Orchards

If you have plenty of space and time, you can reap big rewards by planting a back-yard orchard. An orchard can supply you with ample quantities of fresh produce to eat or share, and you'll probably have lots left over for preserving, too. Orchards, however, take work to stay healthy and productive, so it's smart to plan carefully before you make the commitment. Here are some planning pointers to help you make a sane, sensible start.

## Find the Right Site

A key part of planning a healthy, productive orchard is finding a good planting site. An ideal site would get full sun and have well-drained soil. Good fertility and steady soil moisture are pluses, but you can work around them if your site is lacking. A north-facing slope or northern exposure is also beneficial but not required.

Also look for sites that are as far as possible from wild fruit trees (which can harbor many fruit pests and diseases). While some shelter from wind is desirable (perhaps from a hedge or a vine-covered trellis), try to avoid sites near tall walls or woodlands. These features will block air circulation and increase the chance of disease problems.

## Pick Your Plants

As with any garden, one of the most fun parts of planning an orchard is deciding what to grow. Start with

If you don't have room for a whole orchard, consider planting a fruit garden full of bush fruits and strawberries.

a wish list of all the plants you'd like to have. Maybe you'd like to concentrate on heirloom apples, specialize in nut trees, or start a collection of uncommon fruits, such as pawpaws and persimmons. Or perhaps you'd like to grow a little bit of everything to have a season-long supply of fresh produce.

At this point, your list probably contains far more crops than you have the time or space to grow. Check to see what kind of growing conditions and climate each crop needs, and eliminate those that don't match your site. At the same time, mark down how much

---

## Some Suggested Spacings

While it's tempting to cram in as many crops as possible, your orchard plants will grow best when you give them the space they need to spread out and up without crowding. Following is a list of suggested spacings between plant centers for some common fruit crops. (If you need spacing information for a crop that's not covered here, check the individual plant entries later in this book.)

You may want to allow extra space for paths between planted rows. If you intend to use large machinery, such as mowers, to help maintain the orchard, make the paths broad enough to accommodate your equipment. To save space, you could alternate wide equipment paths with narrow foot paths.

- **Apples:** 6 to 8 feet (1.8 to 2.4 m) apart for dwarfs; 12 to 15 feet (3.6 to 4.5 m) apart for semidwarfs; 25 to 30 feet (7.5 to 9 m) apart for full-sized trees
- **Blackberries:** 3 to 6 feet (0.9 to 1.8 m) between plants; 8 to 10 feet (2.4 to 3 m) between rows
- **Peaches, Pears, and Plums:** 8 to 12 feet (2.4 to 3.6 m) apart for dwarf types; 15 to 20 feet (4.5 to 6 m) apart for standard (full-sized) trees
- **Raspberries:** 2 to 3 feet (0.6 to 0.9 m) between plants; 7 to 8 feet (2.1 to 2.4 m) between rows
- **Strawberries:** 1 to 2 feet (0.3 to 0.6 m) between plants; 1 to 4 feet (0.3 to 1.2 m) between rows

Orchard-style plantings can make maintenance easier, since all of your crops are in one spot.

Leave plenty of space around each plant to allow for good air circulation, as well as easy access for maintenance.

space each crop on the remaining list will take up and whether it needs a partner for pollination. ("Deciding What to Grow" on page 33 explains about pollination requirements and has a handy table that lists the widths of many common fruit and nut crops.)

## Make an Orchard Map

Now it's time to see how many plants you can fit into the space you have available. First, make a scale drawing of the space you've chosen for the orchard. Depending on how big the space is, a scale of 1 inch on paper to 1 or 2 feet of garden space should give you a manageable map with room for details.

Next, divide the space up among all your prospective crops. This step is easier if you cut out pieces of paper that represent the width of each fruit tree or shrub you want. (Use a different color for each kind of plant.) Cut out circles or squares for trees and shrubs; use rectangles for strawberry rows. Make the paper pieces to the same scale you used for your map, so you can see just how much space each plant will take up.

Shuffle the paper pieces on your orchard map until you find the layout that looks the best to you. If you like, you can arrange the fruit trees, bushes, and vines in rows with access paths between them. This makes mowing and installing irrigation lines much easier. Stretch the rows

A site map will show you how much space you have available.

from north to south to encourage maximum sun exposure, or have them run in the direction of the prevailing wind to discourage diseases. For more efficient use of space, set the plants in a staggered arrangement, so plants in one row are across from the space between two others in the neighboring row.

"Some Suggested Spacings" gives you guidelines on how much room to leave between the centers of several common fruit crops. For other crops, space them so their edges just barely touch. Leave occasional access paths here and there through the planting sites so you can get in with mowers and other equipment.

Training fruiting plants on trellises is a little extra work, but it gives you more room and makes picking easier.

# PLANNING YOUR PLANTINGS

The secret to successful fruit growing is choosing crops that will thrive in your climate and site. While many crops—including apples, grapes, and raspberries—will adapt to many parts of the country, some fruits have very special needs (such as acid soil or frost-free winters). In this chapter, you'll learn how to identify the resources your yard has to offer and then match them with the crops that are best suited to the site and to your needs.

In "Understanding Your Site" on page 28, you'll find out which features can make an area super or unsuitable for most fruit crops. This section includes tips on avoiding spots where frost may linger, damaging early-flowering plants and possibly wiping out your entire year's harvest. You'll also learn simple tests for finding out what kind of soil you have and how well it drains. Other important factors covered in this section include identifying your climate conditions and spotting sunny and shady areas.

Once you know all about your site, you can start on the most fun part: picking your plants. There are plenty of luscious possibilities, especially if you have a good growing site. "Deciding What to Grow" on page 33 covers some of the considerations you'll want to keep in mind as you make your selections. For an overview of the needs, sizes, and uses of the 20 most popular fruit and nut crops, refer to the "Favorite Fruits and Nuts at a Glance" table on page 34.

As you finalize your plant list, take time to consider the harvest times of your chosen crops. Whenever possible, try to organize fruit plantings to spread the harvest through the season. You can do this by choosing a number of different crops and planting cultivars that mature at different times. That way you'll always have some fresh fruit ready for picking and won't be overwhelmed by the bounty of your fruit garden. For detailed tips on extending your harvest, see "Planning for Season-long Harvests" on page 36.

Picture-perfect fruit is a sign of good planning. When you select plants that are suited to the growing conditions your site has to offer, they will naturally be less prone to pest and disease problems.

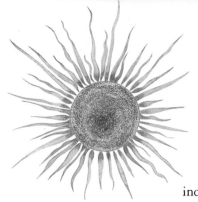

# Understanding Your Site

Before you get your heart set on growing a particular crop, you need to evaluate your site carefully. The four key factors to consider include climate, sun, soil, and slope. You can learn much of what you need to know in one day by going out into your yard and taking notes of your observations. But to get a real handle on the available growing conditions, you'll have the best results by repeating your investigations several times over one or two growing seasons.

## Check Out Your Climate

Your climate sets the stage for the kinds of fruits and nuts you can grow. It seems there's a limiting factor to every climate; nobody can grow every kind of fruit to perfection. Fortunately, there are delicious kinds of fruits that will grow in each climate.

Since climate has such an important influence on successful fruit growing, gathering climate statistics is a good place to start in learning about your site. The most commonly used system for judging a crop's chance of success in a particular climate is the hardiness zone. The United States Department of Agriculture has put together a map that divides the country into many different zones, based on average low winter

Cherry trees flower and set fruit early in the season, so avoid low-lying areas that are prone to late spring frost.

temperatures. These zone recommendations are commonly listed in catalog descriptions and on plant labels. A rating of Zones 5 to 8, for instance, means that a particular crop should be able to survive an average winter in Zones 5, 6, 7, and 8.

Keep in mind, however, that the hardiness zone rating is a guideline, not a guarantee. If you grow a plant rated for Zones 5 to 8 in Zone 5 and have a colder than normal winter, the plant may not survive. To be on the safe side, it's best to stick with crops and cultivars that are hardy to one zone colder than yours (to Zone 4, for example, if you garden in Zone 5). To find out what hardiness zone you live in, see the USDA Plant Hardiness Zone Map on page 154.

Of course, winter cold isn't the only factor you'll need to know. Some crops and cultivars need longer growing seasons than others to ripen their fruits. (You can find out the length of your growing season by counting the number of days between your average last spring and first fall frosts.) If you have mild winters, you'll also need to consider how many hours of the season are below 45°F (7°C)—the temperature some crops require for a cold rest period. For help in gathering these statistics, call your local Cooperative Extension

Fuzzy kiwi is hardy only in the South, but there are hardier species that can grow as far north as Zone 3.

European plums, such as 'Damson', tend to flower later than Japanese plums, so they are less prone to damage from late spring frosts.

If you have a short growing season, look for early-ripening cultivars.

Service or weather bureau. Then keep all of this information in a notebook so you can refer back to it when choosing your crops.

## Observe Sun and Shade Patterns

Most crops require ample sunlight to produce a generous supply of flowers and fruit. Abundant sunlight also is important for crops such as grapes and strawberries because it helps to keep the plants dry and reduces risk of disease problems.

On a fairly open lot, without many tall trees or buildings nearby, you're pretty much assured of full sun. But if you're trying to fit fruiting plants around your existing landscape, you'll need to consider how much shade your crops are likely to get.

Start your sun-and-shade survey as soon as you can—today, if possible. Watching the light patterns through one whole growing season before planting is best. A site that is sunny in early spring or fall may be in deep shade by midsummer. One sunny day a month, for at least several months before planting, watch your proposed planting sites through the day.

Unlike many fruit crops, which tend to prefer full sun, gooseberries can grow well in light shade.

### Understanding Organic Matter

Along with sand, silt, and clay, soil also contains organic matter: decaying leaves, twigs, animal manure, and other plant and animal leftovers. Organic matter, which gives soil a dark, spongy appearance, helps loosen up clay soil and enrich sandy soil. It releases nutrients, holds moisture, and supports soil life, including earthworms and beneficial bacteria. Healthy soils should contain at least 5 percent organic matter.

Using generous amounts of compost as soil amendments and mulch will help to build soil organic matter and keep it at the right level. If you want to be sure that your soil contains at least 5 percent organic matter, ask for this test when you get your soil analyzed (as explained in "Soil Texture") on page 30.

Currants will grow fine in average to good garden soil that's evenly moist but not waterlogged.

Crab apples thrive in the same conditions as regular apples: full sun and well-drained soil.

Record when the sun first strikes the ground and when shadows take its place.

To grow most fruiting plants successfully, you need a site that gets at least 6 hours of sun a day through the whole growing season. If you have slightly less than that, you can still grow light shade-tolerant plants such as gooseberries, elderberries, and currants. Darker spots will give disappointing results for nearly every fruit crop.

## Dig into Your Soil

As you're investigating the aboveground characteristics of your yard, don't forget to look below the surface as well. Fruit trees can develop root systems that span as much as three times beyond the spread of their branches. If not obstructed by poor or packed soil, the roots may also dig down one and one half times the height of the tree in clay soil and up to three times the tree height in sandy soil. Roots anchor your plants, interact with other soil life, and absorb water and dissolved nutrients.

The health and productivity of your fruiting plants depend on good root growth, and good root growth depends on loose, fertile, well-drained soil. Knowing the texture, pH, and drainage characteristics of your soil will help you choose the crops that are best suited to your site.

**Soil Texture**  Understanding soil texture is the key to unlocking your soil's secrets. The way soil allows water and air to flow through it, the speed with which it warms up, the depth to which it allows roots to grow, and the amount of nutrients it holds are all closely related to soil texture.

The texture of the soil, just like the texture of a nail

file, depends on the size of the mineral particles in it. Large sand particles, which you might compare to the coarse surface of a nail file, feel rough in your hand. They also break apart easily. A high sand content makes a loose, dry soil that's low in nutrients but quick to warm up in spring and easy for roots to dig into deeply.

Clay particles lie on the other end of the size spectrum. They are fine textured, like the smooth "finishing" surface of a nail file. Clay soil holds nutrients and moisture, but it can become dense enough to limit root growth and the movement of water and air.

### Foiling Frost

While most fruiting plants need some kind of winter cold period for good growth, sudden, late frosts can wreak havoc with your harvest. A good way to reduce the risk of frost damage on early bloomers is to plant on a site that is slow to warm up after winter. As the snow melts in spring, look for spots where it lingers the longest—usually on the north side of buildings, walls, or hedges. Cooler soil delays spring growth, sometimes sparing young flowers and leaves from frost.

Blueberries require acid soil to thrive. If your soil isn't naturally acid, you'll need to prepare a special area or grow your plants in containers.

European plums tolerate clayey soil better than Japanese and American types.

Most soils are loams that fall somewhere between these two extremes. Loams contain varying percentages of sand or clay blended with intermediate-sized particles called silt.

You can conduct a simple home test to get a rough idea of your soil's texture. Take a handful of moist soil 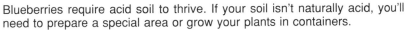 and squish it into a ball; then try to squeeze it into a ribbon by flattening it between your thumb and the side of your forefinger. If the soil won't hold together to make a ribbon, it's on the sandy side. If the soil molds easily into bits of ribbon over 1 inch (2.5 cm) long, you have clay soil. Intermediate-length ribbons range from sandy loam to loam and clay loam, depending on their percentage of sand, silt, and clay.

Strawberries appreciate rich, moist soil. You can improve average soil before planting by digging in lots of compost.

This simple test will give you a rough idea of your soil's texture, so you'll be able to pick plants that are best suited to your site. Apricots and peaches, for instance, thrive in loose, sandy loam soils, while European plums and strawberries grow better on fertile, moist soils that are on the clayey side. To get a more detailed picture of your soil's texture, you can have your soil analyzed by a soil-testing laboratory. Your local Cooperative Extension Service probably sells kits for collecting soil samples for analysis. You can also get tests done by private soil-testing laboratories; some garden centers even offer testing services to their customers.

**pH** The pH of your soil refers to its natural acidity or alkalinity. While some crops can adapt to a range of soil pH, others, like blueberries, have very specific needs. The pH has a great effect on which nutrients are available for plant growth. While you can adjust the pH of your soil, you'll get the best results for the least work by picking naturally adapted crops.

The pH scale ranges from 0 to 14, although values of 4 to 9 are most common for soil. Soil that has a pH of 7 is said to be neutral. Acid soil has a pH below 7; alkaline soil has a pH above 7. Most fruit crops grow best in neutral or slightly acid soil, which allows plants access to the widest range of nutrients. A couple, including blueberries and cranberries, require especially acidic soils, down to a pH of 4.5. Few fruit plants grow well in alkaline soils.

Apricots prefer loose, well-drained soil, but they can tolerate somewhat heavier soil when grafted onto plum roots.

You can test soil pH yourself with a simple home test kit or have the test done as part of a more complete soil analysis. If you find out your soil does not have a suitable pH for the fruit crops you want to grow, it's possible to change it. (Most test results come with recommendations of materials and amounts to apply to adjust pH.) However, it's a long-term process that you'll have to continue for the life of the plant.

**Soil Drainage**  Just like you, plant roots need fresh air to live, but theirs must be available in the soil. That's why nearly all fruiting plants demand well-drained soil. Soils with poor drainage fill up with water, squeezing out the air and suffocating plant roots.

Poor drainage occurs most often in heavy clay soil, where the tiny soil particles are too tightly packed to allow rainfall to move between them. It also happens if mineral particles in any soil pack into a hard underground layer that traps water near the soil surface. Even sandy soils can be poorly drained if underground water seeps up into the planting area.

To tell how well your soil drains, dig a hole 1 foot (30 cm) deep and wide in your potential planting area. If you strike thick, gray clay or if water wells up when you dig, that soil is waterlogged—not well suited for planting. Brown or yellow-brown subsoil usually indicates good drainage. To double-check, try this simple test.

1. Fill the hole with water.

2. Wait 30 minutes, then check the hole.

3. If all of the water is gone, refill the hole with water to see how the soil will handle excess moisture.

4. Wait another 2½ hours, then check the hole again. If all the water has seeped out of the hole by the end of Step 4, the drainage is good enough to grow fruit trees. If the hole still contains water at the end of Step 3 or 4, your soil will stay too wet for good root growth in most crops. In that case, you have several options.

• Stick with the few fruit crops—such as cranberries—that can take poor drainage.

• Look for a different site.

• Build a raised bed to give roots well-drained soil to spread out in.

• Give excess moisture a place to go by breaking up hard underground layers or installing culverts or underground drainage pipes.

As with all of the other site factors, you'll get the best results with the least amount of work by picking plants that are adapted to your soil's natural drainage. But if your soil is poorly drained, that doesn't leave you with many options. If you don't have any other possible planting sites, raised beds are probably the best way to go. For details on constructing them, check out "Building Raised Beds" on page 43.

## Consider the Slope

One final factor to watch for is whether your proposed planting site is on a hilltop, on a slope, or in a low spot. Low-lying areas collect cold air; they tend to get frosted first in fall and latest in spring. This can be a real problem for early-blooming fruit crops, such as apricots, peaches, and strawberries, since a late-spring frost can damage the flowers and prevent them from setting fruit that year. Sheltered valleys also tend to have poor air circulation, so plant leaves stay wet longer after rains, giving diseases a better chance to get established.

A position slightly uphill or in the middle of a gentle slope with cultivated earth around it is ideal for fruit crops. (Open earth tends to radiate more heat than turf and can keep frost away a little longer.) Hilltops are least prone to frosts, and they also have the best air circulation. They can also be quite windy and dry, though, so you may want to stake your trees and plan for some kind of irrigation system.

A sloping site is ideal for strawberries, since their early-blooming flowers can be damaged by spring frosts.

# Deciding What to Grow

With all the information you've gathered about your site and climate, you're well on your way toward making the best possible planting decisions. Now you need to compare the growing conditions your site has to offer with the fruit and nut crops you want to grow and see where you can match them up.

### Pick from the Possibilities

Even before you started planning your fruit planting, you probably had at least a mental wish list of what you wanted to grow. But before you limit yourself to just those, skim through the later crop chapters in this book, including "Fruit Trees," starting on page 78, "Fruiting Vines and Bushes," starting on page 100, "Nut-bearing Plants," starting on page 116, and especially the "Uncommon Fruits, Berries, and Nuts," starting on page 124. When you come across a crop that sounds appealing, jot it down on your wish list.

---

### Pollination Planning Pointers

It's a basic principle of botany: To produce a fruit, a flower needs to be pollinated. From there, though, it gets a little trickier. You see, sometimes the flowers on a particular plant can be fertilized by pollen from the same plant, so you can have just one plant and still get a good crop. Peaches, nectarines, tart cherries, strawberries, some plums, and some citrus crops fall into this group.

Other fruit and nut trees need pollen from another plant or cultivar of the same crop. Examples of plants that need (or at least benefit from) cross-pollination include sweet cherries, pears, pecans, walnuts, most apples, and some plums and apricots.

Because different cultivars can bloom at different times, you can't just buy two trees and assume they'll pollinate each other. Mail-order catalogs that sell fruit trees will suggest pollinators for the crops that need them; follow these guidelines when you buy to get the best results.

---

Most sweet cherries need cross-pollination, so make sure you have enough space to grow at least two trees.

### Make the Perfect Match

Once you finish your wish list, go through it crop by crop to see if the plant in question will fit your growing conditions. Consider each crop's sun, moisture, and temperature requirements, as well as its size and maintenance needs. You can find this information in the crop chapters and "Uncommon Fruits, Berries, and Nuts." You'll also find "Favorite Fruits and Nuts at a Glance" on page 34 helpful; it's an easy-to-follow table with basic growing and size information for 20 popular crops. You may also want to refer to mail-order fruit catalogs to find out all the special features and needs of specific cultivars.

### Fine-tune Your Crop Choices

The last step between your wish list and your shopping list is reviewing your crop choices. If space is a limitation, you may need to drop some crops. Don't forget that some fruits and nuts require (or benefit from) cross-pollination for good production, so you'll need to allow room for at least two plants of those. (For more details, see "Pollination Planning Pointers.") If a long picking season is important to you, you will also want to check out the tips in "Planning for Season-long Harvests" on page 36. Once you've finalized the list of the fruit and nut crops you want to grow, you're ready to move on to "Buying and Planting Fruits and Berries," starting on page 38.

## Favorite Fruits and Nuts at a Glance

As you gather information about the crops you want to grow, you can save lots of time by referring to this handy table of 20 popular fruits and nuts. In here, you'll find all the basic information you need to know about each crop, including sun and soil preferences, hardiness, average height and spread of the plant, bloom time, harvest time, uses, and storage.

Keep in mind that this information can vary somewhat, depending on which crop cultivars you choose and where you live. For instance, some fruits, such as ever-bearing strawberries and raspberries and day-neutral strawberries, will bloom in spring and then again in summer. Hardiness zones are also rather general guidelines about where you can expect a particular crop to perform well. Some plants that are listed for warmer zones—including citrus and figs—can also grow farther north if you select super-hardy cultivars or grow the plants in containers and bring them indoors in winter.

| Crop Name | Exposure | Soil Fertility | Hardiness | Height | Spread |
|---|---|---|---|---|---|
| Almond | Full sun | Average to poor soil | Zones 6–9 | 15–30 feet (4.5–9 m) | 15–30 feet (4.5–9 m) |
| Apple | Full sun | Average soil | Zones 3–9 | 8–30 feet (2.4–9 m) | 8–30 feet (2.4–9 m) |
| Apricot | Full sun | Average to poor soil | Zones 5–9 | 8–24 feet (2.4–7.2 m) | 16–24 feet (4.8–7.2 m) |
| Blackberry | Full sun | Average to rich soil | Zones 5–9 | 4–7 feet (1.2–2.1 m) | 3–6 feet (0.9–1.8 m) |
| Blueberry | Full sun | Average to rich soil | Zones 3–9 | 2–15 feet (0.6–4.5 m) | 3–10 feet (0.9–3 m) |
| Cherry, sour | Full sun | Average to rich soil | Zones 4–8 | 8–20 feet (2.4–6 m) | 8–20 feet (2.4–6 m) |
| Cherry, sweet | Full sun | Average to poor soil | Zones 4–9 | 15–30 feet (4.5–9 m) | 15–30 feet (4.5–9 m) |
| Chestnut, Chinese | Full sun | Average to rich soil | Zones 5–9 | 40 feet (12 m) or more | 20–40 feet (6–12 m) |
| Citrus | Full sun to light shade | Average to rich soil | Zones 8–10 | 10–30 feet (3–9 m) | 10–30 feet (3–9 m) |
| Figs | Full sun | Average soil | Zones 8–10 | 10–25 feet (3–7.5 m) | 10–25 feet (3–7.5 m) |
| Filbert, European | Full sun to light shade | Average to poor soil | Zones 4–8 | 15 feet (4.5 m) or more | 15 feet (4.5 m) |
| Gooseberry | Full sun to light shade | Average soil | Zones 3–7 | 3–6 feet (0.9–1.8 m) | 3–6 feet (0.9–1.8 m) |
| Grape | Full sun | Average to rich soil | Zones 4–10 | 4–6 feet (1.2–1.8 m) | 8–15 feet (2.4–4.5 m) |
| Kiwi | Full sun to light shade | Average to poor soil | Zones 3–9 | 4–6 feet (1.2–1.8 m) | 15 feet (4.5 m) |
| Peach | Full sun | Average to poor soil | Zones 5–9 | 8–15 feet (2.4–4.5 m) | 10–20 feet (3–6 m) |
| Pear | Full sun | Average to poor soil | Zones 4–9 | 8–20 feet (2.4–6 m) | 8–20 feet (2.4–6 m) |
| Pecan | Full sun | Average to rich soil | Zones 6–9 | 50–150 feet (15–45 m) | 35–50 feet (10.5–15 m) |
| Plum | Full sun | Average to rich soil | Zones 4–10 | 8–20 feet (2.4–6 m) | 8–20 feet (2.4–6 m) |
| Raspberry | Full sun | Average to poor soil | Zones 3–9 | 4–6 feet (1.2–1.8 m) | 2–4 feet (0.6–1.2 m) |
| Strawberry | Full sun | Average to rich soil | Zones 3–10 | 10 inches (25 cm) | 12–24 inches (30–60 cm) |

As you fine-tune your plant list, take time to consider the harvest times of your chosen crops. Try to organize your fruit plantings to spread the harvest through the season by choosing several different crops and planting cultivars that mature at different times. That way you'll always have some fresh fruit ready for picking and won't be overwhelmed by bushels of fruit that you don't have time to eat or preserve. (For more details on extending your harvest, see "Planning for Season-long Harvests" on page 36.)

In the "Pollination Requirements" section, you'll find out whether the crop is usually self- or cross-pollinated. To get fruit from cross-pollinated crops, you'll need to grow at least two plants of different but compatible seedlings or cultivars. If a plant is both self- and cross-pollinated, that means it can set some fruit on its own, but it will produce higher yields with at least one partner. Self-pollinated crops are ideal for small gardens, since you can get a harvest from just one plant.

| Bloom Time | Harvest Time | Uses and Storage | Pollination Requirements |
| --- | --- | --- | --- |
| Early spring | Midsummer to fall | Eat fresh; dry for storage | Cross-pollinated |
| Midspring | Midsummer to fall | Eat fresh; keep for several weeks in refrigerator; preserve for longer storage | Cross-pollinated |
| Early spring | Early summer | Eat fresh; keep a week or two in refrigerator; dry for storage | Cross- and self-pollinated |
| Midspring | Midsummer | Eat fresh; keep a week or two in refrigerator; preserve for storage | Self-pollinated |
| Midspring | Mid- to late-summer | Eat fresh; keep a few days in refrigerator; preserve for storage | Cross- and self-pollinated |
| Midspring | Early summer | Eat fresh; keep a few days in refrigerator; preserve for storage | Cross- and self-pollinated |
| Midspring | Early summer | Eat fresh; keep a few days in refrigerator; preserve for storage | Cross-pollinated |
| Late spring | Late summer to fall | Eat fresh; freeze for storage | Cross-pollinated |
| Varies | Varies | Eat fresh; keep a week or two in refrigerator; make into marmalade for storage | Self-pollinated |
| Varies | Varies | Eat fresh; keep a few days in refrigerator; freeze for storage | Self-pollinated |
| Early spring | Late summer to fall | Eat fresh; keep for weeks in refrigerator; dry for storage | Cross-pollinated |
| Midspring | Midsummer | Eat fresh; keep a week or two in refrigerator; preserve for storage | Self-pollinated |
| Midspring | Midsummer to fall | Eat fresh; keep a week or two in refrigerator; preserve for storage | Self-pollinated |
| Midspring | Fall | Eat fresh; keep for several weeks in refrigerator; preserve for longer storage | Cross-pollinated |
| Early spring | Midsummer | Eat fresh; keep a week or two in refrigerator; preserve for storage | Self-pollinated |
| Midspring | Late summer to fall | Eat fresh; keep for several weeks in refrigerator; preserve for longer storage | Cross-pollinated |
| Early spring | Fall | Eat fresh; keep for several weeks in refrigerator; dry for longer storage | Cross-pollinated |
| Early spring | Midsummer | Eat fresh; keep a week or two in refrigerator; preserve for storage | Cross- and self-pollinated |
| Midspring | Midsummer to fall | Eat fresh; keep a few days in refrigerator; preserve for storage | Self-pollinated |
| Midspring | Early- to mid-summer | Eat fresh; keep a few days in refrigerator; preserve for storage | Self-pollinated |

# Planning for Season-long Harvests

If you're planning to stock a roadside stand or do plenty of preserving, you might prefer to choose crops that all ripen about the same time. Otherwise, it makes sense to spread out your harvests. As you're working on your list of crops to grow, check the prospective harvest times of all the crops you've chosen to see if they are fairly well spread out. (The actual harvest time can vary each year, depending on the weather, but the spread of time between the peak for each crop should remain fairly consistent.) If the harvest times aren't evenly distributed through summer and fall, try some or all of the approaches outlined below to get the longest possible picking season.

## Make a Mixed-fruit Garden

Some home gardeners prefer to grow a few each of several different kinds of fruit, so they have prime produce to pick and enjoy at any time during the growing season. Choosing one or two crops for each season from the following list will help you make sure you have all your harvesting times covered.

- **Late spring (in warm climates):** Citrus fruit and apricots
- **Early summer:** Apricots, sweet cherries, early

Oranges, peaches, and several other fruits have cultivars that ripen at different times, extending your harvest.

blueberries, and June-bearing strawberries
- **Midsummer:** Early apples, early peaches, midseason blueberries, blackberries, summer-bearing raspberries, day-neutral strawberries, and gooseberries
- **Late summer:** Grapes, late blueberries, elderberries, hardy kiwi, filberts, ever-bearing strawberries, midseason apples, midseason peaches, and plums
- **Fall:** Late apples, late peaches, fall-bearing and ever-bearing raspberries, cranberries, persimmons, chestnuts, walnuts, and pecans

## Pick Different Cultivars

Even if you only concentrate on one or two crops, you can still have a longer harvest season by choosing different cultivars that mature at different times. For

By planting both summer-bearing and ever-bearing raspberries, you can enjoy the fruit from midsummer to frost.

Spread out your apple harvests by choosing cultivars that bloom at the same time but ripen in different seasons.

Day-neutral strawberries produce small amounts of berries at any one time, but they yield over a long season.

Ripe nectarines and peaches don't last long, so you'll need to eat or preserve them soon after picking.

instance, you could start out the strawberry season with June-bearing cultivars, continue picking all summer with day-neutral cultivars, and keep on harvesting into fall with ever-bearing strawberries. The same technique works to spread the raspberry season: Plant summer-bearing types for midsummer picking, then get another sweep of berries in fall on ever-bearing and fall-bearing raspberries.

Any time you have to plant two or more compatible cultivars of a particular fruit for pollination, look for those that flower at the same time but mature at different times. With apples, for instance, you could choose the cultivars 'Liberty' and 'Prima'. They will bloom in time to cross-pollinate each other, but 'Prima' ripens near the end of August while 'Liberty' ripens around the end of September.

## Choose Your Harvest Carefully

By keeping an eye on natural variations in ripening times, you can sometimes extend the harvest time for a particular crop by a month or more. When you're picking apples, for instance, take the early-ripening ones on the sunny outer portions of the tree first, followed a couple weeks later by the inner apples. Pick some ripe rabbiteye blueberries or grapefruits when they first become sweet, then let the others linger on the plant a little longer. If you want an extended harvest of currants,

for instance, grow black currants (which ripen over several weeks) instead of simultaneously ripening white and red currants.

## Select Different Planting Sites

If you're determined to grow two crops that ripen at the same time but are afraid you'll be swamped with produce, you can try to alter their timing a little. Plant one on a south-facing slope or in front of a south-facing wall to speed up its flowering and fruiting times. To delay flowering and fruiting on the other plant, site it on a north-facing slope or beside a north-facing wall, and leave mulch on the soil in spring to keep the roots cooler longer. Remember that if you're growing a crop that needs cross-pollination, you'll have to plant compatible companions in each area.

Apples growing on the outer parts of the tree tend to ripen first, followed by those toward the inside.

# BUYING AND PLANTING
# FRUITS AND BERRIES

To get generous harvests of sweet, juicy fruit, you need to start with healthy, vigorous plants. Weak, diseased, aged, or malformed plants, even when pampered for years, simply will not produce high yields of the top-quality fruit you're looking for. This chapter is your guide for getting off to a good start by purchasing great plants, preparing a super growing site, and planting properly for healthy future growth.

Whether you plan to shop at a local nursery or through a mail-order catalog, "Buying the Best Plants" on page 40, is your guide to getting the most value for your money. You'll learn all kinds of smart-shopping secrets, so you'll begin with high-quality, problem-free trees that are likely to produce the best crops.

Your fruiting plants will be living in the same spot for several years, so giving them a good planting site is a critical step in helping them succeed. If you have the time to plan ahead, it's ideal to start preparing the site a year or two before planting by loosening the soil and planting cover crops. But even if you aren't that organized, you can still get good results by setting up the planting site the same season you buy your plants. You'll learn all the down-and-dirty details in "Preparing the Planting Site" on page 42.

When the time comes to put your purchases in the ground, you'll need to know the best ways to plant them. In "Planting Fruit Trees, Shrubs, and Vines" on page 44, you'll find step-by-step directions for getting bareroot and container-grown nursery stock off to the best possible start. You'll also get tips on caring for your fruits, nuts, and berry-bearing plants just after planting, so they can easily settle into their growing site.

Once you know what crops you want to grow, it's time to get your fruit garden started. Begin with healthy, young stock and plant it carefully, and you'll be on your way to high-quality harvests.

# Buying the Best Plants

By the time you're ready to purchase your plants, you've already spent some time and effort on the planning process. Make sure you spend your money as wisely to get healthy, high-quality fruit trees, shrubs, and vines. Follow the smart-shopping tips below to help you get your money's worth!

## Know What You're Getting

When you're shopping for an appliance, it's easy to see what you're paying for. Buying good plants, however, is a little trickier, especially by mail. That doesn't mean that you can't get excellent, high-quality plants through the mail; it just means you want to check the age and condition of the plants before you buy.

**Buying Young Plants** Many fruit plants take several years to reach fruiting age, so buying tiny plants will only prolong your wait for the first harvest. But

The stems of young plants are thin and flexible, so they are easy to train as you wish.

you also want plants that are relatively young so they'll have an easier time adapting to life in your garden. When buying fruit and nut trees and fruiting vines, look for 1-year-old plants (in the case of trees, these are sometimes called whips). Trees and vines at this stage are vigorous, adaptable, and ready to begin training. For shrubby fruits, such as blueberries, 2- or 3-year-old plants will get off to a faster start.

**Bareroot vs. Container Plants** Depending on when you buy and what source you buy from, your new plants may be bareroot or growing in containers.

Bareroot plants are sold when they're dormant (not actively growing), without any soil around the roots. One disadvantage of buying bareroot stock is that it is only available at certain times of the year (usually late fall and early spring). It also needs to be planted as soon as possible after arrival. But it is also the most practical way for mail-order nurseries to ship plants; otherwise, you'd have to pay shipping on a lot of heavy soil!

Local nurseries most often sell their plants growing in containers. The disadvantages of container-grown plants are that they tend to be more expensive than bareroot stock, and you'll have a much more limited selection. On the plus side, though, container-grown plants are available through the year, and they can be planted any time the ground isn't frozen. If you can't plant them right away, you can keep them growing in their pots until you're ready to set them in the ground. Container stock is quite easy to plant, and it tends to have a lower failure rate than bareroot stock.

## Understanding Guarantees

When you buy a television or a toaster, you want one that comes with a guarantee. You need to know that you're getting the product that you paid for and that it will perform as promised. Well, the same is true when you're buying a tree, shrub, or vine from a nursery. You want an assurance that the plant you're getting is the cultivar it's supposed to be and that it is healthy and capable of good growth.

Before you buy, look to see if the seller offers such a guarantee. Most mail-order catalogs print their guarantee (if they have one) prominently near the front or back cover or order form. Local nurseries may or may not have a written guarantee posted: Ask the manager or a knowledgeable salesperson about it. You need to know what the nursery will guarantee, how you can make a claim if you're dissatisfied, and what sort of compensation you can expect. Sometimes you have to show the original sales slip and/or plant label to prove your purchase, so it's wise to file these in a safe place soon after planting.

If you're willing to pay more, you may be able to get already trained fruiting plants, such as this potted gooseberry standard.

For fruit trees, you'll get the best results by starting with young, single-stem plants.

## Don't Buy Problem Plants

Buying disease- and pest-resistant plants is important to the future health of your fruit plantings. But it's just as important to avoid buying plants that have problems right now. Otherwise, you may bring home serious problems, such as bacterial and viral diseases, that can affect all your crops.

To reduce the risk of purchasing pest and disease problems, buy only from nurseries that offer certified disease-free plants. This means that the plants have been checked and approved by nursery inspectors.

If you can find a source, it's even better to buy "virus-indexed" plants. Virus-indexed plants come from laboratories that test stock plants and grow only those that are virus-free. These laboratories sell young plants to commercial nurseries, who propagate and grow them under controlled conditions that prevent virus infection. Virus-free stock is available for most fruit trees, as well as for grapes, raspberries, blackberries, and strawberries.

It's also smart for you to examine any plant carefully before you take it home or plant it out in your yard. On bareroot plants, check that the roots and base of the plant are firm and healthy looking and that there are no unusual swellings (other than the graft union near the base of the trunk). Look for plump, healthy buds and bark that's clean, free of suspicious holes, and evenly colored. On container-grown plants, check that the foliage is a bright, uniform green color. Look underneath the leaves and at the base of stems to be sure that no insects or egg clusters are hiding there. If possible, remove the plant from its container to make sure the roots aren't tightly matted or circling the outside of the root ball. If you find a problem, send the plant back or don't buy it; you don't want to risk spreading pests or diseases to your other plants.

### Accept No Substitutes!

Be aware that mail-order nurseries will occasionally substitute another cultivar if they are sold out of the one you want. While the substitute may be of equal or greater monetary value, it may not have the right balance of flower and fruit timing, flavor, disease resistance, and climate adaptation you need.

As you fill out your order form, read the sales information carefully to find out the substitution policy. Some companies provide lines or boxes where you can indicate if substitutions are acceptable. If the form does not give you a place to mark your wishes, write "no substitutions" below your order.

Preparing the site several months before planting will give you time to test and amend your soil for good plant growth.

## Preparing the Planting Site

You've chosen a good spot, and you've picked the perfect plants. Now follow through with creating the best possible planting site, so your plants will get off to a great start.

### Deciding When to Dig

*When* you prepare the site depends on how organized you are and when you plan to plant. Ideally, you should start a year or two before planting by clearing the site and planting cover crops to improve the soil. (See "Improving Your Soil with Cover Crops" for more details on growing cover crops.) But if you don't have the time or inclination to plan so far ahead, you can prepare the site the same season you plant. Whenever possible, have the planting site ready at least a week or two before your plants arrive.

### Clearing the Site

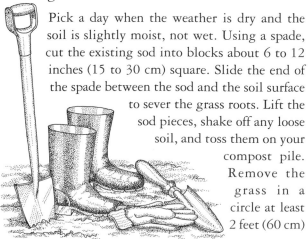

Pick a day when the weather is dry and the soil is slightly moist, not wet. Using a spade, cut the existing sod into blocks about 6 to 12 inches (15 to 30 cm) square. Slide the end of the spade between the sod and the soil surface to sever the grass roots. Lift the sod pieces, shake off any loose soil, and toss them on your compost pile. Remove the grass in a circle at least 2 feet (60 cm)

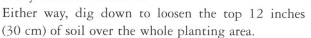

across for vines, 3 feet (90 cm) across for shrubs, and 5 feet (1.5 m) across for trees.

If the exposed soil is fairly loose, you can break it up easily by digging with a spade or shovel. If the exposed soil is hard and compacted, you may choose to use a rotary tiller to loosen it. Either way, dig down to loosen the top 12 inches (30 cm) of soil over the whole planting area.

This is also a good time to work in any nutrients that your soil is lacking. If you haven't already done so, have a soil sample tested to check its pH and fertility level. ("Dig into Your Soil" on page 30 has more information on soil testing.) You can add needed nutrients before planting, working them down into the soil where they'll be accessible to plant roots. You can also begin to adjust soil pH as recommended in the test results.

At this point, you have three options. If the soil is now in good condition and you're ready to plant, move on to "Planting Fruit Trees, Shrubs, and Vines" on page 44. If you don't plan to plant for at least several months, consider growing a cover crop in the area to protect and build the soil; see "Improving Your Soil with Cover Crops." Or, if the soil is poorly drained or too hard to dig, construct raised beds to provide a good layer of soil for root growth; see "Building Raised Beds" for details.

A deeply dug growing bed provides ideal conditions for root formation, so your fruiting plants will thrive.

Removing grass from the planting area will prevent it from competing with young trees for water and nutrients.

Most fruiting plants don't thrive in waterlogged soil; try planting in raised beds if your soil is soggy.

## Improving Your Soil with Cover Crops

When you have the chance to wait several months between soil preparation and planting, it's smart to sow a cover crop in the planting area. As it grows, the cover crop will protect the soil from erosion, add organic matter to the soil, and discourage weeds from sprouting.

While all cover crops can be beneficial, some work better for particular purposes than others. In Cornell University field trials, for example, researchers found that both marigolds and sudan grass were particularly good at suppressing weed growth the year after they were tilled into the soil. (Marigolds kept down grasses and nutsedge, while sudan grass controlled broad-leaved weeds.) If you especially want to increase the soil's fertility, consider fast-growing legumes (such as clover and vetch) and cereals (such as oats and winter rye), which will add abundant organic matter to the planting site after you till them in. This is especially beneficial for shallow-rooted, moisture-loving crops such as strawberries, recommends Cornell University researchers.

Plant a cover crop as soon as you've prepared the growing site, so it can get established before weeds take over. Scatter the seed over the prepared soil, rake the area lightly, and then keep it moist until the seeds sprout. Dig or till the cover crop into the soil in late summer (if you're planting your fruit crops in fall) or in late fall to early spring (if you're planting your fruit crops in spring). If the crop is more than a few inches tall, mow or cut it down first to make it easier to dig or till. Allow a week or two between turning under the cover crop and planting your fruiting trees, shrubs, and vines.

## Building Raised Beds

If your soil is very hard or poorly drained, don't despair! You can still grow a wide variety of fruiting plants if you build raised beds to give your plants extra room for good root development.

You can mound soil up to about 12 inches (30 cm) high without surrounding it with some kind of frame. To raise a bed higher, support the soil with structures such as timbers, stone, or brick. Fill the beds with good-quality, well-drained topsoil that's similar in texture to the underlying soil. (If your garden soil tends to be clayey, for instance, don't choose a very light or sandy soil to fill the bed; otherwise, the plant roots will have difficulty making the transition.)

Once installed, raised beds are easy to plant and maintain. They do, however, tend to dry out more quickly than in-ground plantings, so pay close attention to the soil moisture during dry spells.

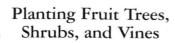

# Planting Fruit Trees, Shrubs, and Vines

It's always exciting when planting day arrives. All the effort you've put into choosing the best cultivars, deciding where to put them, and preparing the soil will pay off as you make the transition from plans to plants.

## Deciding When to Plant

When is the best time to plant your fruit garden? The answer is not always a simple one. It depends on the kind of soil and climate you have, the kind of plants you're planting, and the time your plants are available.

**Fall Planting** If you live in a moderate to warm climate—Zones 6 to 10—fall is a good time to plant most fruit and nut crops. Dormant, bareroot, mail-order plants will come in late October to early November (even later in the Deep South). Nurseries and garden centers may also offer container-grown stock in time for fall planting.

If you live in Zone 5 or north and you have light, well-drained soil and winters that aren't severely cold, you can plant currants, gooseberries, and hardy Concord grapes in fall; save the rest of your planting for spring.

In warm climates, the planting season extends well into winter. In California, bareroot apricots go in the ground from January to March. In Florida, midwinter is the best time to plant blueberries and strawberries.

**Spring Planting** In cool climates (Zone 5 and north), early spring is a better time to plant most fruits and nuts.

Bareroot mail-order plants will arrive early, so prepare the planting site in fall so it will be all ready when your plants come. You'll want to get the plants in the ground as soon as possible, so they can get their roots established before the heat and drought of summer. If you don't have the time to deal with your bareroot plants when they arrive or if the weather in your area is still dropping well below freezing at night, you may need to hold the plants indoors for a few days. For information on giving them the right conditions while you're waiting to plant, see "Dealing with Planting Delays."

---

### Dealing with Planting Delays

When you buy bareroot fruit plants through the mail, they will probably arrive at the ideal time for your climate—but not necessarily when you and your garden are ready. If you can't plant for a few days, you can store the dormant plants in several ways.

- Put them in the refrigerator (at 35° to 40°F [1.6° to 4.4°C]). Make sure you don't store apples in the same refrigerator—they give off ethylene gas, which can kill young trees.

- Leave packaged bareroot plants outdoors in a shaded, cool place for a couple of days. Open the box to let fresh air in, and sprinkle the plants with water occasionally to keep them moist.

- Unpack the plants and set the roots in a tub of water. (Keep them this way for no more than 2 days.)

To store bareroot plants for more than a few days, plant them temporarily in an out-of-the way spot. Choose a site that has well-drained soil and is sheltered from sun and wind. Dig a 2-foot (60 cm) deep trench with one vertical side and one outward-sloping side. Lay the plants against the sloping side, with the tops out of the trench. Cover the roots and graft unions with soil, and keep the area moist. As soon as you can, uncover the roots and move the plants to their permanent spots.

---

Walnuts and other nut trees are often sold bareroot. Set out the dormant plants in late fall or early spring.

Plant citrus trees in late winter, when the soil is cool but all danger of frost has passed.

Apples and other trees that are grafted onto dwarfing root-stocks need to be staked after planting.

If you're buying your plants locally, they'll most likely be growing in containers. While it's ideal to plant them early, container-grown fruit trees, shrubs, or vines are much more forgiving of planting delays than bareroot plants. They can wait for weeks or even months before you plant them, as long as you keep them well watered.

## Planting Bareroot Plants

If you've never seen a bareroot plant before, you might be in for a surprise when you unpack your box from the nursery. Bareroot plants are just what they sound like—tentacle-like naked roots topped with bare branches or merely a single stem. They can look rather pathetic, but don't be dismayed. As long as you bought the plants from a reputable nursery and give them proper care, they can grow beautifully. (If you lose one or two plants right after transplanting, which is not all that uncommon, contact the nursery right away for a refund or replacement.) Refer to the following steps to get your bareroot plants off to a good start.

1. When you're ready to plant, cut off any damaged, sickly, or exceptionally long roots. Leave healthy roots alone. Give most fruit and nut plants, except blueberries, a preplanting booster by soaking their roots in a bucket of compost tea. (To make compost tea, fill a loosely woven bag with compost and soak it in a big tub of water until the water turns tan. Use the soggy compost as mulch, or throw it back into the compost pile; save the liquid left in the tub.) Soak the roots of strawberries and grapes for 20 minutes, and soak bush and tree roots for 2 hours.

2. While the roots are soaking, dig a hole deep enough to hold the roots without curling them up at the end. Slice into the walls of the hole with a shovel to make them easy for roots to penetrate. Make a tall cone of soil in the center of the hole and firm it well.

3. Remove the roots from the compost tea, then dip them in a blend of 1 part bonemeal and 1 part powdered kelp. If the bacterial disease crown gall is a problem in your area, this is also a good time to apply a preventive treatment. *Agrobacterium radiobacter* (sold as Galltrol-A and Norbac 84) is a benign bacterial dip that prevents crown gall from infecting clean plants. Dunk your bareroot fruit plants in it before planting to prevent later crown gall infection.

4. Put the crown of the plant (the place where the roots come together and the shoots emerge) on top of the soil cone in the planting hole.

5. Check that the crown or graft swelling is at the right height by comparing the location of the crown or graft with the surface of the soil. ("Getting the Height Right" on page 47 has details on the needs of different kinds of plants.) If your soil tends to sink slightly as it settles, you may want to elevate the plant a little to adjust. If your plant sits too high or too low on the soil cone, lift it out, add or remove soil to change the height of the cone, and try again.

Spread the roots of bareroot plants over a mound of soil in the planting hole.

Soak bareroot plants in compost tea before planting to promote vigorous growth.

Planting in containers is easy, since you don't have to dig. Just make sure you pick a planter big enough to hold the roots without bending them.

6. When you have the right crown or graft height, spread out the roots evenly over the soil cone. Holding the plant with one hand, fill in around the roots with the soil you removed from the hole. When the hole is half-filled, add some water so the planting site is thoroughly soaked; then finish filling the hole. Firm the soil gently, and add a plant label if you haven't noted the cultivar name on a garden plan elsewhere.

### Planting Container-grown Plants

Plants grown in containers come with a complete set of roots snugly situated in a pot. They seldom suffer problems after transplanting. Follow these simple planting steps for best results.

1. Dig a hole the same depth as the nursery container in your prepared planting site. Leave the soil in the bottom of the hole undisturbed so it won't shift after planting; just rough it up a little with a shovel or hoe. If your soil is especially heavy (clayey) or light (sandy), dig some composted pine bark or peat moss into the area around the planting hole, using gradually less farther from the hole. (This makes a transitional zone that will help the new roots spread from the pot's peat-based mix into your natural soil.)

2. Double-check that your plant will sit at the proper depth, as explained in "Getting the Height Right." To make measuring easier, lay a stake across the planting hole, and use a yardstick to measure from the bottom of the hole to the stake. (This will save you from having to lift the pot into and out of the hole.) If your soil sinks slightly when it settles, place the container plant slightly higher than ideal so it's perfect after the soil settles.

3. Remove the plant from its pot. To do this, put one hand on the surface of the planting mix to support the top of the plant. Then put your other hand beneath the container, squeezing the sides gently to separate it from the roots. Turn the pot upside down and carefully slide the plant out. If the pot still won't come off, you could cut it loose.

4. Take a close look at the roots. If the plant has been growing in the pot for a long time, the roots will be matted on the outside of the root ball. Use a sharp knife or pruning shears to cut off matted portions. Loosen circling roots with your fingers.

5. Set the plant in the hole, spreading loose roots in different directions so each has its own space.

6. Refill the hole with soil, then water thoroughly to settle the roots.

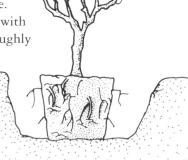

Set container plants at the same depth they were growing in their pot.

Cut the canes of bareroot brambles to just above the ground after planting to reduce the spread of cane-borne diseases.

## Getting the Height Right

When setting out bareroot plants, it can be tricky to tell exactly how deep to set them. Here are some pointers to make the job a little easier.

- Set strawberries so the crown is nestled in the soil and the shoots are emerging just above it.
- For vines and shrubby fruits, set the crown at the soil surface.
- For grafted plants—such as grapes and fruit or nut trees—set the swollen graft union 2 to 3 inches (5 to 7.5 cm) above ground level. (An exception is plum trees grown on virus-susceptible rootstock. With them, you may want to place the graft below the soil. For more details, see "Choosing Your Plants" on page 98.)

## Planting Aftercare

Once your young plants are safely in the ground, give them special care until they grow strong on their own.

**Trimming**  A little post-planting pruning will get your new plants off to a vigorous start. On year-old fruit trees, cut back the main trunk to about 2 feet (60 cm) high to encourage it to develop new branches for later training. On hickories and walnuts, cut the young tree back by half, leaving several buds on the trunk to form new branches. On bareroot fruit bushes, cut back up to half of the stems to compensate for the roots lost. Remove all but the base of the old canes from raspberries and blackberries to eliminate any diseases they may carry. And on grapes, remove all but the strongest stem to prepare the vine for future training.

On strawberries, blueberries, raspberries, and blackberries, also remove all the flowers the first spring after planting to encourage good growth. Pinch off grape flowers for 2 years after planting.

**Watering**  Regular watering is especially critical during a plant's first year of growth. To funnel the water down to the roots, make a shallow saucer in the soil around the base of the tree and mound up a slight rim beneath the branch tips. Let a hose or irrigation system trickle into the saucer when you water. For more information on knowing when and how to water, see "Watering Wisely" on page 56.

**Weeding**  Help your plants grow to their potential by keeping the planting site free of weeds. Otherwise, the weeds will compete for—and usually win—a bigger share of the site's water, nutrients, and light. To discourage weed seeds from sprouting, spread mulch in a circle around the base of the plant to just beyond the outermost reach of the branches. Use a 2-inch (5 cm) thick layer of decayed pine bark or compost or up to 4 inches (10 cm) of straw or bark chips. Once a week, pull up any weeds that emerge through the mulch.

After planting a grapevine, remove all but the strongest stem. Insert a stake next to the vine to direct it to the trellis.

# FRUIT CARE BASICS

Some fruiting plants need more care than others, but they all benefit from at least a little attention. In this chapter, you'll learn the basics for keeping your plants healthy and vigorous—from mulching and fertilizing to watering and pruning. You'll also learn how to collect and store your harvest, so you can—literally—enjoy the fruits of your labors. And if you get the urge to expand your fruit plantings, you can refer to this chapter to discover the secrets to propagating many kinds of fruit-bearing trees, shrubs, and vines.

Mulch is one of the most important additions to any home fruit planting. This multipurpose material is invaluable for maintaining steady soil moisture, adding nutrients and organic matter, and discouraging weeds from sprouting. "Mulching Basics" on page 50 explains all you need to know about choosing the best mulches for your needs, applying them correctly, and maintaining them to enjoy their many benefits.

Fertilizing is also an important part of fruit care, since your plants need a balanced supply of nutrients to grow and bear generous quantities of sweet, juicy produce. In "Fertilizing for Fruitful Growth" on page 54, you'll learn how to tell if your plants would benefit from a nutrient boost and how to select the right organic fertilizer for their needs.

Watering, of course, is another critical part of good plant care, especially if you live where rainfall is undependable. Even if you normally get a steady supply of rain through the growing season, you still need to be ready for those occasional dry spells. "Watering Wisely" on page 56 takes the guesswork out of the process by explaining when and how to irrigate effectively.

By meeting the growth needs of your fruiting plants, you've provided ideal conditions for maximum productivity. The last step in helping your plants reach their potential is with proper pruning and training. In the "Pruning Primer" on page 58, you'll learn how different kinds of pruning cuts will influence plant growth and how you can use these cuts to train young plants and maintain older ones. Once you gain confidence with these basic pruning methods, you may want to try your hand at the fun and fanciful techniques explained in "Easing into Espalier" on page 61.

Once your fruits grow ripe and sweet, you'll need a bushel of ideas for picking and keeping them. "Harvesting and Storing Fruit" on page 62 tells when and how to pick different kinds of fruit and how to store the extras that you're sure to have.

When you find out how fun and rewarding fruit growing can be, you may want to plant even more! "Making More Plants" on page 64 covers the techniques you can use to reproduce all your favorite fruits, from sowing seed to basic grafting. With this know-how, you'll be able to fill your yard with a variety of great fruit trees, shrubs, and vines for little or no cost.

Care needs for fruiting plants will vary greatly, depending on the kind of the fruit and where it's growing. Espaliered pears, for instance, need more careful pruning than regular pear trees, but they're also easier to pick from.

# Mulching Basics

Mulch is an invaluable part of almost any home fruit planting. For the relatively small amount of time and money you invest in mulching, you'll get big rewards—in reducing future maintenance, minimizing weed problems, and promoting healthy plant growth.

## How Mulch Helps

With the single step of applying mulch, you can encourage better growth in a number of ways.

- **Mulch conserves moisture.** Mulch shields the soil surface from drying winds and sun, reducing evaporation.
- **Mulch minimizes weed seedlings.** Mulches keep light from reaching the soil, discouraging weed seeds from sprouting. (They usually won't stop weeds that emerge from perennial roots, such as dandelions or thistles.)

Mulches help the soil stay moist, promoting good root growth.

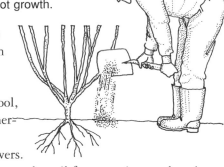

- **Mulch keeps the soil cool.** In spring, a thick layer of mulch keeps the soil cool, delaying the emergence of early, frost-prone flowers.

In summer, it keeps the soil from getting too hot; in winter, it keeps soil stable and frozen. (Soil that freezes and thaws can shift and damage plant roots.)

- **Mulch enriches the soil.** Compost, shredded bark, and other organic mulches break down over time, releasing nutrients and humus and making the soil more fertile and productive.

## Options for Mulch Materials

When you're faced with dozens of mulching materials, how do you decide which one is best for your plants? In flower gardens, the mulch's appearance is usually most important, since you want a fine, dark background to show off the colorful blooms. While good looks are nice in fruit plantings, it's more important to consider other mulch characteristics—such as coarseness, durability, and nutrient value.

For maximum mulch benefits, you'll want to stick with

Shredded bark makes an attractive, effective, and long-lasting mulch for many kinds of fruiting plants.

---

## Grow Your Own Mulch

If you have many fruiting plants, you may be looking at quite an investment to buy enough mulch to cover the ground around all of them. Fortunately, you have another option—using living plants as a groundcover to protect and enrich the soil.

Perennial cover crops are great for growing between rows or outside the mulched root zone of individual fruit trees. You can walk or drive on them all year when you need to get to your plants. For this purpose, pick cover crops that grow slowly and have modest nutrient needs. They should also be low-growing or easy to mow. Some good selections include slow-growing selections of hard fescue, creeping red fescue, perennial ryegrass, and Canada bluegrass. Dwarf white clover is also useful, since the flowers can attract beneficial insects that prey on fruit-eating pests.

Like regular mulches, cover crops prevent the soil from radiating as much heat as bare ground. In summer, this keeps the growing area cooler, benefiting heat-hating crops such as day-neutral strawberries, currants, and gooseberries. In spring or fall, however, mow permanent groundcovers short so the soil can release some heat and possibly reduce frost damage.

Make your own mulch by composting yard waste, garden trimmings, and kitchen scraps.

As they break down, organic mulches release some nutrients into the soil. For good fruit production, though, you'll still need to fertilize.

organic materials, such as compost, shredded leaves, straw, or bark. Inorganic mulches share some of the same benefits, but they also have several disadvantages as well; see "Plastic and Fabric Mulches" on page 52 for more details. The following list contains some of the most common organic mulches, along with a few notes about the characteristics and uses of each.

**Bark Nuggets** You'll need to apply a thick layer of this coarse mulch—about 4 to 6 inches (10 to 15 cm) deep. The nuggets decompose fairly slowly, which is

good in that you won't need to renew them very often. On the other hand, they won't add much organic matter or nutrients to the soil, so you may want to pull them back each year and apply a layer of compost over the soil before replacing them.

**Bark, Shredded** Shredded bark has a medium texture, so you can apply a thinner layer to get the same benefits. A 2-inch (5 cm) thick layer works well for most fruit crops. Shredded bark may draw some nitrogen from the soil as it breaks down. That's okay if your

Currants and gooseberries have shallow root systems. Protect them from heat and drought with a layer of mulch.

Since blueberries prefer acid soil conditions, they benefit from an acidic mulch, such as pine needles.

soil is very fertile or if you want to discourage rapid, lush growth. But if your soil is not naturally nutrient-rich, you may need to add extra nitrogen to compensate for what the mulch uses. To do this, mix compost or grass clippings with the bark, or spread a layer of compost between the shredded bark and the soil.

**Compost** Most fruits will thrive with a 1- to 3-inch (2.5 to 7.5 cm) layer of compost mulch. In many ways, compost is an ideal mulch, since it releases a balanced supply of nutrients to the soil as it decomposes. This fine-textured material will break down fairly quickly, however, so you may need to add more several times during the year. It may also carry

## Plastic and Fabric Mulches

Inorganic mulches—including plastic sheets and landscape fabrics—are generally less desirable than organic materials for mulching fruit plantings. Inorganic mulches help to maintain soil moisture and control weeds, and they can help you make a low-maintenance strawberry bed, but they won't help to improve soil fertility the way organic mulches do.

Plastic mulches have other drawbacks as well. With long-term use (around trees and shrubs, for instance), plastic mulch will block water and air from entering the soil, damaging root development. Dark plastics help the soil to warm up quickly in spring, encouraging plants to bloom while there is still a good chance of frost damage. Plastic mulches can also increase the spread of diseases—especially on strawberries—by making it easy for raindrops to splash dropped fungus spores onto plants and fruit.

Landscape fabrics are usually better for plants than solid plastic sheets because they allow water and air to reach the soil. The main drawback, besides the fact that they don't help to improve the soil, is the relatively high price. But if you have just a few fruit trees or bushes and are willing to pay for extra-special treatment, you may choose to buy landscape fabric to lay under a layer of organic mulch. This combination gives very good weed control and provides healthy conditions for root growth.

weed seeds, which can lead to more weed problems. A good compromise is to apply a layer of compost about 1 inch (2.5 cm) thick, then top it with a longer-lasting mulch such as bark or straw.

**Leaves, Shredded** A 1- to 3-inch (2.5 to 7.5 cm) thick layer of shredded leaves makes an attractive, fine-textured mulch that works well for many fruiting plants. Apply more leaves each fall as they are available.

**Pine Needles** A 2-inch (5 cm) layer of pine needles makes a nice-looking, medium-textured mulch. Pine needles are slightly acidic, which makes them ideally suited for mulching blueberries and strawberries (but not for most other fruit crops).

**Sawdust** This fine-textured, acidic material is best suited for mulching around acid-loving blueberries. Use a layer about 1 inch (2.5 cm) thick. Like shredded bark, sawdust can draw nitrogen from the soil as it breaks down, so mix it with compost or grass clippings or apply it over a layer of compost.

**Straw** Straw is a good, coarse mulch well suited for most fruit plantings. It's rather coarse, so pile it on—up to about 6 inches (15 cm) thick. Top it off once or twice a year to keep the layer even. If you need to improve the soil's fertility, pull back the straw each year and add a layer of compost before replacing it.

Straw is rather coarse, but it makes a light, loose, clean-looking mulch that's ideal for many fruiting plants.

Avoid piling mulch right against the stems; leave a much-free zone several inches wide.

Many fruit trees have tender bark that makes a tasty winter snack for rodents. Prevent damage by pulling mulches away from plants in fall.

## When to Mulch

Start mulching right after planting (as explained in "Planting Aftercare" on page 47). Add to that mulch layer as needed in late fall each year to maintain the right thickness. Add more mulch in spring if the layer has decomposed, especially if weeds are starting to poke through (remove the weeds first). As your fruit trees and bushes grow, increase the diameter of the mulched circle, so the mulch extends beyond the tree branches, where the feeding roots lie.

Add more mulch as needed each year to keep it at the right depth. Expand the mulch circle as the plant grows.

## Managing Mulch to Minimize Problems

It's easy to see that mulch has many advantages, but in some situations, it does have some drawbacks as well. Here are some pointers to help you avoid mulch-related problems in your fruit plantings.

- Avoid mulching soil that's heavy, moist, and not well drained. Under those conditions, mulch can make the soil even soggier and encourage diseases, such as root rots, and pests, such as slugs.

- When applying fine-textured mulches, such as sawdust or sifted compost, keep the layer thin, or mix the fine mulch with a coarser mulch material. Otherwise, the fine-textured mulch may pack into a hard, tight layer that prevents moisture and air from reaching tree roots. This results in poor growth and disease problems.

- If you have lots of rodents around, think twice about winter mulching. These creatures make homes in mulch during fall and nibble the tender bark and roots of your fruit plants during winter. To minimize damage, rake existing mulches away from the base of fruiting plants in early fall; replace the mulch in winter once the soil is frozen.

- Smell wood-chip mulches before you buy and spread them. If they smell sour or foul, they may have fermented in the center of a big mulch pile, accumulating acids that can damage your plants. Use only mulch that has a fresh or earthy smell.

If a soil test indicates that your site is deficient in phosphorus, work some bonemeal into the soil before planting.

A compost mulch may be all your established fruiting plants need to produce steady, productive new growth.

## Fertilizing for Fruitful Growth

To stay in peak productive condition, your fruiting plants need a steady supply of nutrients from the soil. Making sure the soil is stocked with these nutrients will help to ensure that your plants remain healthy and produce high yields.

### Fruit Fertilizing Basics

If you had your soil tested back when you chose your planting site (as explained in "Dig into Your Soil" on page 30), you have a good idea of your soil's general fertility. If there is a balanced supply of nutrients already in the soil, you can follow a simple fertilizer program to maintain the current levels. One or two applications of a balanced organic fertilizer each year will help young plants get off to a good start. For established fruiting plants, a compost mulch (used alone or under another mulch) may be all the nutrients they need.

Of course, there may be some times when you'll need to add extra nutrients to keep your plants healthy. Your preplanting soil test may have indicated that your soil is naturally lacking in one or more nutrients. Or your plants may show signs of nutrient deficiencies, such as yellowing leaves or distorted fruit.

Soil tests will usually suggest how much and what kind of fertilizers to add to balance the fertility level. If you suspect that your fruiting plants are suffering from a nutrient deficiency, contact your county Cooperative Extension Service office for information on taking plant samples for analysis.

### Understanding Your Fertilizer Options

Organic fertilizers, which come from plant, animal, or mineral sources, are a healthy, natural way to provide plants with necessary nutrients. "Complete" or "balanced" fertilizers include nitrogen, phosphorus, and potassium (the elements used most by plants), sometimes supplemented with trace minerals (elements needed only in minute quantities). These are best for routine fertilizing. Other fertilizers are particularly rich in individual nutrients. These materials are helpful for correcting specific soil deficiencies.

When your plants need a general or specific nutrient boost, you can choose between various solid or liquid fertilizers. Some of the most common materials are listed below. The ratios noted here and on fertilizer labels indicate the percentages of nitrogen, phosphorus, and potassium in each product. Balanced fertilizers will have three similar numbers (such as 2-2-2). If one number is higher than the others, as in 5-2-2, it means that the material is especially rich in that respective nutrient. (Fish fertilizer,

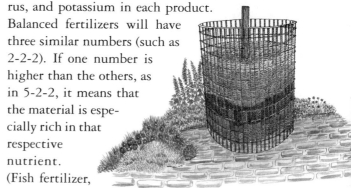

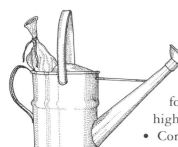
To make compost tea, soak compost in water.

for instance, is particularly high in nitrogen.)

- Compost (1-1-1 or 2-2-2): Compost is made from leftover yard wastes, livestock manure, and wood products. Work it into the soil or use it as a mulch.
- Compost tea (1-1-1): This liquid fertilizer releases a mild dose of nutrients. To make compost tea, fill a loosely woven bag with compost and soak it in a big tub of water until the water turns tan. Apply it to the soil or foliage.
- Cottonseed meal (4-2-2, 6-2-1, or 7-2-2, depending on the brand): This organic material is high in nitrogen but releases that nutrient relatively slowly. Apply it to the soil.
- Fish fertilizer (5-2-2): Use this liquid fertilizer on foliage or apply it to the soil. But keep it out of drip irrigation systems—it can clog them unless you buy refined hydrolyzed formulations.
- Greensand (0.1-1.5-6.7): Greensand is a potassium-rich rock powder that slowly releases its nutrients into the soil.
- Bloodmeal (14-0-0): This nitrogen source is good for encouraging new growth on young trees in spring. Scatter it sparingly over the soil.
- Bonemeal (0-20-0): This soil-applied material provides phosphorus to correct deficiencies.
- Epsom salts/magnesium sulfate (10% magnesium and 6% sulfate): Sprinkle this on the soil or dilute it in water—about 5 ounces (142 g) in 2 gallons (9 l) of water—if needed to correct magnesium shortages.
- Kelp extract (trace elements and plant growth stimulators): Spray this on fruit crops when the buds form and when they open to increase fruit set and frost tolerance. Spray again when fruit are forming or when diseases strike to increase vigor. Drench newly transplanted trees to encourage faster root formation. Be sure to follow package directions carefully. If you use too much, it can inhibit plant growth.

## Applying Organic Fertilizers

Solid, granular fertilizer and rock powders tend to release their nutrients gradually over time. Apply most of them in winter or early spring so the nutrients will be there when the plants need them most. The exception is nitrogen, which can be released fairly quickly from fertilizers such as bloodmeal. If you add nitrogen in late winter, you'll get fast results but also earlier growth and possible frost damage. To get the benefits of nitrogen without the risk of frost damage, apply one-third of the nitrogen early and the rest immediately after the last frost date.

Winter or early spring is a good time to apply most organic fertilizers, except for those high in nitrogen.

Read package directions and sprinkle the amount of solid fertilizer you need under the branch tips where the feeding roots lie. If the plants are mulched, pull back the mulch, sprinkle the fertilizer over the soil, and then replace the mulch.

Liquid fertilizers can be absorbed fairly quickly by plants; they'll make a big impact in a short period of time. Apply them to the soil around the base of the plant or spray them onto the leaves. If you apply liquid fertilizer to the foliage, do it in the cool of the morning, when the leaf pores are open. Add a touch of vegetable oil or liquid soap (1/4 teaspoon of oil or soap per 1 gallon [4.5 l] of fertilizer) to help the fertilizer cling to the leaves.

Spraying fruit trees with kelp extract at bloom time and when fruits are forming can promote higher yields.

# Watering Wisely

Water is the powerhouse for many critical plant functions. It carries dissolved nutrients into the roots and circulates them around the plant, so all parts get the energy they need for healthy growth. But most important—to you, anyway—is that it's a key part of the sweet juice that springs from each bite of a fresh ripe peach, pear, or plum. Making sure that your plants have an ample supply of moisture for all of these functions is a key part of growing tasty, top-quality fruit.

## Deciding When to Water

If you've had luck growing flowers or vegetables, you probably have a good idea of when you need to provide supplemental water for your plants. If you're a beginner, though, figuring out just when you need to water can be a real puzzle. Fortunately, there are some pointers you can keep in mind to help you water wisely.

As a very general rule of thumb, most fruiting plants need 1 inch (2.5 cm) of water each week during the growing season, either from rainfall or irrigation. This is helpful as a starting point, but you'll need to adjust it to fit your particular conditions. If your soil is on the clayey side, for instance, or if you maintain a thick mulch layer, you probably won't have to worry much about irrigating, since the soil will naturally tend to stay moist. But if your soil is sandy or if there's a severe drought, you may need to provide several inches of water a week to keep the soil moistened. You'll also have to water more frequently if you have an interplanted groundcover or cover crop or if you've just recently planted new trees, bushes, and vines.

The 1-inch (2.5 cm) rule is a handy starting point for deciding when to water, but you can see that it needs some fine-tuning. If you're in doubt about whether or not to water, look to your soil for answers. If the top layer of soil is moist, your plants are in fine shape. If the top is dry, dig down about 4 to 6 inches (10 to 15 cm) in the soil near your fruit plants. Loosen the soil at the bottom of the hole, take some in your hand, and squeeze it. If it clings together, it's moist enough

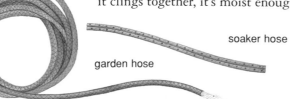

soaker hose

garden hose

Drip or trickle irrigation systems are an efficient way to provide the water your crops need for high yields.

for the next day or two. If it falls apart easily, the ground is dry. Assuming there's no rain in sight, this means you'll have to water your plants.

## Choosing a Watering Method

If you only have a few fruiting plants and droughts are infrequent in your area, you can water plants individually. Water small plants by hand, or let your regular hose trickle near the base of each plant for an hour or so.

When you're dealing with more than a few plants or if your time or inclination for watering is limited, finding an easier watering system becomes more critical.

One of the most common, but least desirable, methods for garden watering is using an overhead sprinkler. Much of the water it flings across garden areas is wasted by evaporation or runoff. This method indiscriminately nourishes weeds and wets plant foliage, making your fruiting plants more susceptible to disease attack. If you still choose to use a sprinkler despite these drawbacks, turn it on low for about 30 minutes, then turn it off. Let the moisture soak in and repeat the process until the top 4 inches (10 cm) of soil are moist.

A much more efficient and effective watering method is soaking the ground beneath fruit plants with trickle or drip irrigation. This approach gently

If you choose crops that are naturally suited to your climate, you should get good harvests without much watering.

Steady soil moisture is critical for young plants, so pay careful attention to watering the first year or two.

moistens the roots without compacting the soil, running off, or evaporating extensively.

For just a few plants, you can buy inexpensive "leaky" or soaker hoses (hoses with small holes that ooze water onto the soil) at garden centers. These kinds of systems are most effective for watering rows of plants or individual trees. Run the hoses straight along each side of a row, or lay them in concentric rings under each tree. When you need to water, run a regular hose from the faucet, attach it to the end of the soaker hose, and turn on the water. Check the soil every hour or so, and turn off the water when the top 4 inches (10 cm) of soil are moist. After they've been used for a while, these kinds of hoses are prone to clogs or leaks that can make the water come out unevenly. Check for and fix leaks regularly. If clogging is a regular problem, add a water filter to the faucet.

If you have a number of fruit plants or live in a dry climate where you'll have to be irrigating extensively, you might want to invest in a more sophisticated irrigation system. Buy from a company that offers professional help to determine how much water you need to apply at any location. In sandy soils, irrigation water will sink deep without much spread, so you need to have more flow and more emitters to wet the soil uniformly. In clay loams, water will stay shallower and spread more widely; you'll need fewer emitters and lower water volume. The company you choose to install the system should work with you to develop a layout that is matched to your particular watering needs.

### Young Plants Need More Moisture

Be especially alert to soil moisture levels around new fruiting plants for the year after planting. When the weather is dry, you need to soak the planting area often (although not deeply) to keep the soil evenly moist. Once the roots begin to spread through the soil, becoming more self-sufficient, you can change to watering more deeply and infrequently. This encourages the roots to spread farther, becoming more effective and strongly anchored.

Cherries need ample moisture during fruit formation so the fruits can swell and develop normally.

Established citrus trees usually don't need much pruning; trim back long branches in early spring to shape the plant.

## Pruning Primer

Pruning is probably the most intimidating part of fruit tree care for any novice fruit grower. It does take some practice, and you likely will make a few mistakes when you start out. Fortunately, plants are very forgiving, so a few mistakes are rarely fatal.

There are three keys to successful pruning: having the right tools, knowing when to prune, and knowing what to prune.

### Choosing Pruning Tools

A few good tools will make your pruning sessions go much easier. Here's a basic collection of tools you'll need to maintain your fruiting trees, shrubs, and vines, along with some tips on how to use them.

**Hand Pruners** Hand pruners (also called pruning shears) are a must for every fruit grower. Use them for cutting small twigs less than about 1/2 inch (12 mm) in diameter. Choose the "bypass" kind, with two curved blades that cut like scissors; they cut more cleanly than the straight-edged blade-and-anvil types. If you have thorny blackberries, raspberries, or gooseberries, look for cut-and-hold bypass shears that hang onto the trimmings so they're easy to pull out.

bypass pruners

**Loppers** Loppers are basically hand pruners with very long handles. They are useful for cutting stems up to about 1 inch (2.5 cm) in diameter, depending on the model you buy. The long handles make pruning thorny-stemmed plants much more pleasant, since your hands will be farther away from the thorns. Loppers are also handy for cutting out the old canes of fruit-bearing bushes, such as blueberries and currants.

saw and loppers

**Pruning Saws** If you need to cut a branch larger than 1 inch (2.5 cm) in diameter, a pruning saw is the tool of choice. A narrow blade will simplify cutting branches in tight spaces.

**Pole Pruners** While not a necessary tool, pole pruners can be handy if you need to prune branches farther than your normal reach. These pruners usually have either shear-type cutting blades or a saw blade (or sometimes both) on a 4- to 6-foot (1.2 to 1.8 m) long pole. Always use care with these tools: Keep them

Pruning shears are the tool of choice for trimming stems less than 1/2 inch (12 mm) in diameter.

Loppers have long handles that extend your reach. They can cut branches up to 1 inch (2.5 cm) in diameter.

Late winter and early spring is the time to prune if you want to promote vigorous new growth.

Summer is a good time to thin out crowded stems and sucker growth, since the plants are less likely to resprout.

away from power lines, and don't cut branches directly over your head. If there are branches that are still out of your reach with a pole pruner, play it safe and hire a professional to do the work for you.

## Deciding When to Prune

The best time of year to prune depends on the results you want to get from your efforts.

**Late-winter and Early-spring Pruning** Pruning dormant (not actively growing) plants in late winter or early spring encourages new growth. This is a plus on young trees, where you want to promote branching and vigorous growth. It's also a good time for cutting out old stems on bush fruits, such as blueberries, to make room for new growth. Another advantage of

dormant pruning is that it's easy to see what you're doing, since there aren't any leaves in the way.

**Summer Pruning** Summer is an ideal time to thin out crowded growth on older trees, improving air circulation and light penetration to reduce disease problems and promote better ripening. The plants will resprout much less vigorously, so there's less chance of ending up with lots of unwanted sucker growth. Pruning during dry summer weather also decreases the

pruning saw

spread of disease-causing fungi and bacteria—a real plus on disease-susceptible fruits such as apricots.

Just one caution—stop summer pruning at least

## Removing Large Branches

Make a cut halfway through from underneath, about 1 foot (30 cm) from the trunk.

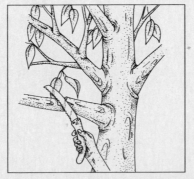

Make the next cut from above, about 1 inch (2.5 cm) farther out; the branch will break.

Finish with a clean, straight cut just outside the branch base (collar).

Pruning fruiting plants carefully when they are young will promote high yields later on.

2 months before the first fall frost to give tender new growth that emerges after pruning a chance to harden off before winter. Otherwise, cold winter temperatures may kill off the new shoots, leaving you with lots of dead wood to prune out. (You can, by the way, safely prune out dead wood and damaged branches any time of year.)

### Making the Right Pruning Cuts

Each pruning cut you make affects the plant differently and helps you direct its growth. With just two different kinds of cuts, you can shape practically any fruiting plant to your heart's content. Once you understand these two types of cuts, you're well on your way to pruning success. (For specific information on using these cuts to shape and maintain fruit trees, nut trees, small fruits, and fruiting vines, see the discussions of individual fruit crops in later chapters.)

**Thinning Cuts** A thinning cut removes a branch where it arises from another branch, the trunk, or the ground. Use thinning cuts to shorten overly long branches, clear out crowded growth, remove a branch that crosses or rubs another, or take out dead and diseased wood. Thinning cuts are especially valuable for rejuvenating older, overgrown fruit trees, where you want to remove a number of smaller branches and suckers and leave the larger branches.

To thin an overly long or poorly placed branch, cut it back to the ground, to a side branch, or to a shoot that's aimed in an uncrowded or desired direction. If you cut back to another branch or to the trunk, make the cut outside the slanted branch collar that forms a small swelling at the base of the branch.

**Heading Cuts** Heading cuts remove shoot tips, encouraging buds farther back on the stem to sprout. You can choose the best new shoots to become main branches on a young tree or to provide productive new fruit-bearing growth on older trees (especially peaches and nectarines).

In most cases, it's best to make a heading cut just above an outward-facing bud to promote outward growth and avoid leaving a stub.

Thinning cuts keep a plant open to air and sun.

# Easing into Espalier

One of the most interesting ways to use your pruning skills is to make espaliers—fruit trees shaped into fanciful two-dimensional patterns to set against a wall or train on a trellis. Espaliered trees tend to produce fewer but larger brightly colored fruit—a real treat for the eyes and the appetite.

Espaliered trees take time to train and maintain. You'll have to shape them carefully, choosing the best main branches and manipulating them into the right position. Then you'll have to thin out side growth and errant shoots to maintain the purity of the pattern you've established. The stunning results, however, more than repay the extra work.

## Picking the Plants

Espalier training works best with dwarf fruit trees, which naturally tend to be less vigorous than full-sized trees. (This is a plus, since less vigor means less pruning!) Trees that bear their fruit on short stem "spurs"—such as pears and many apples—are ideal. Those that bear their fruit near the stem tips, such as peaches and plums, are more challenging, since you have to balance the plant's need for new fruiting stems with your need to maintain the pattern.

## Picking the Pattern

While the options for shaping espalier are really only limited by your imagination, here are a few traditional favorite patterns to inspire you.

**Belgian Fence** For a long wall of diagonally intercrossing fruit trees, try a Belgian fence espalier. Use all one kind of fruit tree for a very formal look, or plant several kinds for a variety of different flowers and fruits. For details on how to make a Belgian fence, see "Grow a Living Apple Fence" on page 84.

**Fan Espalier** For a less formal look, consider a fan espalier, with branches that radiate out from the top of a short trunk. This type of pattern is especially good for peaches. For complete instructions, see "Training a Fan-shaped Espalier" on page 95.

**Palmette Verrier** For a formal-looking espalier, try

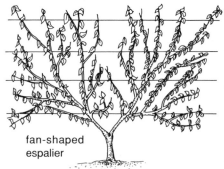
fan-shaped espalier

training a dwarf apple or pear tree in a four-armed, U-shaped pattern known as palmette verrier. Here's how:

1. Before planting, make a framework of wires to attach the stems

Espalier training takes patience and careful pruning, but the result is a unique and beautiful addition to any yard.

to. String the wires between eyebolts screwed into the wall or between sturdy posts set just in front of the wall. Make the first horizontal wire about 18 inches (45 cm) above the ground, and string additional wires every 18 inches (45 cm) above that.

2. Plant your young tree about 8 inches (20 cm) away from the wall. Cut off the top of the tree about 4 inches (10 cm) below the first wire.

3. During late winter or early spring the following year, select three of the new shoots and prune out the rest.

4. Train the center shoot upward to form the next tier of branches. The remaining two shoots will form the lower "arms." Tie them to bamboo canes, and

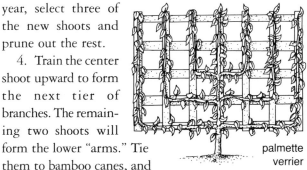
palmette verrier

tie the canes to the wire trellis. Over the growing season, gradually change the position of the canes until the branches are growing horizontally, away from the trunk.

5. During the next dormant pruning, cut off the top of the center shoot, just below the next wire. Remove the side branches from the bamboo canes and fasten them directly to the bottom wire. Attach the canes vertically to the trellis at the tips of the "arms," and start training the tips upward.

6. The next dormant season, train the upper "arms" as explained in Step 4. Continue training the bottom shoot tips upward.

7. In following years, train the tips of the upper "arms" upward, as explained in Step 5. When the vertical shoots reach the top of the trellis, cut them off. Trim the sideshoots as needed so you can see the pattern.

## Harvesting and Storing Fruit

There's nothing like the thrill of picking and eating fresh, homegrown fruit that's still warm from the sun. Get the reward you deserve from your fruiting plants by picking produce at just the right time and storing the surplus to maintain the flavor as long as possible.

### Picking Pointers

Pick fruit in the cool of the morning—just after the dew dries—and store it in a cold place right away. Harvest perishable fruit, such as berries and cherries, every day or two as new fruit ripens. Discard any rotten fruit you find so it won't infect the rest. You can harvest less perishable fruit, such as apples and pears, once or twice a week.

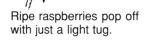

Gather fruit gently to avoid damaging it; cuts and bruises can greatly reduce storage time. When harvesting large fruit, put one hand beneath the fruit to support it. With the other hand, gently work the stem free from the plant. Place the fruit in a soft bag or a bucket, preferably one you can suspend from your shoulder or belt. Empty the bag or bucket frequently when collecting soft fruits,

Ripe raspberries pop off with just a light tug.

such as peaches and raspberries, so the weight won't damage fruit on the bottom of the container. You can gather dropped fruit from the ground, but use it immediately.

As you pick, make sure you keep your safety in mind. Get a sturdy, no-tip ladder if you need to climb up into fruit or nut trees. Or, better yet, check garden-

Ripe figs are soft and tend to be slightly flexible at the stem end; sometimes the skin splits.

supply catalogs for a long-handled fruit picker—basically a small wire basket with curved "fingers" that pull off the fruit and let it drop into the basket. The long handle lets you pick from the safety of the ground.

Wear leather gloves when harvesting from thorny-stemmed plants, such as raspberries, blackberries, and gooseberries. Gloves are also an excellent precaution when picking up dropped fruit, which is a favorite feeding spot for yellow jackets and other insects.

### Storing Your Bounty

Most fruit, nut, and berry plants will produce more fruit than you'll be able to eat right away. If you store

Taste-test a few gooseberries before harvesting; it can be tricky to tell if they're ripe by looks alone.

Ripe peaches and nectarines are quite soft, so handle them gently to avoid bruising the tender flesh.

Berries and other soft fruits don't last long; eat them right away, refrigerate them for a few days, or preserve them.

the produce properly, you can enjoy it over a long period without letting any go to waste.

If you grow grapefruit or persimmons, you can leave them on the plant for weeks in cool weather, harvesting as you need them. Most other fruits require cold storage. The ideal is 32°F (0°C) and 90 percent relative humidity. Under these conditions, late apples and pears will store for months, especially if you wrap them in oiled paper or newspaper or nestle them in shredded paper.

You can make a special fruit storage area in a cold, damp root cellar. Or keep fruit in a second refrigerator with the temperature set low and an open pan of water to raise the humidity.

Perishable berries and soft fruit (such as peaches, cherries, and plums) will only last for a few days in cold storage. An ordinary refrigerator is fine for keeping them. Eat them up as soon as possible and freeze, can, or make preserves out of the extra. Wash berries just before use, not before refrigeration.

After harvesting nuts, keep them dry and cool. Stomp on or thrash the nuts to remove the hulls, husks, or burs. Dry all nuts except chestnuts until the shells are crackling dry. Pop chestnuts and any other hulled nuts into the freezer. Store dry nuts at about 70 percent humidity and 35° to 40°F (2° to 4°C); in warmer temperatures or they can become rancid.

## Clues to Fruit Ripeness

It's important to know how to tell when fruit is ripe, so you can harvest it at its prime. Most fruit is ready when the skin changes to its ripe color and the fruit becomes soft, sweet, and easy to pluck from the plant. A few exceptions are listed below.

- **Apples:** Pick when the fruit is firm but fully colored and the seeds are brown. Take one apple and try it for flavor and seed color before picking them all. Leave the stem on for storage.
- **Blueberries:** Let the berries turn blue, then wait a few days—or for rabbiteye blueberries, a week or two—until the fruit is sweet and comes off easily.
- **Cherries:** Harvest cherries when they're fully colored. Sweet cherries should taste sweet and juicy. Pick tart cherries when they're still firm for cooking, or let them soften on the tree for fresh eating. If rain threatens when cherries are nearly ripe, pick them all to prevent cracking.
- **Citrus:** No matter what the skin color is, evaluate fruit flavor and harvest when it's sweet enough to your taste.
- **Gooseberries:** Berries will remain firm even when ripe, so go by the color to judge picking time.
- **Grapes:** Pick when the fruit turns to its ripe color and is flavorful but still firm.
- **Nuts:** Collect nuts once they've fallen to the ground.
- **Pears:** Pick European pears slightly underripe, when the pores on the fruit surface change from white to brown. The pear will be rounded with waxy skin and brown seeds. Let it finish ripening at room temperature. Allow Asian pears to ripen on the tree until they are sweet but still crisp.

# Making More Plants

Once you've enjoyed your first fruit harvest, chances are good that you'll get the urge to grow more and more. To expand your plantings without depleting your budget, you can propagate a virtually unlimited supply of new plants from your existing stock.

Just one word of caution: Always propagate only from healthy plants. If you start new plants from infected ones, you'll end up with lots of disease-damaged stock—a rather pointless effort!

## Growing from Seed

When you start fruiting plants from seed, you never know what you'll get. Seed will produce offspring of varying quality, most of which will not be as good as the cultivar parents. In most cases, you'll get the best results by sticking with cuttings, layering, division, or grafting—techniques that will produce plants with the same qualities as their parent.

Of course, there are always exceptions. For instance, seed is a great way to start alpine strawberries. You can find good cultivars in most mail-order seed catalogs.

Sow seed indoors in early spring; it germinates quickly at 60°F (16°C) in moist, well-drained, seed-starting mix. Grow the seedlings in bright light, then transplant them outdoors in spring after frosts pass. The young plants will produce fruit the first year.

Another reason you might want to grow from seed is to have rootstocks for grafting. (When you graft part of one plant onto another, the top part is called the scion and the bottom part—the part with the roots—is called the rootstock.) For fruit trees, it's probably better to buy rootstocks that have been selected for specific characteristics, such as dwarfing or disease tolerance. But for grafting nut trees, homegrown rootstocks work fine. Start with large, heavy, and healthy nuts that have uncracked shells. Enclose them in a resealable plastic bag with dampened perlite or peat moss. Label the bag with plant name and date, then toss it into the refrigerator for a couple of months until you see roots beginning to emerge from the nuts. Plant the nuts on their side in the site where you want them to grow or in a nursery bed. Cover them lightly with soil. If you grow the plants in a nursery bed, dig them up and replant them several times while they are young to make the tap root branch out into a more versatile fibrous root system.

## Do-it-yourself Grafting

Walnuts, pecans, and almonds bear fruit sooner when a piece of a desirable cultivar (called a scion) is grafted onto an established rootstock. (See "Growing from Seed" for details on growing your own rootstocks.) If you want to experiment with your own grafting, here are basic instructions for a simple splice graft:

1. Gather scions from shoots in early spring, when the temperature has been above freezing for 2 days. Store the cut scions in a plastic bag at just-above-freezing temperatures until spring.

2. As your rootstocks begin to grow, choose a rootstock and 4- to 6-inch (10 to 15 cm) scion piece that are the same diameter, and make a matching sloping cut on each.

3. Match up the inner bark areas of both cut sections and bind the rootstock and scion together with ties or grafting tape.

4. Once the scion begins to grow, cut off any shoots that arise from the rootstock.

Make a matching sloping cut on the scion and the rootstock.

Match the cuts and secure the area with ties or grafting tape.

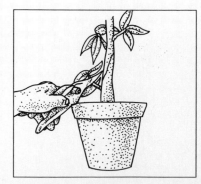

Remove any shoots that sprout below the graft union.

Layer strawberries by pinning a runner into a sunken pot. When the plantlet has rooted, clip it from the parent.

## Layering

Layering is an easy way to propagate small quantities of some fruit- and nut-bearing plants. Filberts, trailing blackberries, muscadine grapes, and lowbush blueberries will sprout roots if you bury a portion of a young stem in the soil.

In spring or fall, stretch a healthy, flexible branch down to the ground. Remove the leaves from the part of the stem along the ground, and make a small nick in the bark on the side touching the soil. Cover the portion of the stem with about 2 inches (5 cm) of soil (and weight the whole thing down with a brick or stone, if necessary). Leave 10 to 18 inches (25 to 40 cm) of leafy branch tip exposed; it'll be the top of your new plant. Depending on the species, the buried stem will take several months to several years to root. Cut the rooted stem from the parent plant, and transplant it to where you want it to grow.

You also can layer many brambles, including black raspberries and boysenberries, by bending down the long canes and burying the tips in the soil. The tips will sprout new shoots that should be ready to cut free and move the following spring.

## Dividing

Upright blackberries and raspberries spread on creeping roots. It's a snap to dig up any of the spreading roots in spring and move the sprout to a new location. Cut the top growth back by half to ease the transition. Strawberries are even easier to divide. Just cut off and move the rooted plantlets.

## Taking Cuttings

Taking cuttings is a common propagation technique that's used for many kinds of shrubby and vining fruiting plants. You can take either hardwood or softwood cuttings, depending on what kind of plant you're dealing with.

**Hardwood Cuttings**  You can take hardwood cuttings from firm, dormant (nongrowing) stems of currants, figs, and quinces. Cuttings also work for nongrafted grapes. Cut 8- to 10-inch (20 to 25 cm) pieces of healthy growth from low sideshoots in winter. Cut off an inch or two from the tip, and make a diagonal cut at the bottom so you'll know which end is up. Bundle cuttings from the same plant together, label them, and bury them (with the tops up) outdoors in a trench of moist sand. When the weather has warmed up in spring, dig up the cuttings and bury the bottom half in good garden soil. The cuttings should start growing and rooting in about a month. Move them to their final growing spot the following spring.

**Softwood Cuttings**  Softwood cuttings are easy to take from any bush fruit in early summer. Cut off quickly growing shoot tips, making the pieces 4 to 6 inches (10 to 15 cm) long with at least two sets of leaves. Remove the lower leaves from each stem, and insert the bottom half of the stems into pots filled with moist sand or a moistened mixture of half perlite and half vermiculite. (Perlite and vermiculite are available in garden centers.) Cover the pots with clear plastic (support the plastic with small stakes to keep it from resting on the cuttings) and set them in a spot with bright but indirect light. Water as needed to keep the soil evenly moist. The cuttings should begin to send up new growth in about a month. Transplant them into individual pots when they are well rooted.

## Grafting

Grafting part of one plant onto the stem and roots of another is a challenging but rewarding skill to develop. It is the method of choice for propagating most kinds of fruit and nut trees. Grafting generally works best between closely related plants (between peaches and peaches or peaches and apricots, for instance). For detailed information on this exciting technique, see "Do-it-yourself Grafting."

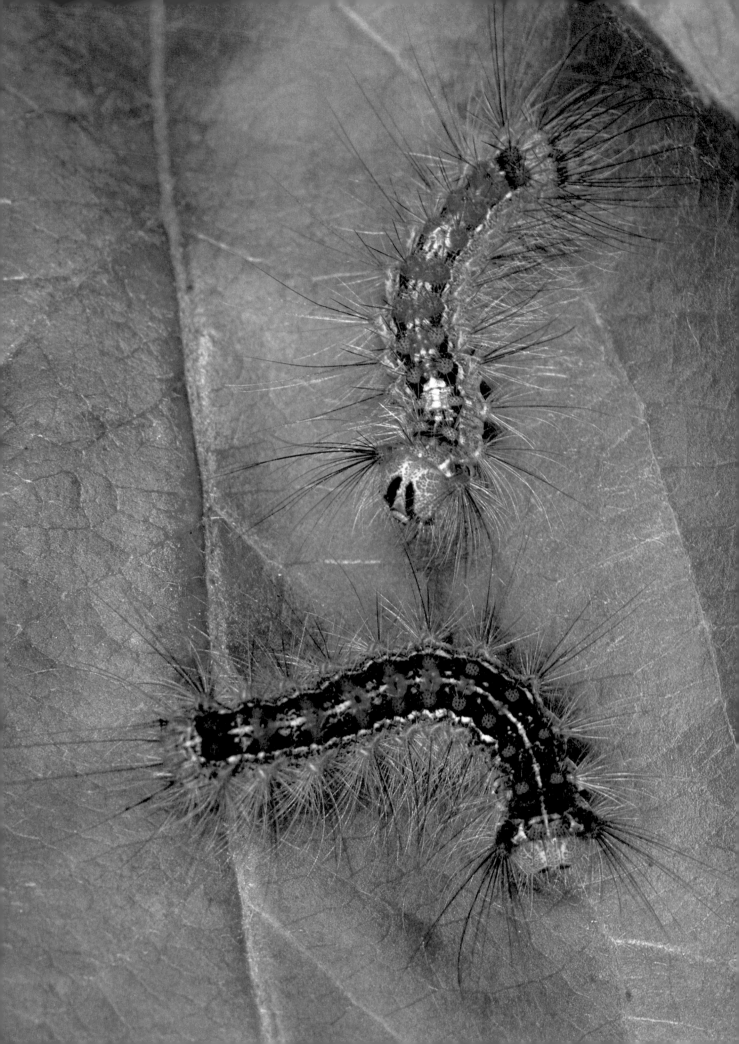

# DEALING WITH FRUIT
# PESTS AND DISEASES

The shiny perfect apples and spotless peaches you find at the grocery store can be enticing—until you think about all the chemical sprays that went into producing them. When you grow fruit at home, you can skip the dangerous chemicals and grow fruit organically. Your harvest may not be perfect and blemish-free, but you're sure to get plenty of good fruit for your efforts.

Growing fruit organically is easiest with berries and disease-resistant cultivars of apples. Once you can handle those, you can move on to more difficult fruit crops with confidence. With all fruit and nut crops, growing a high-quality harvest starts well before planting, with choosing the right kinds for your conditions and preparing a good planting site. After planting, there are other steps you can take to stop pest and disease problems before they start. "Preventing Pests and Diseases" on page 68 offers complete details on choosing disease-resistant cultivars, using traps to monitor pests and lure them away from crops and encouraging beneficial insects to control the pests for you.

Sometimes, however, pests and diseases can sneak past even the best defenses. If problem signs and symptoms appear, follow the suggestions in "Managing Minor Problems" on page 70. You'll find tips for using traps to control pests and pruning cuts to discourage diseases. Other tactics covered include releasing beneficial insects (to supplement those already living in your garden) and using beneficial microorganisms to counteract plant-attacking pests.

If the pests or diseases are still damaging your plants after you try these nontoxic techniques, you have a choice to make: Either give up or get out the last-resort controls. Giving up may be the best (or the only) option if the problem has seriously weakened the plant or if there is no way to cope with the problem (as with plant-attacking viruses). But if you want to try to save your crop from insects, fungi, and bacteria, you do have some controls to try, including insecticidal soap, horticultural oil, botanical pesticides, sulfur, and copper. In "Handling Serious Problems" on page 74, you'll learn when and how to use these options safely and effectively.

As you watch your healthy, bountiful fruit crops ripening in the sun, don't forget that you're not alone—hungry birds, mice, and other wildlife may be ready to race you for dinner. "Coping with Animal Pests" on page 76 is loaded with tips for protecting your produce so you can keep your harvest for yourself.

Just like any garden plants, fruiting trees, bushes, and vines can be attacked by insects, diseases, and animal pests. Stack the odds in your favor by growing resistant cultivars, which are less prone to damage.

Aphids may cause reddish blisters on currant leaves. Encouraging beneficial insects can minimize aphid problems.

## Preventing Pests and Diseases

Stopping pests and diseases before they start is the key to easy fruit growing. When you learn how to work with nature—by choosing naturally problem-resistant plants, encouraging beneficial insects to control pests for you, and keeping the garden clean—you can look forward to a largely trouble-free fruit garden.

### Choose Resistant Cultivars

Plants that naturally resist infection by diseases and attack by insects are the stars of an organic fruit garden. With them, you don't have to worry about what to spray; you head off trouble before it begins. If you know your soil is on the clayey side, for instance, you could plant cherries that are grafted on 'Stockton Morello' roots, which are less susceptible to root rot. These "designer" plants allow you to grow high-quality harvests without hassling with common problems.

It's important to remember that a cultivar described as "disease-resistant" will not resist all the possible diseases that could attack. Usually, that phrase means that the plant resists one or more of the most serious problems. To get the right plant for your conditions, you first need to know which problems are most prevalent in your area. (You can find this out from other fruit growers in your area or from your local Cooperative Extension Service office.) Then you can read catalog descriptions to find cultivars that resist those specific problems.

### Try Monitoring Traps

Another part of problem prevention is knowing which pests are present. If you know that aphids are around, for instance, you can keep a close eye out for any signs of damage and be prepared to control the pests before they get out of hand.

Using monitoring traps is an easy way to keep an eye on pest populations. Check them every few days for signs of pests. (Other insects may get stuck, too, so don't assume that they're all pests.) Here are some traps that work for common fruit-attacking insects. The "Apples" entry, which starts on page 80, also has specific information on a trap for plum curculios, a common fruit pest.

**Apple Maggot Traps** Catch apple maggots and cherry fruit flies by hanging a red ball covered with sticky coating in your fruit trees. Leave the trap out from early summer until frost. When the adult flies stop to feed on the fake apple, they will stick to it. Buy already-made traps through garden-supply catalogs, or make your own by smearing an apple-sized red ball with sticky coating. (Purchase commercial sticky coating, or mix equal parts

Round, red sticky traps are useful for catching apple maggots.

of petroleum jelly or mineral oil with liquid dish soap.) Hang one trap in a small planting to monitor pest numbers. Renew the sticky coating as needed.

**Colored Sticky Traps** White plastic rectangles covered with sticky coating (as explained previously) can attract tarnished plant bugs and flea beetles. Hang the traps about 3 feet (90 cm) above the ground from early spring until the flowers open. Take down the

Mulches provide a cool, moist hiding place for slugs and snails. If these pests become a problem, remove the mulch.

traps when plants start to flower; otherwise, the traps may catch beneficial pollinating insects as well.

Yellow sticky traps can catch aphids, pear psyllas, whiteflies, leafhoppers, and young apple maggot flies, which get stuck when they investigate. If you need to keep an eye on thrips, try blue sticky traps. Leave the traps out all season. One or two colored traps should be fine for a few trees.

**Pheromone Lure Traps** Insects communicate with others in the same species by releasing chemicals called pheromones. You can take advantage of this by using synthetically produced pheromones to lure insects to sticky traps. Pheromone lures are available (usually through mail-order suppliers) for many common fruit-attacking pests, including peach tree borers, cherry fruit flies, gypsy moths, red-banded leaf rollers, lesser apple worms, oriental fruit moths, green fruit worms, and codling moths. These lures generally attract males of whatever species you bought the lure for.

Set out the traps a few weeks before plant growth begins. One trap for each of your common pests is usually fine for a home fruit planting. It's smart to hang the traps in landscape plants that aren't attacked by whatever pest you're trying to trap; otherwise, you may actually help the pests find your fruit trees! If you find many males in your trap, there are probably lots of egg-laying females around, so watch your plants for damage and take control measures if necessary.

## Encourage Beneficial Insects

In an organic garden, you can count on problem-preventing help from beneficial insects. Beneficial insects are those that attack pest insects. Some beneficial insects—including praying mantises and lady beetles—feed directly on other pests, taking

Pheromone lures entice pests away from plants and into the trap, where they're caught on the sticky material inside.

Reduce codling moth damage on your apples by growing dill and other plants to attract beneficial predators.

care of many problems before you even notice them. Other beneficials, such as the many tiny parasitic wasps, lay their eggs in pests; the eggs hatch into larvae, which consume and kill the pests.

You can encourage beneficial insects to hang around your garden by growing a variety of plants that provide varying kinds of shelter for them. Many beneficials feed on pollen or nectar for part of their life, so they are attracted to flowers with plenty of pollen or large clusters of small flowers. A border of daisies, dill, yarrow, parsley, catnip, sage, thyme, and other food and shelter plants will attract a bevy of beneficials to protect your fruit plantings.

To keep beneficial predators and parasites thriving, avoid spraying them with toxic chemicals. Even organic pesticides, such as pyrethrin, can harm beneficial and pest insects alike. Whenever possible, try to use less toxic controls, such as insecticidal soap. If you must spray heavy-duty controls, avoid spraying open flowers as much as possible.

## Keep the Garden Clean

General good-gardening practices will go a long way toward keeping any fruit planting healthy. Clean up fallen fruit, nuts, or leaves—especially those that drop early—since they may harbor pests or diseases. To make fall cleanup easier, rake mulch away from the base of your plants in late summer to early fall. Clean up the dropped leaves from the bare soil in late fall to early winter, then replace the mulch.

## Managing Minor Problems

Proper advance planning and problem prevention tactics minimize the difficulties you'll encounter, but even the best-planned fruit garden may occasionally fall prey to problems. The specific fruit entries later in this book will give you details on dealing with the particular problems that are common for each crop. But the basic control steps outlined here will work for just about any problem, no matter what the cause or what crop it's on.

### Identify the Problem

If you don't know what's damaging your plants, the chances of choosing an effective control are slim. By keeping a close eye on your crops, you're more likely to know what your healthy plants look like, and you'll know if something looks different than usual. Every few days, take the time to look at the upper and lower surfaces of a few leaves on each plant. Also check a few fruits and flowers. Check the base of the trunk, too. During your inspection, look for anything out of the ordinary—strange colors, unusual spots or markings, or stunted, damaged, or distorted growth.

If you see any of these odd features, look around for signs of possible pests. Insects lingering in the area may or may not be the ones that actually caused the

Identifying the problem is the first step to choosing the right control. Tiny purple dots indicate cherry leaf spot.

damage; beneficial insects may have already come along to deal with the problem. Make a note of what damage you see, what part of the plant it's on, and what insects you see in the area.

Now it's time to figure out what the problem might be. Turn to the fruit entries in this book to find out which problems are likely to occur on that particular crop, what they look like, and what damage they cause. If your cherry tree leaves are yellowish with purple dots, for instance, you'd go to the "Problem Prevention and Control" section of the "Cherries" entry on page 89. There you'd find that the symptoms on your tree match those for a fungal disease called cherry leaf spot.

If you can't find a clear match between the symptoms discussed in the crop entry and the symptoms you see on your plant, it's time to get help. If you can, take a sample of the damage (along with a sample of any insects you found near the damage) to your county Cooperative Extension Service office for assistance. Some garden centers, botanical gardens, and arboreta also offer plant clinics where you can get help. Nutrient imbalances can cause symptoms similar to those caused by diseases, so you may need to have some leaves or shoots tested by a lab.

### Handpick Pests

If you know an insect is the culprit, you can take the simple and direct measure of killing the pests by

Hand picking is a fast and effective control.

> ### Know Your Enemy
> Identifying fruit pest and disease problems accurately is a key part of choosing the correct control. It's also a vital step in planning an effective prevention program to minimize problems in the future.
>
> Once you know what's causing the damage, you can learn more about it. Find out where the pest hides during winter, so you can clean up those places and destroy the dormant spores or insects that otherwise would attack again next year. Learn when your plants are susceptible to problem attack and when in their life cycle pests or diseases are easy to control. Gather the control supplies you need in advance, and note on your calendar when you need to apply them. That way you can head off common pests and diseases before they damage your fruit crop.

Some problems are so common that they're easy to identify. Gooseberries, for instance, often get powdery mildew.

Pruning out crowded stems to keep plants open to light and air will minimize fungal diseases, such as rust.

hand. (It's okay to wear gloves if you're squeamish!) This approach is really only practical when all—or at least most—of the plant is within your reach. But when you can easily reach the leaves and stems, handpicking is a fast and effective way to immediately reduce pest damage each time you inspect your plants. Pick off large, slow-moving pests such as caterpillars and drop them in a bucket of soapy water. (When the pests are dead, dump them on your compost pile.) Crush small pests and egg masses with your fingers.

## Prevent Disease Spread with Pruning

When disease is the problem you're dealing with, pinching and pruning can be your first line of defense. If you notice disease symptoms—such as spots or discolorations—starting to develop on a few leaves, pinch off the infected leaves right away and dispose of them. Sometimes this is enough to stop further spread of the disease. Keep a close eye on the remaining leaves, though, and consider taking more serious control measures if more symptoms develop.

You can stop the spread of some serious diseases, such as fire blight and crown gall, by actually pruning off infected areas. "Fighting Fire Blight" on page 73

Nutrient deficiencies often look like diseases; have some leaves tested if you suspect a nutrient imbalance.

Thinning out crowded growth allows better air circulation and discourages diseases such as botrytis (gray mold).

If a few shoots show aphid damage, you could crush the pests with your fingers; serious infestations need spraying.

BT sprays help control caterpillar damage, but apply them carefully; they kill desirable species as well as pests.

has more details on pruning to control that bacterial disease. If crown gall causes knobbly, swollen growths on plant stems, pruning out infected stems as soon as you spot them may reduce the spread of this disease. To sanitize pruning shears when working around diseased plants, soak a rag in a 10 percent bleach solution (1 part chlorine bleach in 9 parts water) and use it to wipe the blades between cuts. On any fruiting plant, you can reduce diseases by thinning out crowded stems and branches to increase air circulation and sun penetration. This helps wet foliage dry fast and makes disease development less likely.

## Try Trapping Pests

The same sticky traps you use to monitor pest populations (as explained in "Try Monitoring Traps" on page 68) can be effective at reducing pest damage. The trick is to put out more of each trap so you catch as many of the pests as possible. For example, hang two apple maggot traps for each large tree or one trap for each dwarf tree to minimize damage from apple maggots and cherry fruit flies. Put one or more yellow sticky traps for each 25 square feet (2.25 sq m) of fruiting plants to control aphids, whiteflies, and leafhoppers.

Replace sticky traps when they get full to keep them effective.

Use sticky trunk wraps (one per tree) to surround tree trunks and capture ants (which carry aphids), snails, or gypsy moth and codling moth caterpillars as they climb toward the leaves.

To attract more pests to the traps, use pheromone lures or make your own bait. You can attract apple maggot adults, codling moths, and oriental fruit moths with a solution of 1 part molasses in 9 parts water and a little yeast. Pour the solution into cans and hang them on sunlit parts of each tree, about 5 feet (1.5 m) above the ground. After each rain, dump the can contents on your compost pile, then refill the cans. To lure cherry fruit flies to a yellow sticky trap, hang a small, screen-covered jar below the trap. Fill the jar with a mixture of equal parts of ammonia and water.

You can entice slugs that are damaging small fruit plants to take a swim in a beer trap. Sink a plastic margarine tub in the soil so the top is level with the soil surface. Fill it with 1 inch (2.5 cm) or more of beer. Check traps daily and remove pests; refill traps every few weeks or after each rain.

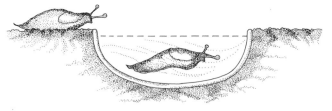

Trap slugs and snails by sinking shallow dishes of beer into the soil. Check the traps daily and remove any pests.

## Fighting Fire Blight

One of the worst problems that can attack apples and pears is called fire blight. This bacterial disease attacks succulent young shoots, often while they are blooming. Infected shoots wilt from the tip downward and turn black, with the tip shriveled into a hook shape. The bacteria spread downward, eventually forming dark, sunken cankers on branches. These cankers may kill the branch outright or just provide an overwintering spot for the bacteria.

Once fire blight gets started, it's hard to control. Your best bet is prevention. Since tender new growth is an easy target for infection, take steps to discourage lots of soft shoots. Avoid using high-nitrogen fertilizers around susceptible trees. And prune only lightly in winter; heavy pruning may promote a mass of soft regrowth in spring. If fire blight is common in your area, you may want to try preventive sprays of streptomycin. Start just as the blooms open, and spray again every 4 days while the blooms are open. Then spray every 5 to 7 days until the tiny fruits appear.

If you do notice fire blight damage in summer, cut it out using the "ugly stub" method developed at the University of Maryland. In the past, the standard advice was to cut off the canker along with at least 1 foot (30 cm) of healthy branch tissue. However, recent research has shown that the fire blight bacteria can exist in seemingly healthy parts of a branch. If you make a cut, the remaining bacteria may just form a new canker at the surface of the cut. Sometimes the canker will be so small it resembles dried bark, but it will be there, says Paul Steiner, of the University of Maryland. And it will reinfect more plants.

So instead of making a nice, neat cut, cut back infected branches to leave an ugly, 4- to 5-inch (10 to 12.5 cm) long stub. Remove the stub during regular dormant season pruning, when it's too cold for a new canker to develop. By spring, new growth seems to seal off the cut so infection is no longer a problem.

No apples or pears are immune to fire blight, but some cultivars and rootstocks are less susceptible than others.

## Consider Biological Controls

If the beneficial insects in your garden aren't keeping up with the pests, you can buy and release more beneficials to help out. Many organic gardening–supply catalogs now sell beneficial insects. Read the catalog descriptions, and buy the insects that are appropriate for your problems. Order the beneficials as soon as you spot a problem developing, so they'll have a chance to do their job before pests cause serious damage. (In fact, if you know a certain pest is a problem every year, it's smart to place your order ahead of time, so your beneficials will arrive at the ideal time for your needs.) For more information on attracting and protecting these helpful creatures, see "Encourage Beneficial Insects" on page 69.

Beneficial microorganisms aren't as visible as beneficial insects, but they can do an equally good job at minimizing pest problems. *Bacillus thuringiensis*—commonly known as BT—is a bacterial control that works against several kinds of insects. One kind, called BTK (*B. thuringiensis* var. *kurstaki*), affects many kinds of leaf-feeding caterpillars. When caterpillars eat leaves coated with BTK, they stop feeding within a day and die a few days after. Apply BTK according to package directions. It will not harm most beneficials, but it can kill butterfly larvae, so only spray it on plants that you know are infested by pests.

# Handling Serious Problems

If you've done all you can to keep your plants healthy but the problems still keep coming, you may choose to take a stand with spray gun in hand. Sprays are generally considered only as a last resort, since they can wipe out beneficial insects as well as pests. Some can also be harmful to you if you don't apply them carefully, so always read and follow all safety directions on the package before using any spray or dust.

## Controlling Pests

A number of organic products can help you control pests in your fruit garden. Here are some of the best.

**Insecticidal Soaps**  Most insecticidal soaps will kill soft-bodied insects such as aphids, mites, and leafhoppers without much damage to beneficial insects. Mix commercial soaps as directed on the label with "soft" water (water that is low in calcium, such as rainwater or water that has been treated in a home water softener). Or make your own soap spray with 1 teaspoon of pure liquid dish soap (not detergent or soap with additives) in 2 quarts (2 l) of water.

**Horticultural Oils**  Refined petroleum oils can be very useful for controlling difficult pests. They work by smothering and killing pests and their eggs. Products labeled as "dormant" oil are only suitable for spraying in winter to kill over-wintering insects. The newer, more-refined oils contain fewer impurities and are less likely to damage plants, so you can apply them at any time. During the growing season, use them to control aphids, immature bugs, mites, scale, pear psylla, and other pests. Buy commercial brands and apply according to package directions, or make your own oil spray with 2 tablespoons of vegetable oil, $^1/_2$ teaspoon of

It's smart to wear protective clothing while using any kind of pest- or disease-control sprays.

Sulfur sprays from spring through midsummer can help prevent apple scab from ruining your crop.

liquid soap, and 2 quarts (2 l) of water. Oil sprays react badly if mixed with sulfur sprays, so if you apply one, wait for at least 30 days to apply the other.

**Botanical Pesticides**  Some plants produce protective compounds that organic gardeners can use to kill pests. These compounds, called botanical pesticides, hit problem pests hard and then break down quickly. Neemix, one formulation of a botanical insecticide extracted from seeds of the neem tree, is a repellent that also disrupts insect growth. It is approved for use on citrus, apples, pears, peaches, plums, and some other fruits. It's effective and fairly gentle on beneficial insects. If necessary, you can also use pyrethrin, which is effective against a wide range of pests.

Before applying any botanical pesticide, check the label to make sure the product is suitable for the pest you want to control. Read the application instructions carefully, and apply the product according to the suggested rates. To protect yourself while spraying, wear rubber gloves, rubber boots, long pants, a long-sleeved shirt, a hat, goggles, and a respirator to avoid contacting or inhaling the product. Spray on a calm day, and keep children and pets out of the way. Check the product label for the "reentry time": the length of time you should stay out of the area after spraying. To minimize damage to beneficial insects, spray only plants that you know have pest problems.

## Controlling Diseases

Handling diseases organically is more a matter of prevention than control. Most organic sprays can't actually cure a plant of a disease; they usually just discourage existing infections from spreading to other parts of the same plant or to other plants.

Part of coping with diseases effectively is spotting the symptoms early so you can apply controls to stop the spread. The other secret is keeping track of problems your plants have had in the past so you can try preventive sprays. (Remembering past problems will also remind you to buy disease-resistant cultivars next time you go plant shopping!)

Here are some of the products that are available for organic disease control. As you would when handling botanical pesticides, always read and follow the label directions on these products carefully to avoid harming yourself or your plants.

**Sulfur** This commonly used organic fungicide protects against apple scab, powdery mildew, brown rot, mites, rust, and scab. There are many formulations, but flowable or wettable sulfur (a type that mixes easily with water) is generally the most effective. When sprayed, the protective layer of sulfur only lasts for about 7 to 10 days; reapply often while diseases are actively spreading. Keep sulfur sprays off the soil, and never use them on 'Concord' or other sulfur-sensitive grapes. Always wait for at least 30 days between applications of sulfur sprays and oil sprays. Don't apply sulfur when temperatures are over 80°F (27°C).

**Lime-sulfur** Adding lime to sulfur increases its fungus-killing ability. Lime-sulfur is so strong that it may even kill disease spores that have already started

If gray mold strikes each year, try a preventive spray of sulfur when the fruit starts to turn red.

to infect the plant. But this added power comes with a price: Lime-sulfur is more likely to damage plant tissue than plain sulfur sprays. Save it for dealing with difficult disease problems.

You can apply full-strength lime-sulfur to dormant raspberries and blackberries to control anthracnose. Use milder-strength dilutions for growing-season control of brown rot, peach leaf curl, and scab. (Follow the mixing instructions on the label for suggested rates.) Some organic-certification programs don't approve of lime-sulfur, so check with your program if you are growing fruit for sale.

**Copper** This is another highly toxic natural fungicide that can kill plants as well as prevent diseases. A milder, more suitable fungicide that uses copper is bordeaux mix, which combines copper sulfate and lime. It protects against downy mildew, leaf spot, anthracnose, fire blight, leaf blights, brown rot, and Botrytis. The safest time to apply bordeaux mix is just before plants leaf out in spring.

Before treating a whole plant with copper or bordeaux mix, test the spray on a single branch and wait a few days to make sure it doesn't cause any visible leaf or shoot damage.

Good-quality equipment will help you spray safely.

Black rot is a serious problem on grapes. Try a copper spray in early spring, followed by sulfur every week or two.

## Coping with Animal Pests

If you love the fruit you raise, think of what a treat it must be for wild animals. When the weather is hot and dry and your fruit is starting to mature and color, birds find it nearly irresistible. They'll flock out of nearby woodlands or hedgerows and start to work on the closest fruit they can find. Deer and smaller animals also get into the act. Squirrels, for instance, can be serious competitors for your nut crops. Rabbits and rodents, attracted initially to fallen fruits and nuts, may hang around to nest in mulch or tall groundcovers and chew on roots and bark during the winter.

rabbit tracks

You can use a variety of barriers and deterrents to keep these animal pests away. Some tactics will control a variety of animals; others are specifically geared toward one certain animal. Not all of these techniques are effective in all situations, so experiment to see which work best for you.

### Netting and Bagging

To keep birds and deer away from ripening fruit, cover individual fruit plants with plastic netting with ³/₄-inch (18 mm) or narrower openings. Netting is easiest to use on shrubs and dwarf trees, especially if you only have a few of them. Use clothespins to close any gaps that birds may be able to sneak through. Fasten the bottom edges to the lowest stems with twist-ties to anchor the net to the plant. When you're ready to harvest, remove the net carefully so you don't bruise the fruit or damage the plant stems. Nets are not cheap but you can reuse them for years if you take care of them.

If you have a utilitarian fruit garden or orchard, you

Protect your strawberries from birds by covering the whole patch with plastic netting.

might consider installing a permanent wire mesh cage around the most enticing fruit bushes. This is expensive and not particularly attractive, but it saves you the trouble of messing around with nets.

Another strange-looking but effective way to guard large fruits—such as peaches, apples, and grape clusters—is to enclose the ripening fruit in paper bags. Secure the top of the bag to the branch firmly but without cutting into the bark. Peek in one or two bags every day or so as harvest time approaches. Remove the bags and harvest as normal.

Enclosing grapes, peaches, apples, and other fruits in bags can help prevent animal damage during ripening.

---

### Send Animal Pests Packing

Eliminate wild animals' favorite nesting and hiding areas to encourage them to move elsewhere. Block the openings to deer trails. Eliminate piles of rocks, lumber, or other debris so rabbits and rodents won't have a ready-made hiding place. Close doors and windows tightly on little-used outdoor structures. In fall, rake mulch away from fruit plants and mow groundcovers short so they don't make attractive nesting areas for rodents. You can move the mulch back under plants in winter.

Caging your fruiting plants can help to shield them from hungry deer.

## Fencing

To keep out deer, rabbits, and rodents, install a fence around your fruit garden. An 8-foot (2.4 m) tall fence is an expensive but effective option for keeping deer out. Properly designed electric fences can also work. Talk to local gardeners or your county Cooperative Extension Service to find out which fence styles are most effective in your area.

To rabbit-proof a garden area, install a wire mesh fence with openings 1 inch (2.5 cm) wide or smaller. The fence should be at least 18 inches (45 cm) above the ground and extend 6 inches (15 cm) below the ground to prevent rabbits from tunneling under.

To keep rabbits and rodents away from the tender bark on fruit plants, wrap the trunk loosely with a strip of wire hardware cloth at least 18 inches (45 cm) tall. If you have deep snowfall in winter, make the wrap higher. (Loosen the wrap every year or two if needed to keep if from cutting into the bark.) Surround potted nut seeds and planted seedlings with wire mesh cages to keep squirrels away until the young trees start growing strong.

## Deterrents

There are many ingenious devices you can buy or make to chase birds away from ripening fruit. Dangling aluminum pie pans, iridescent bird tape, owl balloons, and hawk kites are just a few scare tactics frustrated fruit gardeners have come up with. Space these deterrents every 6 feet (1.8 m) or so for thorough coverage. Scare balloons are especially effective if allowed to swing in the wind a few feet above the tree. Moving deterrents around every few days can help to keep pests from getting used to them.

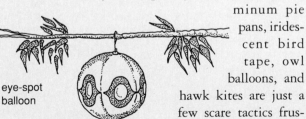

eye-spot balloon

Keep squirrels off lone nut trees by wrapping the trunk with a 2- to 3-foot (60 to 90 cm) wide sheet of slippery aluminum. (This won't work if the squirrels can climb up nearby trees and jump over to your nut tree.)

Squirrels are fond of newly planted nuts and nut seedlings. Guard your plants with wire mesh cages.

You can discourage deer and rabbits by spraying your fruiting plants with foul-scented repellents. Plan to spray them often to keep the odor strong. But don't get the spray on the fruit or you might be repelled, too! Buy commercial repellents or experiment with home remedies. A spray of a dozen eggs mixed with 5 quarts (5 l) of water is said to discourage deer. Other possible deer deterrents include bars of bath soap or mesh bags of human hair hung about 4 feet (1.2 m) above the ground. Sprinkling bloodmeal, hot sauce, or hot-pepper dust around plants may discourage small creatures from coming close to your crops. Keep in mind that deterrents may not be effective if animals are very hungry. If you can't find a deterrent that works, you may need to resort to sturdy fences to protect your fruiting plants from damage.

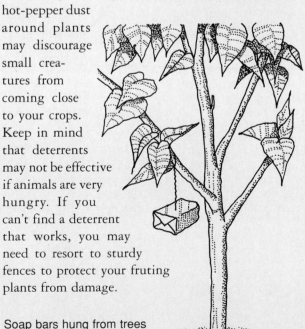

Soap bars hung from trees and bushes may deter deer from feeding there.

# FRUIT TREES

Gone are the days when you needed lots of space for trees to produce generous harvests of high-quality fruit. Today, fruit trees can be small enough to fit in any yard, making them easy to handle without a lot of special equipment. They bear fruit in a great variety of colors and flavors. Some resist diseases and are as close as fruiting plants can come to low maintenance. When carefully pruned, fruit trees are graceful and handsome—as beautiful as any strictly ornamental trees. They please us with flowers in spring, treat us with colorful fruit in summer, and make us proud of their carefully crafted shape in winter.

When you grow your own fruit, you can select cultivars with the flavors and colors of fruit you like best. You also can grow your trees organically, so you don't have to worry about eating fruit that has been repeatedly doused with synthetic chemicals. You can fertilize your trees with natural products, prevent problems by outwitting pests and diseases, and spray—as a last resort—with the mildest organic preventives.

In this chapter, you'll learn the best ways to grow the healthiest, most productive trees possible as you read about each kind of luscious fruit: apples, apricots, cherries, citrus, figs, peaches and nectarines, pears, and plums. Each entry will tell you how to handle the crop's special needs—such as pollination, spacing, and pruning—and help you choose the right cultivars for your conditions. Plus, you'll find out exactly when and how to harvest, so you can enjoy your rich reward at the peak of freshness and flavor.

Apples, cherries, and other fruit trees look great in any landscape, with prolific flowers in spring and colorful, tasty fruits later in the season. Try them in place of ornamental flowering trees.

# Apples

The old saying, "An apple a day keeps the doctor away," is just as valid today as in centuries gone by. Modern medicine confirms that the fiber in apples discourages digestive system problems and helps lower cholesterol levels. In addition, apples are packed with vitamins, minerals, and good flavor. So there are plenty of reasons to keep lots of apples around the house.

Apples are just as rewarding to grow in the garden as they are to use in the kitchen. That's partly because you have so many cultivars to choose from—over 1,000 different cultivars are available in the United States. For extra-high yields, you can choose spur-type trees, which are so heavily loaded with short fruit-bearing spur branches that they stay about 25 percent smaller than the same cultivar without spurs. You can also choose grafted trees with different combinations of rootstocks, interstems (short pieces of trunk), and tops to make just about any kind of apple tree you can imagine.

Green-skinned 'Granny Smith' is popular for its crisp, juicy, white-fleshed fruit. It lasts well in storage.

## Best Climate and Site

Apples can grow in Zones 3 to 9, but you need to pick a cultivar that's suited to your area. In warm climates, look for apples with short chill hour requirements. This is a measurement of the number of hours at 45°F (7°C) or cooler that cultivars need to be ready to start growing again in spring. For example, 'Mollies Delicious' grows well in Zones 6 to 8 and needs 400 to 500 chill hours. 'Rome Beauty' does well in the middle of the country and needs 700 to 1,000 chill hours. In very cold climates, look for extra-hardy cultivars such as 'Scott Winter' and 'Redwell', which can survive as low as −40°F (−40°C).

Apple trees need full sun. They prefer well-drained soil, although you can select different rootstocks if your soil conditions aren't ideal. Look for a site that's free from late-spring or early-fall frosts and that has free air circulation.

## Choosing Your Plants

With so many options to choose from, picking out the best apple plants can be a real adventure. Begin by identifying cultivars that are resistant to the diseases most common in your area. "Disease Resistance in Apples" gives you an overview of some common cultivars. For more specific recommendations, check nursery catalogs or ask your local Cooperative Extension Service.

Apples need pollination from a second compatible cultivar that flowers at the same time. 'William's Pride', 'Dayton', 'Freedom', and 'Redfree', for instance, flower at similar times and will pollinate each other. 'Liberty' is an early bloomer but ordinarily overlaps

---

## Disease Resistance in Apples

You can prevent many apple problems by planting only disease-resistant cultivars. Here's a sampling of some excellent apple cultivars and their relative resistance to apple scab (scab), cedar-apple rust (rust), fire blight (blight), and powdery mildew (mildew). "Res." means the plant is resistant (rarely infected); "M.res." plants are moderately resistant (seldom infected); "Susc." cultivars are susceptible (often infected); "Tol." plants are tolerant (productive despite infection).

| Name | Scab | Rust | Blight | Mildew |
|---|---|---|---|---|
| 'Dayton' | Res. | — | M.res. | M.res. |
| 'Enterprise' | Res. | Res. | Res. | M.res. |
| 'Freedom' | Res. | Res. | M.res. | M.res. |
| 'Jonafree' | Res. | Res. | M.res. | Susc. |
| 'Liberty' | Res. | Res. | Res. | Res. |
| 'Redfree' | Res. | Res. | Tol. | Tol. |
| 'Prima' | Res. | Res. | Res. | Res. |
| 'William's Pride' | Res | Res. | M.res. | M.res. |
| 'Wolf River' | Res. | Res. | Res. | Res. |

To get high yields from your apples, you'll need to grow at least two compatible cultivars for cross-pollination.

Spur-bearing apple trees tend to be more compact than tip-bearing types, making harvesting much easier.

with the others enough to be pollinated. You also can pollinate apples with crab apples, such as early- to mid-season-blooming 'Manchurian' and late-blooming 'Snowdrift'.

If you have room to plant more than two trees, look for apples that ripen at different times to extend the harvest season. Among the disease-resistant cultivars, 'Prima', 'Dayton', and 'William's Pride' are early ripening; 'Jonafree', 'Freedom', and 'Liberty' ripen in midseason; and 'Enterprise' ripens late.

If your space is limited, look into spur-bearing cultivars, which are more compact-growing forms of standard apple cultivars. They have the same great flavor as the parent plant but are 25 to 30 percent shorter. You can find spur forms of 'Red Delicious', 'Granny Smith', 'Winesap', 'McIntosh', 'Golden Delicious', and other popular cultivars.

## Planting and Care

Plant full-sized apple trees 25 to 30 feet (7.5 to 9 m) apart, semi-dwarfs 12 to 15 feet (3.6 to 4.5 m) apart, and dwarfs 6 to 8 feet (1.8 to 2.4 m) apart (or closer if you're using them for hedges or espalier).

Most dwarf and some semidwarf apple trees have short or brittle roots that easily break and let the tree tip over, so provide extra support to prevent this problem. If you have a row of dwarf trees, tie them to a wire trellis. Otherwise tie the main trunk of each tree to a metal pipe or wooden orchard stake using a soft tie that will rot before it cuts into the growing wood.

Paint the trunk of 2- to 4-year-old trees with white exterior latex paint diluted with an equal amount of water to keep the bark from splitting in cold weather. This also makes the bark less appealing to rodents.

Provide plenty of moisture and nutrients to keep young apple trees growing fairly quickly. Mulch with compost in spring, and make sure the soil is moist around mature trees when they're in bloom and close to harvest. Each year, healthy young trees will grow 6 to 12 inches (15 to 30 cm) if they're spur-type cultivars or 12 to 24 inches (30 to 60 cm) if they're regular cultivars. Older trees will grow 6 to 10 inches (15 to 25 cm) of new growth a year. If growth is slower, take a soil test or have the foliage analyzed for nutrient deficiencies; apply fertilizers as needed to correct the problem. If growth is too vigorous, hold off on fertilizing and plant a cover crop to use up some of the nutrients. Propagate apple trees by grafting.

In early summer, thin young apple fruits to about 6 inches (15 cm) apart, leaving no more than one fruit per spur.

Dwarf trees tend to have small root systems, so you'll need to stake the trunk to keep the plant upright.

## Pruning and Training

Apple trees grow best when trained into a pyramidal, central leader form with one trunk and several sets of branches emerging off of it. Here's how to do it.

1. Start training young trees just after spring planting (or in the spring following fall planting). Use sharp pruning shears to snip off the top of the main trunk, leaving a stem about 24 inches (60 cm) tall. Cut back any side branches by one-third to one-half.

2. As the tree grows through the summer, select four branches that are growing in opposite directions and spaced 4 to 8 inches (10 to 20 cm) apart. These will be the lower scaffold branches. Remove all other side branches.

3. The next winter or early spring, make the scaffolds branch by heading them back by one-third to one-half. Snip out any extra sideshoots coming off the main stem.

4. When the main trunk grows about 2 feet (60 cm) over the lower set of scaffolds, pick four new shoots to become an upper tier of branches. Each branch should emerge from the trunk in a different direction so it won't shade the branches below.

5. Continue in this manner each year, thinning back unnecessary growth and selecting new tiers of scaffolds until the tree reaches full height. When the tree matures, thin out crowded, old, or unproductive branches each summer.

## Training to a Central Leader

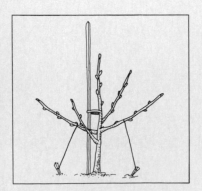

The first summer, select four branches. Use spreaders or ties to promote wide branch angles.

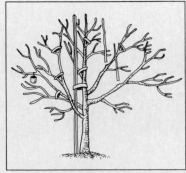

When the trunk is 2 feet (60 cm) above the lower branches, choose another set of four branches.

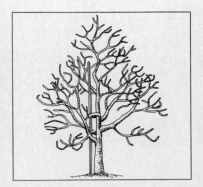

As the tree matures, thin out old, crowded, or unproductive growth each summer.

Apples get sweeter as they mature on the tree, so you can spread out your harvest over a few weeks.

Throughout the training process, most apple trees will need a little help developing strong, fruitful branches. Your goal is to have the branches emerge from the trunk at a 45 degree angle or slightly wider. At this angle, the branch base will be sturdy and unlikely to snap off when loaded with heavy fruit or ice. Narrow-angled branches have a weaker connection to the trunk and tend to grow upward quickly without producing much fruit.

Each year, when you select a new set of scaffold branches, use one of the following procedures to correct narrow branch angles:

- For small branches, hang a fishing weight or a couple of clothespins on the branch to pull it down, or stick

Check ties on staked trees every few months to make sure they're not cutting into the wood; loosen them if needed.

## Choosing Rootstocks

Some catalogs give you a choice of apple rootstocks; others only indicate whether the plant is dwarf or not. Before you buy, it's worth taking the time to find out exactly which rootstocks grafted trees are growing on. There are over 100 different kinds of apple rootstocks available; here's a sampling of some of the most common size-controlling rootstocks suitable for different situations:

### Well-drained Soil, Moderate Climate

- M.106 reduces tree size by 35 to 45 percent and is less likely to sprout root suckers.
- MM.26 reduces tree size by 60 to 70 percent with few root suckers. It is, however, very susceptible to fire blight and needs staking.

### Moist Soil, Moderate Climate

- M.111 is a semidwarf that reduces tree size by 15 to 35 percent and withstands heavy soil and drought.
- M.9, which reduces tree size by 65 to 75 percent, does best in moist soil but tends to develop a lot of sprouts (suckers) from the rootstock. It's resistant to collar rot but very susceptible to fire blight.

### Cold Climates

- MARK reduces size by 60 to 70 percent and seldom needs staking. It has, however, been linked to an early decline in some apple trees.
- P-2 and P-22, dwarfing rootstocks developed in Poland, have good winter hardiness.

### Fire Blight–prone Areas

- 'Geneva 65' is a dwarfing rootstock that resists crown rot and is almost immune to fire blight.
- 'Geneva 30' is a semidwarf with similar resistance and little tendency to produce root suckers.

a toothpick between the trunk and branch to push the branch out.

- For a larger branch, push the branch down with a board that's cut on both ends to fit snugly between the trunk and branch. Or hang a mesh bag of pebbles on the branch to pull it down.

After a season or two, the branch should hold the desired shape by itself, so you can remove the weights or spreaders.

### Harvesting

Apples will start producing fruit in 2 to 5 years, depending on the rootstock and growing conditions. Pick apples when they develop full color and flavor but are still crunchy and crisp. You can leave late-maturing apples on the tree as long as the temperature remains above 28°F (–2°C); below that, they'll freeze. Use bruised or damaged fruit right away. Store unblemished apples at 32°F (0°C) and 90 percent humidity.

### Problem Prevention and Control

You can stop many apple problems before they start by selecting disease-resistant cultivars and choosing a

'Golden Delicious' apples tend to have a soft skin, so handle them carefully during harvest to avoid bruising.

good planting site. Here's a rundown on some of the problems that might occur, along with suggestions on how to deal with them.

**Apple Maggots**  Apple maggots are larvae of the apple maggot fly. These $1/4$-inch (6 mm) long, cream-colored larvae ruin fruit by tunneling through the flesh. Infested apples often drop early. Pick up and destroy early drops at least weekly. To minimize infestations, trap the adults with red sticky traps (as explained in "Apple Maggot Traps" on page 68). Put the traps out in mid-June; use two traps per tree for control.

**Codling Moths**  Codling moth larvae also tunnel within fruit, damaging the flesh. The plump, pinkish to white larvae are nearly 1 inch (2.5 cm) long. In early spring, scrape loose bark from the trunk and limbs to remove overwintering cocoons, then apply an oil spray. Pick up and destroy any fruit that drops

---

### Grow a Living Apple Fence

You can train a series of side-by-side dwarf apple trees into an interwoven lattice framework called a Belgian fence. This systems looks great, and the plants tend to bear extra-large fruit. Start with three to five 1-year-old apple trees, and plant them 2 feet (60 cm) apart along a 6-foot (1.8 m) tall wire trellis. The trellis should have strands of 10-gauge wire set at 2, 4, and 6 feet (60, 120, and 180 cm) above the ground.

Head the young trees back to 15 inches (37.5 cm) at planting time. When branches sprout, find two that grow flat against the trellis and rise from the trunk at a 45 degree angle; remove the others. To keep them growing at this angle, tie the branches frequently to the trellis or to other branches they pass. Use soft natural twine; it will decay before it gets too tight.

In a few years, when the branches reach the top of the trellis, cut back the shoot tips to stop upward growth, and thin out side branches to show off the lattice pattern.

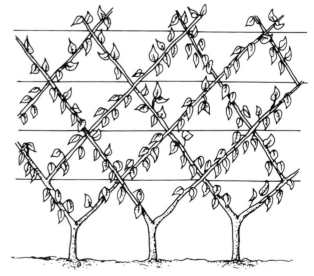

Training dwarf apple trees into a Belgian fence makes an attractive and useful landscape feature.

Cedar-apple rust is a problem where juniper trees are common. Prevent problems by planting resistant cultivars.

Crumbly looking scars on the skin is a sign that codling moth larvae have been feeding within the fruit.

early. You can also try trapping the male flies with pheromone traps; set them out a week or two before the buds open. Heirloom cultivar 'Arkansas Black' is moderately resistant to codling moths.

**Plum Curculios** Plum curculios are brown, long-nosed beetles that cause crescent-shaped scars in fruit. Severely damaged fruit may drop; otherwise, they will be scarred but still edible. To control the pests without sprays (which usually don't do much good anyway), tap the apple tree limbs with a padded stick once or twice a day for 2 weeks after the petals drop to make adult plum curculios fall down before they can reproduce. Catch them on a white cloth—they'll be easily visible—and dump them in a bucket of soapy water to destroy them. You can also catch the pests on the same apple-shaped traps as apple maggots, but use green traps instead of red. (See "Apple Maggot Traps" on page 68 for details on making the basic traps.)

The University of Georgia has had great success catching plum curculios in peach orchards on a "Tedder's trap." This is a 4-foot (1.2 m) tall, dark gray pyramid with a small, funnel-shaped trap in the top to catch the curculios. Dan Horton, entomologist for the University of Georgia, speculates that the trap appeals to curculios' desire to climb up and down tree trunks in spring. Use several traps around each tree from the time growth begins in spring until 3 or 4 weeks after petal fall. Make your own traps or check garden-supply catalogs for commercially produced traps.

**Rust, Scab, and Mildew** Several fungal diseases attack apples. Cedar-apple rust causes yellow to orange spots on leaves and fruit. Powdery mildew produces a dusty white coating on leaves and "netting" on fruit. Apple scab causes greenish brown leaf and fruit spots that turn dark and hard. The easiest way to handle these problems is to avoid them with resistant cultivars.

When these diseases do strike, thoroughly rake up all dropped leaves in fall. If the diseases were a major problem last year, spray sulfur as often as once a week from the time growth begins until midsummer. For details on using sulfur sprays effectively, see "Sulfur" on page 75.

**Fire Blight** Fire blight is a difficult-to-control disease that has become an epidemic across the United States. If you don't use blight-resistant cultivars, you're sure to have problems with it at one time or another. Paul Steiner, plant pathologist at the University of Maryland, says that many of the most popular apple cultivars, including 'Jonathan', 'Fuji', 'Gala', and 'Rome', are highly susceptible. Orchards planted in these crops often suffer 30 to 50 percent losses in 3 to 5 years. Two of the most widely used rootstocks, M.9 and M.26, are also extremely susceptible. One small fire blight infection on the end of a branch can move through the tree and kill M.9 or M.26 roots within 6 months.

It's smart to avoid problems with fire blight by growing resistant cultivars. For more prevention and control techniques, see "Fighting Fire Blight" on page 73.

# Apricots

Apricots are delicious and rich in nutrients. You can grow apricots with golden, orange, or red-blushed fruit. Many have flesh that separates easily from the seed, a trait called "freestone." For the greatest chance of success with apricots, look for disease-resistant cultivars, such as 'Harval' and 'Harcot'.

Ripe apricots are so soft that they don't ship well. The way to enjoy them at their peak is to grow your own.

## Best Climate and Site

Most apricots grow in Zones 5 to 9 if you select a cultivar appropriate for your climate. Try 'Katy' for Zones 7 to 9 or 'Sweetheart' for Zones 5 to 8. The heirloom cultivar 'Moorpark' grows as far north as Zone 4. 'Hope' is a drought-hardy cultivar for the southwestern states. 'Manchurian Bush Apricot', which produces small, juicy fruit on a 10-foot- (3 m) tall bush, grows in Zones 2 to 9.

Give apricot trees full sun and well-drained soil. Find a place where the early opening flowers will be sheltered from frost. Avoid low parts of your yard, where frost collects. A northern exposure with mulched soil stays cooler longer in spring and encourages later bloom. But when the flowers open, pull the mulch back to let the soil radiate heat. If a frost is predicted, cover up the tree—as much of it as you can—with a thermal blanket, heavy-duty floating row cover, or a large sheet of plastic to keep frost off the flowers. It also helps to select later-blooming cultivars, such as 'Harglow', or more frost-tolerant 'Alfred' and 'Manchurian Bush Apricot'.

## Choosing Your Plants

Many apricots are self-fertile and will produce some fruit if planted alone. But most will produce more abundant yields with a second cultivar for cross-pollination. Cultivars such as 'Goldrich', 'Sundrop', and 'Perfection' are not self-fertile.

Apricots grown on apricot rootstocks are durable but climb to about 30 feet (9 m) tall. Apricots grown on peach rootstocks reach 20 feet (6 m) tall. In soil infested with root knot nematodes, try 'Nemaguard' peach rootstocks. Or in heavy soils, you can use fairly compatible plum roots such as those from the 'Marianna' series. Many catalogs advertise dwarf apricots—under 10 feet (3 m) tall—but they might not live as long as larger trees.

## Planting and Care

Plant full-sized trees 25 feet (7.5 m) apart and dwarf trees 12 to 15 feet (3.6 to 4.5 m) apart. Mulch with compost in spring, keep the soil moist through the growing season, and fertilize as needed to maintain 12 to 20 inches (30 to 50 cm) of growth a year. Propagate apricots by bud grafting.

## Pruning and Training

You can train upright-growing dwarf apricots with the central leader system (as explained in "Pruning and Training" on page 82). For taller or more outward-growing plants, use the open-center system (as explained in "Pruning and Training" on page 94). When the developing apricots get to be marble-sized on 'Tilton' and 'Royal Blenheim', thin the fruits to leave them 2 inches (5 cm) apart; this will prevent the trees from fruiting only every other year. Thin other cultivars only if the tree is overburdened.

## Harvesting

Apricot trees will begin to bear fruit in 2 to 4 years after planting. Pluck the fruits when they're soft and sweet. You also can eat the seeds of 'Sweetheart' like almonds. Seeds of most other cultivars are not edible. Freeze or dry some of the fruit and store the rest for a week or two at high humidity and near-freezing temperatures.

## Problem Prevention and Control

Apricots have problems similar to peaches; see "Problem Prevention and Control" on page 95 for complete details. They also can suffer from Eutypa dieback, a disease that attacks through pruning cuts and eventually kills the branch. Prune in dry summer weather, when the disease is dormant, to prevent infection. Treat scale, mite, and aphid infestations with oil sprays.

Unlike most fruit trees, cherries don't need thinning to produce high-quality fruit.

Sweet cherries tend to need a compatible partner for cross-pollination. Sour cherries are self-fertile, so you can get a harvest from just one tree.

# Cherries

If you don't have your own cherry tree, store-bought cherries seem like such a treat. They're only available for about 6 weeks, and then they're gone until next year. Homegrown cherries won't give you a much longer season, but they do have a peak-of-freshness taste that is even better than the store-bought ones. If you're a cherry fan, you owe yourself the luxury of having your own cherry trees.

You can grow either sweet or sour cherries (or both). Sweet cherries, of course, are famous for their succulent fruit. You can find a range of fruit colors, including purple 'Black Tartarian', black 'Sam', and yellow 'Golden Emperor Francis' or 'Rainier'. As their name implies, sour cherries stay tart until they are extremely ripe, but they're great for pies, cobblers, and preserves. If you don't have room for a full-sized tree, consider growing bush cherries; see "Cherry, Nanking" on page 133 for growing guidelines.

## Best Climate and Site

Sweet cherries grow best in sun and well-drained soil. They prefer arid climates, such as cooler regions of California—the home of most commercial cherry orchards—but they will grow elsewhere. They're hardy in Zones 5 to 9 and can withstand winter temperatures down to about −16°F (−27°C) without damage to flower buds. The flowers are more vulnerable when they bloom early in spring and often suffer frost damage unless protected. Sweet cherry trees also suffer from heat, which reduces fruit size and, when combined with humidity, increases disease problems. Ask local nurseries or your Cooperative Extension Service office to suggest cultivars that are appropriate for your climate. 'Royal Ann' and 'Hedelfingen' are good in Zones 5 to 7; 'Bing' and 'Stella' perform well in Zones 6 and 7; and 'Lapins' is a good choice for Zone 8.

Sour cherries grow in Zones 4 to 8. Compared to sweet cherries, they're more tolerant of summer heat and a little later to bloom, so they are less likely to suffer frost damage. 'North Star' and 'Montmorency' are tough cultivars that can adapt to both heat and cold.

## Choosing Your Plants

Height and rootstock can be an issue when selecting cherry cultivars. Most sweet cherries reach about 25 feet (7.5 m) tall; sour cherries top out at 15 feet (4.5 m) tall. Both can be slightly smaller if grown on dwarfing rootstocks, but be sure to choose the right rootstock for your conditions.

In full bloom, cherry trees can rival some of the finest ornamental trees; they have a sweet, fresh fragrance, too.

If you have very well-drained soil and a fairly dry climate, you can grow slightly compacted cherry trees on 'Mahaleb' roots. Otherwise stick with 'Mazzard', which tolerates moister soils and often grows better in eastern states. 'Stockton Morello' sour cherry rootstock withstands even heavier soils but may carry a virus; it often needs staking for extra support. You'll also find 'Colt' used for dwarfing, but it suffers occasional graft incompatibility problems and is only hardy to −10°F (−23°C). The New York State Agricultural Experiment Station has released a new series of cherry dwarfing rootstocks called 'Gisela'. These rootstocks reduce tree size by 40 to 50 percent, tolerate richer soil, and produce heavier crops of larger fruit earlier than 'Stockton Morello'.

Sour cherries are self-fertile, so you only need one tree to get a crop. A few sweet cherries—such as 'Stella', 'Lapins', 'Starkcrimson', and 'Sunburst'—are also self-fertile, but most other sweet cherries require another compatible cultivar for cross-pollination. When it comes to pollination, sweet cherries fall into several different groups, which cannot pollinate others in their group but can usually pollinate outside the group. For example, you cannot pollinate 'Bing' with 'Lambert' or 'Napoleon'—they're all in the same group. But you can pollinate 'Bing' with 'Windsor'. 'Seneca', 'Vega', and 'Vista' are compatible pollinators for most cultivars. Check catalog descriptions for recommended pollination partners. If you don't have room to grow extra trees for pollination, graft shoots of the appropriate pollinators onto your main tree.

Light-skinned, yellow cherries tend to be less inviting to birds than the regular red-skinned kinds.

## Planting and Care

Space standard sweet cherry trees 20 to 30 feet (6 to 9 m) apart, sour cherries 20 feet (6 m) apart, and dwarf cherries 10 feet (3 m) apart. Mulch with compost in early spring. Expect full-sized cherry trees to grow 12 to 20 inches (30 to 50 cm) a year; dwarf trees should grow 5 to 10 inches (12.5 to 25 cm) a year. If growth is slower, have the soil or foliage tested for nutrient deficiencies and fertilize accordingly. If your trees are overly vigorous, hold off on the fertilizer, and plant a cover crop to use up some of the extra nutrients.

In cooler climates, you may have to protect cherry flowers from frost. Avoid planting in low parts of your yard, where frost collects. A northern exposure with mulched soil stays cooler longer in spring and encourages later bloom. But when the flowers open, pull the mulch back to let the soil radiate heat. If a frost is predicted, cover up the tree—as much of it as you can—

Cherries won't ripen more after harvest; taste test a few before picking. For best storage, leave the stem attached.

A cage of netting is an easy and effective way to protect small cherry trees from birds.

with a thermal blanket, heavy-duty floating row cover, or a large sheet of plastic to keep frost off the flowers.

Keep the soil evenly moist during the time cherries are swelling so they reach full size. If you need to irrigate, provide water that's not high in salt, boron, or chlorine. Propagate by grafting.

## Pruning and Training

You can train sour cherries and naturally spreading sweet cherries (such as 'Somerset') to an open-center form, as explained in "Pruning and Training" on page 82. For more upright-growing sweet cherries, use a central leader system, as discussed in "Pruning and Training" on page 94. Try slow-growing dwarf trees on a wire trellis, training the scaffolds to grow almost horizontally so they're easier to handle. Thin out older growth on mature trees to give productive young branches and spurs plenty of sun and space.

## Harvesting

Cherries begin to bear fruit in 3 to 7 years after planting. Get a tall harvest ladder—one with a no-tip-tripod structure is handy—so you can reach high into tall trees. If the weather is dry, let cherries ripen completely on the tree for best flavor. They should be fairly soft and very sweet. If heavy rain falls when the fruit is nearly ripe, you may have to pick it early to prevent splitting. You can refrigerate cherries briefly and freeze, can, or dry the rest for storage.

harvest ladder

## Problem Prevention and Control

When you grow cherries, the major problems you'll face are birds, cracked fruit, and some diseases.

Birds can be a real nuisance when your cherries start to ripen, although they're less attracted to yellow cherries such as 'Stark Gold'. Be prepared to either net the trees to keep the birds away or frighten the birds off; see "Coping with Animal Pests" on page 76 for details.

To limit losses from ripe fruit cracking, grow cultivars that are less susceptible to cracking, such as 'Seneca', 'Vista', 'Black Tartarian', 'Sam', 'Stella', 'Sweet Ann', 'Van', and 'Viva'.

To reduce the incidence of disease problems, eliminate wild cherry and choke cherry trees growing nearby. Brown rot is a fungal disease that causes soft, brown, fuzzy patches on fruit. If it has been a problem in the past, spray lime-sulfur when buds begin to turn

Brown rot commonly attacks fruit, producing a fuzzy mold, but it can also cause leaves and blossoms to turn brown.

green in spring. During bloom, spray with sulfur when the weather is humid or rainy and above 70°F (21°C). When fruit begins to change color, spray again with sulfur if the weather is rainy or humid and below 80°F (27°C). You will find some resistance to brown rot in 'Windsor' sweet cherry and 'North Star' sour cherry.

Cherries are susceptible to black knot, a fungus that covers tree limbs. When pruning in the dormant season, remove any dark, knobby growths, along with about 12 inches (30 cm) of healthy wood. To prevent disease spread, spray with lime-sulfur when the buds swell and again a week later.

Some cultivars are susceptible to cherry leaf spot, a fungus that causes dark leaf spots and early leaf drop. If the disease strikes, rake up and destroy fallen leaves. The following year, spray swelling buds with lime-sulfur, and continue to spray with sulfur every 1 to 3 weeks in wet or humid weather until the end of the growing season. Cherry leaf spot resistance is available in 'Lambert', 'Hedelfingen', 'Valera', 'Viva', and 'North Star'.

cherry leaf spot

Cherry fruit flies may lay eggs in developing fruits. The larvae tunnel in the fruit; infested cherries are malformed and shrunken and drop early. Pick up and destroy infested fruit to prevent larvae from leaving the fruit and entering the ground to pupate. Monitor and control adult fruit flies with sticky red balls (as discussed in "Apple Maggot Traps" on page 68). Set the traps out shortly after the flowers fade. For a small orchard, use at least four traps.

# Citrus

Citrus fruits wrap up sweet, sour, tangy, or juicy flesh in a neat green, orange, yellow, or ruby package. One factor common to all citrus fruits is the rich vitamin C content. Lemons and limes have the power to perk up the flavor of most dishes; oranges and grapefruit are refreshing as snacks and in salads. These and other citrus fruits can be a rewarding addition to your edible garden.

## Best Climate and Site

Most citrus fruit grows outdoors year-round from the southern part of Zone 8 to Zone 10. Frost will damage the fruit of any citrus plants and sometimes the rest of the tree. This restricts the most tender citrus trees—limes, lemons, and oranges—to the Deep South. If you occasionally get surprise frosts, plant these trees near a south-facing wall that will radiate heat on cold nights. For other frost protection ideas, see "Best Climate and Site" on page 86.

Farther north, you can grow calamondin and kumquat trees, which can tolerate temperatures to 15°F (–9°C). 'Dunstan' hybrid grapefruit survives to 5°F (–15°C). Some citrus can live even farther north, if you protect them during winter; see "Growing Citrus in Containers" for details.

Along with their varying cold tolerances, citrus plants also have different heat needs. For example, lemons do better in areas with cooler summers, but grapefruit need long, hot summers to get sweet and develop color in red- or pink-fleshed fruits. All citrus trees flower and produce ripe fruit earlier in warmer climates.

Provide full sun for citrus trees, unless you live in a climate with very hot and dry summers. In that case, give your trees a little light shade in the afternoon. Container-grown citrus plants also do well with some light shade. Avoid areas prone to strong winds, which can tear branches or leaves. Slightly acidic and moist but well-drained soil is best.

Fruit color is not a reliable indicator of ripeness with citrus, so taste one fruit before you harvest the rest.

## Choosing Your Plants

Citrus trees are nearly all self-fertile, so you only need to plant one to get a good harvest. (Check cultivar descriptions in nursery catalogs for exceptions.) Make sure the rootstock used is appropriate for your needs. The most common nondwarfing rootstock for many species is 'Troyer' (actually a citrange—a cross between a sweet orange and trifoliate orange [*Poncirus trifoliata*]). In areas with nematode problems, try citrange 'C32' or 'Carrizo'. In cold areas, look for trees grafted on dwarfing trifoliate orange (good for clay soils) or super-dwarfing 'Flying Dragon' rootstock (hardy to 5°F [–15°C] or below).

Full-sized trees, such as lemons, can grow to 20 feet (6 m) tall; grapefruit can reach 50 feet (15 m) tall. If you need a smaller tree, choose one that has been grafted onto a dwarfing rootstock or look for dwarf cultivars such as 'Meyer' and 'Snow' lemon or 'Valencia' oranges.

Citrus trees seldom need much pruning; just trim out crossing branches and head back long shoots in late winter.

## Planting and Care

Space large citrus trees at least 25 feet (7.5 m) apart and dwarf trees 10 feet (3 m) apart. Paint the trunk with white latex paint (diluted with an equal amount of water) to prevent sunburn. Keep the soil moist to prevent early fruit drop. Mulch with compost, adding a fresh layer several times during the year as the old layer breaks down. Fertilize as needed to encourage good tree vigor. If the plants are growing slowly, have the soil or foliage analyzed and correct any nutrient deficiencies. Propagate citrus trees by bud grafting.

To reduce cold-weather injury in the northern part of the citrus range, stop fertilizing and pruning in late summer to encourage new growth to harden before winter. If frost is predicted, cover the plant—or as much as possible—with a large cloth or big pieces of cardboard. You also can make a mini-greenhouse by setting up a rectangular wooden framework around the tree, covering it with clear plastic, and putting some electric light fixtures inside. (The heat from the bulbs will keep the tree warm.) If an unexpected frost damages a tree, leave the plant alone for a while; it may resprout in spring.

## Pruning and Training

Citrus trees generally don't need much pruning. Remove damaged or diseased branches and upright-growing sprouts that emerge from the roots. Trim back long branches to shape the plant. Wear gloves when pruning thorny types to protect your hands.

## Growing Citrus in Containers

Just because you don't live in the South doesn't mean you can't grow citrus trees. They're fun in any climate because they're so easy to keep in a pot. They have handsome glossy leaves, often-fragrant flowers, and colorful fruit. Use dwarf trees such as calamondin; 'Meyer Improved' or giant-fruited 'Ponderosa' lemon; 'Mexican' or 'Dwarf Orange' lime; 'Otaheite' orange; 'Moro' blood orange; 'Oro Blanco' grapefruit; or 'Formosa' kumquat.

Plant your tree in a 5-gallon (23 l) container. (Refer to "Fruits for Containers" on page 22 for details on types of pots and soils.) Keep the plant outdoors in light shade in the summer and bring it indoors for winter. During winter, keep the plant in bright light and moderate humidity. Turn the thermostat down to 20°F (−6°C) at night. Keep the soil evenly moist and fertilize lightly once a month.

## Harvesting

Most citrus trees produce fruit 3 or 4 years after planting. Finding out when the fruit is ripe can be tricky, since you can't rely on the skin color. For example, some oranges remain green when they are ripe unless the temperature falls to below 45°F (7°C). Other cultivars color up early, well before the fruit is ready. The only way to know for sure when fruit is really ripe is to taste it. Even when they're ripe, many citrus fruits can linger on the tree for weeks without losing quality. The exception is mandarin oranges; pick these fruits promptly before the flavor deteriorates. Store citrus fruit in the refrigerator for up to a couple weeks.

## Problem Prevention and Control

Start with virus-free, disease-resistant plants and provide good growing conditions to minimize problems. Keep an eye out for scale (small, hard-shelled insects on leaves and stems), whiteflies (small white flies on leaf undersides), thrips (tiny insects that cause scarring on leaves and fruits), and mites (tiny insects that cause yellow-stippled leaves). Use beneficial insects, traps, and insecticidal soap for prevention and control.

# Figs

If you've only ever tasted dried or processed figs, you're in for a real taste treat if you grow your own fresh figs. You can try yellow-skinned figs such as 'Blanche', green figs such as 'King', brown figs such as 'Brown Turkey', and black figs such as 'Pasquale'. The flesh is a contrasting color, often flushed with pink or red.

## Best Climate and Site

Grow figs outdoors in Zones 8 to 10 or in protected areas as far north as Zone 6. Be certain, however, to choose a cultivar appropriate for your climate. Figs such as 'Genoa', 'Panachee', and 'Conadria' need long, hot summers; cultivars such as 'Osborne Prolific' and 'Venture' do better in areas with cooler summers. Some of the hardiest cultivars include 'Brown Turkey' and 'Celeste', which are hardy to about 5°F (–15°C).

Give fig trees full sun and average, well-drained garden soil. In cool climates, you also can plant figs in large containers, then move them indoors during winter.

## Choosing Your Plants

Select self-pollinating cultivars, such as 'Brown Turkey', 'Celeste', and 'Texas Everbearing'; others rely on a rare wasp to pollinate the flowers, which are inside the fruit. You can choose full-sized cultivars that grow 20 feet (6 m) tall or smaller growers, such as 'Celestial' and 'Brown Turkey', that stay under 10 feet (3 m) tall.

## Planting and Care

Space large cultivars up to 25 feet (7.5 m) apart; smaller trees can go as close as 5 feet (1.5 m) apart. Mulch with compost as needed. The tree should produce about 1 foot (30 cm) of new growth a year. If the growth is too slow, have the soil or foliage tested for nutrient deficiencies, and fertilize as needed to correct them. Mature trees can tolerate some drought but still need irrigation in arid areas. Propagate by cutting rooted suckers off the roots or taking hardwood cuttings.

To protect figs during winter in Zone 7, wrap the entire plant in burlap or old blankets. Farther north, cut the plant back to 6 feet (1.8 m) tall in late fall and tie

Figs are productive and generally easy to grow. They are seldom troubled by pests, except for birds.

the branches close to the trunk. Dig a trench about 2 feet (60 cm) deep and 6 feet (1.8 m) long, with one end next to the roots. Dig to sever the roots on the opposite side of the plant, then gently bend the plant down into the trench. Fill in around the stems with mulch and soil. Dig the tree up gently and replant it in spring when frosts are over. Or keep your fig in a pot and move it to a frost-free area indoors during winter.

## Pruning and Training

Thin out excess growth as needed to control plant size and allow for good light penetration into the center of the plant. You also can train figs as espaliers to grow on walls.

## Harvesting

Fig trees produce their first crop a year after planting. Where the winter is mild, you can have an early-summer harvest on year-old wood. In mild and colder areas, you'll get a late-summer harvest on new growth.

Ripe figs are soft, with a slightly flexible "neck"; sometimes the skin splits. You can keep figs for a few days in the refrigerator, or cut them into sections and dry them for longer storage.

## Problem Prevention and Control

Figs generally have few problems. Place netting over trees to discourage birds, or grow green-fruited cultivars, which are less appealing to birds.

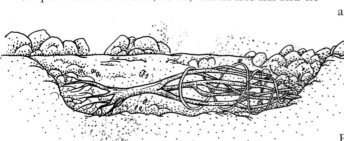

In the North, you can grow fig trees outdoors if you're willing to bury them in the ground for the winter.

Nectarines are basically "fuzzless" peaches—they have the same succulent, sweet, juicy flesh inside.

Both peaches and nectarines are attractive as fan-shaped espaliers. Growing them on a wall provides extra warmth.

# Peaches and Nectarines

Peaches and nectarines are delicious to eat dripping ripe right off the tree. When you've had enough fresh fruit, you can use them in many other ways—baked, sauced, stewed, roasted, pureed, and more. Both fruits are great to can, freeze, and make into preserves.

Peaches and nectarines are very similar—the main difference is that peaches have fuzzy skin. Most modern cultivars are "freestone," which means the fruit flesh separates easily from the seed. But you can still find a few "clingstone" cultivars such as 'Sims', a great one for canning. In addition to yellow-fleshed peaches and nectarines, you can try white-fleshed cultivars such as 'Belle of Georgia' and heirloom 'Early Violet'.

## Best Climate and Site

Peaches and nectarines can generally grow in Zones 5 to 9, but it's best to choose cultivars that are adapted to your particular climate. In cold areas, try extra-hardy cultivars such as 'Reliance' peach (hardy to −25°F [−32°C]) and 'Mericrest' nectarine (hardy to −20°F [−29°C]). In Southern areas, you can grow less-hardy cultivars such as 'Desert Gold' peach (for Zones 8 and 9).

While excess cold is harmful, peaches and nectarines do need some chilling to flower properly. The cultivar you grow must be compatible with your region's winter chill hours, the number of hours of cold weather (45°F [7°C] or under). Chill hour requirements determine when the tree will flower in spring. Cultivars with a short chill hour requirement will bloom in early spring once they've gotten their quota of cold. Those with high chill hour requirements need to go through a lot more cold before they flower, which helps delay bloom until milder weather in Northern climates. Cultivars that only need a brief cold winter period include 'Gulf Queen' (150 chill hours), 'Desert Delight' (100 to 200 chill hours), and 'Sam Houston' (500 to 650 chill hours). In contrast, cold-tolerant 'Reliance' needs 1,000 chill hours.

Give your tree full sun, sandy, well-drained soil, and a site seldom bothered by late frosts. Don't replant in soil where another peach tree grew recently; the decaying roots emit a chemical that will kill the new tree roots.

## Choosing Your Plants

Peaches and nectarines come in a variety of sizes. The smallest are 4-foot (1.2 m) tall genetic dwarfs such as 'Honeyglo' nectarine and 'Sensation' peach. Some genetic dwarfs with especially good fruit flavor include 'Nectar Babe', 'Bonanza', and 'Southern Flame'. Trees that are grafted onto dwarfing roots get to be 8 to 10 feet (2.4 to 3 m) tall. Full-sized trees reach 15 to 20 feet (4.5 to 6 m) tall.

Most peach and nectarine trees are grafted on peach seedlings such as 'Lovell' or 'Halford', which need light, well-drained soil. For cold areas, try 'Bailey' or

'Chui Lum Tao'. For soils troubled with root knot nematodes, try 'Chui Lum Tao' or 'Nemaguard'.

Most peaches and nectarines are self-pollinating, so you can get a full crop from just one tree. Exceptions include miniature 'Garden Sun' peach and 'Nectar Babe' nectarine, which will pollinate each other.

## Planting and Care

Plant full-sized trees 15 to 20 feet (4.5 to 6 m) apart, dwarf trees 8 to 12 feet (2.4 to 3.6 m) apart, and genetic dwarfs 2 to 3 feet (60 to 90 cm) apart or in 2-foot (60 cm) wide containers. Depending on the size of the plant, peaches will grow from 6 to 36 inches (15–90 cm) a year—vigorously enough to keep producing new, year-old, fruit-bearing wood. If they grow less, have the soil or foliage tested for nutrient deficiencies, and apply amendments as needed.

Fertilize with compost in early spring and again with a balanced organic fertilizer when the fruit first forms. Spray the leaves with liquid kelp every 3 to 4 weeks during the growing season. Protect flowers from frost; see "Best Climate and Site" on page 86 for frost-protection measures. Propagate by bud grafting.

Peaches tend to bloom early in spring, so avoid planting in low-lying, frost-prone spots; a sloping spot is ideal.

## Pruning and Training

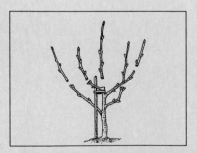

Train peaches and nectarines to an open-center form, as follows:

1. After planting, cut the young tree back to 24 to 30 inches (60 to 75 cm) tall. New shoots will spring up below the cut.

2. When the new shoots get to be 1 foot (30 cm) long in summer, select three or four that emerge in wide angles from the trunk. They should grow in different directions and be separated from each other by 4 to 8 inches (10 to 20 cm) of trunk. These will be the main scaffold branches. Cut off or gradually cut back other branches.

3. During the dormant season for the next several years, head each scaffold branch and side branch back by about one-third of its length to develop a webbed framework of side branches. (For peaches, you can delay dormant pruning until the tree is in bloom to discourage canker diseases and cold damage.)

4. Thin young trees lightly in summer to remove unneeded branches. Spread young branches (as explained in "Pruning and Training" on page 82) to develop a strong 45 to 60 degree branch angle.

5. When the tree is mature, cut half of the older branches back by about half of their total length during the dormant season so they'll resprout productive new wood.

If fruit set is heavy remove the smaller fruit after the June drop—the time when the tree naturally drops some of its excess fruit. Thin the remaining peaches to leave 6 to 8 inches (15 to 20 cm) of stem between each fruit to allow for even ripening.

## Training to an Open Center

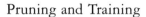

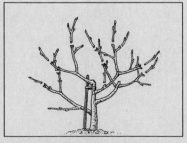

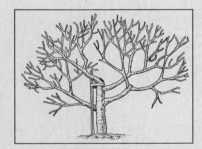

The first year, remove the center shoot and trim side branches.

In following years, remove shoot tips to promote side branching.

On bearing trees, cut half of the older branches back by half.

Most peaches and nectarines are self-pollinating, so you only need one tree to get a harvest.

## Harvesting

Peach and nectarine trees begin producing fruit in 2 to 4 years after planting. Harvest when the fruit is well colored, tender, and sweet. Refrigerate peaches up to a few days for fresh eating; freeze, can, or dry the rest for longer storage.

## Problem Prevention and Control

To make your job easier, start with disease-resistant cultivars if you live in an area that's prone to peach tree diseases. Discourage canker and borers by removing or spreading branches that emerge from the trunk at a narrow angle. Cut out any oozing cankers during winter and cover the cut with lime-sulfur.

If you don't start with disease-resistant cultivars, you may have to spray to control diseases. Brown rot attacks flowers and shoots, then spreads to cause rotten brown areas in fruit. To control brown rot, spray lime-sulfur when buds begin to turn green in spring. (This also reduces problems with bacterial leaf spot and peach scab, both of which can cause spots or cracks on leaves and fruit.) During bloom, spray with sulfur when the weather is humid or rainy and above 70°F (21°C). When fruit begins to change color, spray again with sulfur if the weather is rainy or humid and below 80°F (27°C).

Several kinds of pests like to tunnel in peach trees and fruits. Oriental fruit moths produce white or pink, brown-headed larvae that burrow in shoots and fruits. Peach twig borers are brown caterpillars that cause similar injury, damaging fruits and causing wilted shoot tips. Peachtree borers are whitish, brown-headed caterpillars that tunnel into the inner bark, near or just below the soil level; their feeding weakens the whole tree. Vigorous trees are less prone to borer damage. Avoid injuring the trunk so you don't make it easy for borers to enter. Use pheromone traps to monitor and control adult males. Cut off and destroy infested shoot tips. Plum curculios may cause crescent-shaped scars on fruit; see "Plum Curculios" on page 85 for suggested controls.

# Pears

Whether fresh, dried, or canned, pears are versatile and delicious. You can grow European pears, which develop soft, sweet flesh in traditional pear-shaped fruits. Go for the standard large-fruited, gold-skinned types, or try ruby-skinned cultivars such as 'Red Bartlett' or 'Scarlet Comice' or tiny but spicy-sweet 'Seckel'. For a change of pace, try Asian pears, which are round and crunchy like apples but extra juicy and uniquely flavored.

## Best Climate and Site

Pears can grow in Zones 4 to 9, but few thrive over that entire range. One exception is 'Kieffer', which is thoroughly hardy in Zone 4 and tolerates the heat and short winters in Zone 9. For the far North, try 'Patten', hardy to −40°F (−40°C). 'Comice' and 'Bartlett' grow best in Zones 5 to 7, while 'Stark Jumbo' prefers Zones 6 to 8. 'Florida Home' stretches even farther south to Zones 8 to 10. Most Asian pears are best in Zones 6 to 9.

Give pears moist, rich, slightly acid soil and full sun. Avoid sites prone to spring frosts. But don't despair if a frost arrives; open pear flowers can tolerate temperatures just under freezing.

## Choosing Your Plants

Most pears require cross-pollination for fruit set. Occasionally 'Bartlett' and 'Red Bartlett' will be partly self-pollinating if grown in arid western states; 'Kieffer' and 'Turnbull' also can be self-pollinating. In most cases, though, you'll need to plant at least two trees for a good crop. Check nursery catalogs for suggestions of compatible pollinators.

To extend your harvest, plant pear cultivars that

Pears bear fruit on long-lived spurs, so they adapt well to training in formal espalier patterns.

Most pears require cross-pollination to set fruit, so you'll need to plant at least one compatible companion.

will mature over an extended period of time. For example, 'Moonglow' and 'Clapp's Favorite' ripen around mid-August, followed by 'Bartlett' in late August or early September, 'Seckel' and 'Magness' around mid-September, 'Comice' in early October, and 'Kieffer' in mid-October. (In the South, these cultivars ripen about a month earlier.)

Pears come in a variety of heights, thanks to a broad selection of good rootstocks. Most pears are grafted on fire blight-resistant OH x F ('Old Home' x 'Farmingdale') roots. Some, such as OH x F 97, produce full-sized trees that reach 20 feet (6 m) tall or more. You can get half-sized trees with OH x F 333 and OH x F 513. Quince rootstock gives a dwarfing effect but is incompatible with some pear cultivars.

## Planting and Care

Space full-sized trees 15 to 20 feet (4.5 to 6 m) apart and dwarfs 8 to 12 feet (2.4 to 3.6 m) apart. Water and mulch as necessary to keep the soil moist and prevent damage to foliage and fruit. Mulch with compost in spring.

Your tree should produce 1 to 2 feet (30 to 60 cm) of new growth a year. If it's growing less, have the soil or foliage tested for nutrient deficiencies, and fertilize as needed. If it grows more, hold off on fertilizing, and plant a cover crop around the tree to use up some of the nutrients. Propagate by grafting.

## Pruning and Training

Use the central leader system (as explained in "Pruning and Training" on page 82) to shape upright-growing European pears and the open-center system

Pears tend to produce a lot of upright shoots. Use a combination of pruning and branch spreaders to promote productive, outward growth.

European pears ripen best off the tree; pick them when they snap off the branch easily.

(described in "Pruning and Training" on page 94) for more outward-growing Asian pears. If you're in an area with severe fire blight problems, you could train the tree to two trunks in case one is destroyed by disease. Be certain to spread upright-growing branches so they emerge from the trunk at a 45 to 60 degree angle. This helps slow down and toughen up growth, so it's less susceptible to winter damage and pest or disease problems. If a 'Red Bartlett' branch produces golden-skinned fruit, cut it back to a main branch.

Heavy-bearing trees will need some fruit thinning. In June, remove the smaller fruit, leaving one or two of the best fruit per cluster.

### Harvesting

Pear trees generally begin to produce fruit in about 3 to 5 years after planting. Wait to harvest Asian and 'Seckel' pears until they are completely ripe; taste them to tell for sure. Pick European pears when they are mature but not ripe. Mature pears of most cultivars will develop lighter skin and dark seeds, with the stem end snapping easily off the tree. ('Anjou' remains green even when mature.) Experiment to find the perfect harvest time for your tree. Hold pears in cold storage— 33°F (1°C) and 90 percent humidity. Let European pears ripen for several days at room temperature (until the stem end is slightly soft) for fresh eating.

### Problem Prevention and Control

Many pests common to other fruit crops also enjoy pear trees. For information on identifying and controlling apple maggots, codling moth, and plum curculio, see "Problem Prevention and Control" on page 84. For information on cherry fruit flies, see "Problem Prevention and Control" on page 89.

Keep an eye out for pear psyllas, tiny insects that suck sap from tender shoot tips and fruit and spread diseases. If many attack, they can reduce tree vigor— sometimes to the point that the tree dies. Their sugary droppings feed black sooty mold, a dark fungus that grows on the leaves and fruit. During the growing season, use insecticidal soap or horticultural oil sprays to control psyllas. If psyllas were a problem the previous year, use an oil spray before growth starts and again when the buds begin to turn green.

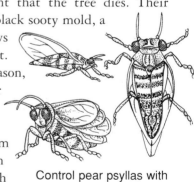

Control pear psyllas with soap or oil sprays.

Pear trees are even more susceptible to fire blight than apples. To avoid blight, plant resistant cultivars such as 'Seckel', 'Magness', 'Orient', 'Kieffer', and 'Hood'. Stay away from Asian pears and highly susceptible European cultivars such as 'Bartlett' and 'Bosc'.

To prevent fire blight infection in susceptible cultivars, you'll have to spray during prime infection times. For more details on coping with this bacterial disease, see "Fighting Fire Blight" on page 73.

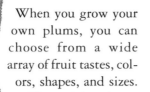

# Plums

When you grow your own plums, you can choose from a wide array of fruit tastes, colors, shapes, and sizes. You might choose sweet, meaty European plums; sugar-filled prune plums; or rich, tart damson plums. The round, heart-shaped, or egg-shaped fruit may be red (as in 'Ozark Premier'), purple (as in 'Stanley'), blue (as in 'Damson'), yellow (as in 'Shiro'), or green (as in 'Green Gage'). Plums range from the size of grapes for American bush plums to baseball-sized 'Elephant Heart'.

## Best Climate and Site

Plums can grow in Zones 4 to 10, but you need to choose a kind that's right for your area. Native American plums are the most cold-hardy; *Prunus americana* grows as far north as Zone 3 and tolerates drought. The fruit is larger in American plum hybrids, such as 'La Crescent', which is hardy to −40°F (−40°C) and bears tender, aromatic, yellow fruit.

European plums, such as 'Stanley' and 'Damson', grow best in cool areas (Zones 5 to 7). They tend to flower later than Japanese plums, so they can escape spring frosts prevalent in some areas. In Zones 6 to 10, you can grow Japanese plums. A few Japanese plums also grow farther north; 'Purple Heart', for example, is hardy to −25°F (−32°C).

Just as with peaches, try to find out the chill hours needed for the plum cultivar you're considering. For an area with a long winter, look for a fairly long chill hour requirement to encourage later blooming; 'Green Gage', for instance, needs 500 to 800 hours of chilling, and 'Italian Prune' and 'Stanley' need about 800 hours. 'Methley' needs only 150 to 250 chill hours and flowers so early in warm climates that the fruit can be ready to harvest in late May.

Give plums full sun and a site not prone to frost. European plums will tolerate moist, clay soils; Japanese and American plums prefer better drainage.

## Choosing Your Plants

When it comes to pollination, plums are a mixed-up bunch. Many European plums and damson plums will self-pollinate, so one tree is enough. But if you plant two compatible cultivars, such as 'Stanley', 'Bluefree', and 'President', they may set more fruit. Japanese and American plums often require cross-pollination with a compatible cultivar. For example, 'Shiro', 'Ozark Premier', 'Santa Rosa', and 'Wickson' can all interchange pollen. To make sure you're getting the right pollinators, check nursery catalog descriptions.

If you have room, plant several trees to extend your harvest season. That way, you can enjoy fresh plums from July (with early cultivars such as 'Earliblue' and 'Shiro') into September (with late-bearers such as 'Stanley', 'Damson', and 'President').

You can choose from a number of good rootstocks, many of which grow well in moist or clay soils. 'Myrobalan' is a popular rootstock that produces a 20-foot (6 m) tall tree; it is, however, susceptible to tomato ring spot virus. (If you choose 'Myrobalan' rootstock, set the graft union 4 to 6 inches [10 to 15 cm] below the soil surface at planting time to encourage the scion to root.)

'Pixie' is a dwarfing rootstock that resists canker and produces trees about 10 feet (3 m) tall. (European plums grafted onto 'Pixie' turn out a little smaller than Japanese plums.) *Prunus besseyi* roots limit height to about 6 feet (1.8 m) and is appropriate for bushy hedge plantings. 'Nemaguard', which needs very well-drained soil, resists root knot nematodes. In moister soils, try 'Marianna' or semidwarfing 'St. Julian GF 655-2', which has moderate resistance to root rot and bacterial canker but also can be susceptible to tomato ring spot virus.

## Planting and Care

Space full-sized plum trees 20 to 25 feet (6 to 7.5 m) apart and dwarf trees 8 to 12 feet (2.4 to 3.6 m) apart.

Plums vary widely in their pollination requirements, so check catalog descriptions carefully before planting.

'Santa Rosa' is a Japanese plum with large, high-quality fruit. It yields best when planted with other Japanese plums.

'Damson' is a late-summer-bearing European plum with heavy crops of dark-skinned, yellow-fleshed fruit.

Mulch with compost in spring and keep the soil moist through the growing season. Apply a complete fertilizer when the petals fall. Expect 12 to 18 inches (30–45 cm) of growth a year. If your tree grows less, have the foliage nutrient levels analyzed and correct nutrient deficiencies. If it grows more, reduce fertilizer and plant a cover crop if necessary. Propagate by bud grafting.

## Pruning and Training

Train upright-growing cultivars (including most European plums) to a central leader, as explained in "Pruning and Training" on page 82. Open-center training (as detailed in "Pruning and Training" on page 94) works better for more spreading plums, including most Japanese types. European plums produce fruit on older spurs, so you don't need to remove as much of the wood as you would on established peach trees; just thin out a few of the oldest branches each year.

Thin the fruit on trees that are overburdened. Remove smaller or misshapen fruit when they are about marble-sized, leaving at least 4 inches (10 cm) between each big plum or about 2 inches (5 cm) between smaller plums.

### Harvesting

Plum trees generally begin to bear in 3 to 4

For fresh eating, pick plums that are fully colored and slightly soft.

years after planting. Pick European plums when they are soft and sweet. Harvest Japanese plums slightly early and let them finish ripening on the kitchen counter. Harvest plums for preserves when they are slightly underripe. Store plums in your refrigerator for up to a few days, or dry, freeze, or can them for longer storage.

## Problem Prevention and Control

Start with good growing conditions and problem-preventing tactics, including planting disease-resistant cultivars. Check with your county Cooperative Extension Service office to find out which plum diseases are most common in your area and which cultivars are recommended. 'AU-Rosa', 'Crimson', and 'Ozark' are a few cultivars that can resist many common plum disease problems.

Plums and cherries share susceptibility to black knot, a fungus that causes dark swellings on tree limbs. When pruning in the dormant season, remove dark, knobby growths and about 12 inches (30 cm) of healthy wood. If black knot was a problem the previous year, spray with lime-sulfur when the buds swell, then reapply a week later.

Bacterial leaf spot causes brown or black spotting on leaves and fruits and early leaf drop. As soon as you notice symptoms, spray with lime-sulfur every 10 to 21 days until leaf drop if the weather is wet or humid. Consider resistant cultivars for new plantings.

Plum curculios cause crescent-shaped scars on fruit; infested fruit usually drops. See "Plum Curculios" on page 85 for control suggestions.

# FRUITING VINES AND BUSHES

Berries—including raspberries, strawberries, kiwis, grapes, and blueberries—generally grow on compact plants that are easier to tend and harvest from than most fruit trees. Because the plants they grow on are smaller than normal trees, these crops are sometimes called "small fruits." But though they may be small in size, there's nothing small about the flavor!

It's hard to beat homegrown berries for taste. You can pick them full-flavored and completely ripe, experiencing them at their best. Most berries don't keep well, but you can enjoy a variety all summer long by planting an assortment of cultivars that ripen at different times. You'll probably even have extras to freeze or preserve for winter cooking.

Another bonus of growing these smaller plants is that they are quick to bear fruit. Nut trees may take a decade to become productive, and fruit trees may take several years, but ever-bearing strawberries and raspberries can produce a harvest the first fall after spring planting. This makes it easy to try new plants and mix and match to find your favorites.

This chapter covers the basics for the most popular small fruits. You'll learn how to find the right cultivars for your climate and how to grow them for high-quality harvests. If bramble fruits are your favorites, check out "Blackberries" on page 102 and "Raspberries" on page 112. Productive, easy-care blueberry bushes are an ideal addition to nearly any landscape; see "Blueberries" on page 103 for growing guidelines. Grapes are great for growing on arbors and trellises; for training tips, see "Grapes" on page 107. Strawberries are super for small-space and container gardening; "Strawberries" on page 114 tells all.

Looking for something a little different? Check out the entries for "Currants and Gooseberries" on page 106 and "Kiwis" on page 111. For information on even more unusual small fruits—such as elderberries, cranberries, or alpine strawberries—see "Uncommon Fruits, Berries, and Nuts," starting on page 124.

Perfectly ripe berries are soft and juicy, so many kinds tend to ship poorly. To enjoy them at the very peak of flavor, you need to grow your own so you can pick and enjoy their sun-ripened goodness immediately.

# Blackberries

Blackberries are exuberant growers with delicious, juicy berries. Try the standard upright, thorny-stemmed types or the floppier, thornless kinds that need the support of a trellis. Or look for the best of both worlds— erect, thornless, and highly productive cultivars such as 'Navaho Erect' and 'Arapaho'.

## Best Climate and Site

Most blackberries grow well in Zones 5 to 9, but some perform better than others in different areas. Choose a cultivar that's right for your area. For the southern end of the range, try 'Rosborough', 'Dirksen', and 'Black Satin'. In cold areas, get a thoroughly hardy cultivar such as 'Illini Hardy' or 'Darrow'.

Find a site with full sun and good air circulation but no high winds. It should be at least 1,000 feet (300 m) from any wild blackberries or similar bramble berries that could spread diseases. Pick a spot with fertile, well-drained soil that hasn't been used to grow bramble berries, tomatoes, roses, or related plants in the past. (These plants may leave behind soilborne disease problems that could attack blackberries.)

## Choosing Your Plants

Always buy certified disease-free plants. They are sold in containers, as bareroot plants, or as tissue-cultured plantlets. For more buying tips, see "Buying the Best Plants" on page 40.

Most blackberry cultivars are self-fertile, but a few need cross-pollination; check catalog descriptions to see if any special pollination needs are mentioned. To extend your harvest season, grow cultivars that ripen at different times, such as 'Choctaw' or 'Cherokee' (early), 'Hull' or 'Illini Hardy' (midseason), and 'Shawnee' or 'Navaho' (late).

## Planting and Care

Blackberries need plenty of space. Within a row, place thorny cultivars 3 to 4 feet (90 to 120 cm) apart and thornless cultivars 4 to 6 feet (1.2 to 1.8 m) apart. Make paths between the rows 7 or 8 feet (2.1 to 2.4 m) wide

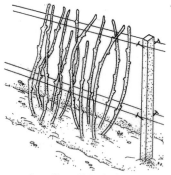
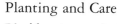
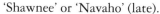

A trellis will help keep canes from sprawling.

Blackberries are at their best flavor when the fruits turn dark and lose some of their glossiness.

for good sun exposure and adequate air circulation.

Keep the soil evenly moist by watering if the weather becomes dry. Mulch with compost to fertilize in early spring. Mow between rows to control weeds and prevent the blackberries from spreading. Propagate blackberries by dividing existing clumps or layering. (See "Layering" on page 65 for details.)

## Pruning and Training

Cut fruit-bearing canes to the ground right after harvest. In early spring, thin to leave seven strong canes per plant. Shorten side branches to about 1 foot (30 cm) long. For maximum yields, train blackberries to a trellis, as explained in "Trellising Brambles" on page 112.

## Harvesting

Blackberries are ready when they turn entirely black and get a little dull, soft, and sweet. Eat them right away, store them in the refrigerator for a day or two, or freeze them.

## Problem Prevention and Control

Watch for distorted growth, sterile canes (mature canes that don't produce fruit as usual), or orange-spotted leaves that drop early—symptoms of incurable viral or orange rust diseases. Remove infected plants immediately. 'Arapaho', 'Chester', and 'Shawnee' are resistant to orange rust.

To discourage other diseases, cut off old canes and rake up fallen leaves. Destroy any that are spotted or off-color. Spray canes with lime-sulfur when the buds begin to turn green in spring to prevent a variety of cane-attacking fungal diseases, including anthracnose.

Blueberries thrive in acid conditions, so add sulfur if needed to lower the pH. A pine needle mulch will help, too.

Some blueberries need cross-pollination, so make sure you check catalog descriptions to get the appropriate partners.

# Blueberries

Blueberry bushes make handsome and colorful garden plants. In spring, blueberry twigs are peppered with white or pink urn-shaped flowers. In summer, the berries change from green to pink or red and finally to blue. In fall, the foliage turns crimson—a display to rival any purely ornamental shrub. And in winter, the twigs can be a warm, glowing red.

You can choose from several different types of blueberries, depending on where you live. As far north as Alaska and Maine, you can grow lowbush blueberries (*Vaccinium angustifolium*) such as 'Early Sweet'. These plants creep close to the ground, safely protected from

To extend your blueberry harvest season by several weeks, choose cultivars that ripen at different times.

frigid temperatures by the snow. Lowbush blueberries produce an abundance of tasty, small berries. In more temperate areas, grow highbush blueberries (*V. corymbosum*), which produce big berries on moderate-sized bushes. You also can plant "midhighs" (such as 'Northblue')—hybrids that combine the hardiness and flavor of lowbush cultivars with the bigger fruit size of highbush blueberries. In warm regions of the South, grow rabbiteye blueberries (*V. ashei*), which grow into large bushes with pink berries that turn blue when ripe.

## Best Climate and Site

Lowbush blueberries grow well in Northern areas, from Zones 3 to 7. Midhighs grow as far north as Zone 4. Highbush blueberries thrive in Zones 5 to 7. Rabbiteye blueberries are normally adapted to Zones 6 to 9, but some cultivars, such as 'Briteblue', can also grow in Zone 10.

Give blueberries full sun for best yields. They can tolerate a little light shade but may not be as productive. Avoid planting in low-lying areas, which are prone to frost and poor air circulation. The soil should be loose and moist but not waterlogged, with a pH around 4.5. If your soil is on the clayey side, try root rot-resistant 'Patriot'. If your soil's pH is higher than 5, you can add sulfur (according to package directions) to bring the pH down to the right level. Prepare the bed a while before you plan to plant, since the sulfur may take 6 to 12 months to become effective. Test the pH again before you plant to make sure it's at the right level. Mulching with pine needles or composted pine bark will help to keep the pH low.

## Choosing Your Plants

Always start with certified disease-free plants. Try to find 2- or 3-year-old plants, which will become productive quickly.

Some blueberries need cross-pollination with compatible cultivars; others can produce crops on their own but set more fruit when planted near another cultivar. Catalog descriptions will usually recommend suitable companions.

Besides improving yields, interplanting cultivars that ripen at different times also lets you extend your blueberry harvest season. In the South, blueberries can ripen from spring into summer; Northern-grown blueberries ripen through the summer. At the New York Agricultural Experiment Station in Geneva, New York, 'Duke' ripens in early July; 'Patriot' ripens in mid-July; 'Northblue' and 'Toro' ripen in late July; 'Bluegold' ripens in early August; and 'Elliott' ripens in mid-August. To further expand your harvest options, you can find cultivars such as 'Toro' that ripen their fruit all at once or those that ripen over a period of several weeks, such as 'Bluecrop'.

## Planting and Care

Plant 12- to 18-inch (30 to 45 cm) tall creeping lowbush blueberries 2 feet (60 cm) apart. Midhigh blueberries grow 18 inches to 3 feet (45 to 90 cm) tall and need to be spaced 2 to 3 feet (60 to 90 cm) apart. You also can plant them in 5-gallon (23 l) nursery containers. Highbush blueberries grow 6 to 12 feet (1.8 to 3.6 m) tall and need to be spaced 6 feet (1.8 m) apart. Rabbiteye blueberries grow 10 to 25 feet (3 to 7.5 m) tall and need to be spaced 8 feet (2.4 m) apart.

After planting, apply a 3- to 5-inch (7.5 to 12.5 cm) layer of organic mulch to keep the soil evenly moist and protect the shallow roots from temperature changes. As the mulch breaks down, the shallow blueberry roots will grow into it. You'll have to continue to add more mulch every year to keep the roots safely

Blueberries may tolerate some drought, but they'll grow and produce better if you keep the soil evenly moist.

covered. Avoid cultivating deeply or raking vigorously beneath the plant so you don't damage the roots.

Keep the soil evenly moist. Although some rabbiteye blueberries can tolerate soil that dries out occasionally, all blueberries produce larger crops and/or bigger berries if constantly supplied with moisture. If you live in a dry area, consider installing an irrigation system to make watering easier.

Blueberries have low nutrient requirements, but they won't grow well if nutrients are lacking. Adding some fresh compost around the plants each spring will meet most or all of your plants' needs. If growth is poor, have the foliage analyzed (contact your county Cooperative Extension Service for information) and correct nutrient deficiencies promptly.

You can propagate blueberry bushes with hardwood or softwood cuttings. Lowbush blueberries are fairly easy to divide when dormant. Blueberries also are propagated commercially by tissue culture.

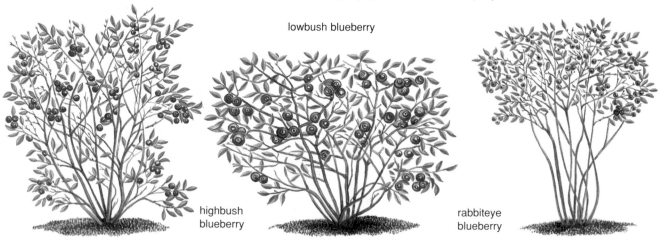

lowbush blueberry

highbush blueberry

rabbiteye blueberry

Thin out a few of the oldest stems each year to promote new growth.

For the best flavor, wait 3 or 4 days after your blueberries turn blue before harvesting them. Underripe berries won't ripen after picking.

## Pruning and Training

Pinch off all of the flowers on a young blueberry bush the first year after planting so the bush will grow strong. The next year, you'll only have to remove dead or damaged wood.

Maintain mature plants of most kinds of blueberries with rejuvenation pruning in early spring. Thin out old, damaged, crowded, or spindly branches to encourage productive new growth and let plenty of sun and air penetrate the entire plant. In Northern areas, you want to have two new branches emerge each year; cut out any other new shoots that come from the base. In Southern areas, you can let three or four new branches grow every year.

Rejuvenate lowbush blueberries by cutting half of the stems (take the oldest ones) to the ground each year.

## Harvesting

Blueberry bushes begin to produce fruit 2 to 4 years after planting. Harvest after the berries turn blue and taste sweet. Don't pick underripe berries; they won't ripen off the plant. Eat ripe blueberries right away, keep them in the refrigerator for up to 2 weeks, or preserve them by freezing, canning, or making jam.

## Problem Prevention and Control

Use sticky red balls (such as apple maggot traps) to catch blueberry maggots before they can tunnel into ripening berries. Set out one trap in each bush before the berries start to turn blue. Leave them in place until all berries are gone. To minimize problems for next year, harvest frequently and destroy infested berries.

If stems begin to die back or show unusual cankers or cracks, cut them back to healthy tissue. To avoid problems with canker, plant resistant cultivars such as 'Blue Chip', 'Cape Fear', and 'Blue Ridge'.

Mummy berry disease makes berries shrivel up or drop early. Reduce the chance of problems by lightly raking or hand fluffing the mulch under the plants in early spring, when the buds are swollen but before they produce new growth. Destroy infected berries that turn white, shrivel, and drop when they begin to ripen. You also can plant resistant cultivars such as 'Bluejay' and 'Spartan'.

If birds are a problem, see "Coping with Animal Pests" on page 76 for control suggestions.

### Blueberry Pruning: Before and After

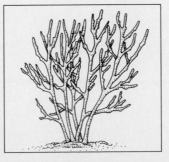

Mature blueberry plants have old, twiggy stems.

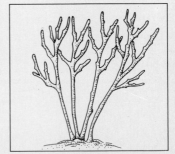

Thin out a few of the oldest stems each year.

# Currants and Gooseberries

These good-looking shrubs are among the few fruit-bearing plants that will thrive in light shade and heavy soil. Try black currants (*Ribes nigrum*), hybrid red or white currants (*Ribes* hybrids), big-berried European dessert gooseberries (*R. uva-crispa*), or smaller-fruited American gooseberries (*R. hirtellum*). Gooseberries have spiny stems, so you'll need to wear heavy gloves to protect your hands when working around the plants.

Some of these plants—particularly black currants—are alternate hosts for white pine blister rust, a disease that also attacks white pines and other five-needled pines. Some states have bans on growing these fruits, so check with your county Cooperative Extension Service to find out if there are any restrictions before you buy and plant.

## Best Climate and Site

Currants and gooseberries thrive in cooler areas, from Zones 3 to 7. Although they may perform better in full sun, they adapt well to light shade, especially in areas with hot summer days.

Find a site that's free of late-spring frosts. You can grow currants and gooseberries in almost any kind of good garden soil, as long as it's moist (but not water-logged) and cool. Add extra organic matter to loosen up clay soil or enrich sandy soil.

## Choosing Your Plants

The flavor of different gooseberries and currants can vary widely, so it's best to sample the fruit of any plant you're thinking about growing to be sure you'll like it.

Most gooseberries and currants are self-pollinating, so you can get berries with only one bush. However, most produce higher yields if interplanted with two or three other cultivars. If you want to grow black currants and white pines or other five-needled pines are growing within 1,000 feet (300 m) of the planting site, choose only rust-resistant cultivars, such as 'Consort', 'Coronet', and 'Crusader'.

## Planting and Care

Currants and gooseberries grow 3 to 7 feet (0.9 to 2.1 m) tall and wide. Space the plants 6 feet (1.8 m) apart. Or, if you're growing them as a hedge, space them as close as 3 feet (90 cm) apart. Mulch around the plants to keep the soil cool and moist and protect

Gooseberries have thorny stems. Hold the stems up with one gloved hand and use the other hand for picking.

the shallow roots. Add compost and a potassium-rich fertilizer in early spring. Water regularly in dry weather. Propagate by hardwood cuttings.

## Pruning and Training

Each winter, remove all shoots that are over 3 years old (or over 2 years old on black currants); then remove all but six of the remaining shoots. You can also train red and white currants and gooseberries to grow in a tree form. At planting time, select one branch to be the main trunk and remove all others. Keep the lower trunk clear of side growth but allow the upper portion to branch out. Each winter, trim the main branches lightly and thin out dead, diseased, or damaged wood.

## Harvesting

For cooking or making jelly, pick gooseberries and currants when they are not quite ripe. For fresh eating, let them ripen on the bush until they taste right to you. Eat them fresh, store them in the refrigerator up to 1 week, or preserve them.

## Problem Prevention and Control

Powdery mildew can devastate gooseberries, and sulfur sprays are not always an effective treatment. Avoid the problem altogether by planting mildew-resistant cultivars, such as 'Hinnomaki Yellow', 'Leepared', 'Pixwell', and 'Poorman'. Mildew resistance is also available in many currant cultivars.

If you find borers tunneling in the stems, cut the stems off below the borer hole. Remove and destroy any fruit that contains insect larvae.

# Grapes

Juicy, sun-warmed, homegrown grapes are a real taste sensation. And once you've had your fill of fresh grapes, you can use the rest to make flavorful wines, juices, and jellies.

Grapes are available in a variety of different types. The hardiest are American, or fox, grapes (*Vitis labrusca*), robust growers with rich flavor for fresh eating, jelly, or juice. Vinifera grapes (*V. vinifera*), also known as European wine grapes, are less hardy but produce top-quality wines. They are also good for fresh eating or drying. French-American hybrids combine the best traits of *V. vinifera* and various American species. Muscadine grapes (*Vitis rotundifolia*) grow into extra-long vines that thrive in the heat and humidity of warm-climate summers. Enjoy these grapes fresh or make them into jelly, juice, or wine.

## Best Climate and Site

Grapes are generally hardy from Zones 4 to 10, but you have to use cultivars appropriate for your area. Here's what you can expect.

**American Grapes** Most American grapes are hardy from Zones 4 to 7 but are most reliable where winter low temperatures seldom reach −10°F (−23°C). They also grow best with a growing season of at least 165 to 180 frost-free days. This allows later-maturing grapes to ripen but is just as necessary for early-ripening cultivars. Cornell University research has shown even early cultivars need a full growing season to harden new growth before winter.

Removing some of the leaves around each fruit cluster in late summer can help discourage disease problems.

**French-American Hybrids** These hybrids have a wide range of adaptability. Before you buy, check catalog descriptions to find those that are best suited to your particular climate and the length of your growing season. Also look for cultivars that are resistant to disease problems common in your area.

**Vinifera Grapes** These disease-susceptible types are best in arid climates with perfect grape-growing conditions. They are hardy from Zones 6 or 7 to 10. For the southern end of the range, look for cultivars that need a short winter rest period. For example, 'Cabernet Ruby' needs only 50 chill hours (hours of winter weather at 45°F [8°C] or colder); 'Thompson Seedless' needs only 100 chill hours.

**Muscadine Grapes** Muscadine grapes grow from Zones 7 to 9. Many cultivars have well-developed disease resistance and can withstand high humidity as well as high heat.

All of these different kinds of grapes need full sun, good air circulation, and deep, well-drained garden soil. Avoid low spots and other sites prone to late-spring frosts. Eliminate any wild grapes growing nearby; they can carry problems that might attack your cultivated grapes.

---

### Expanding Your Options

You can choose from a variety of different grape types. The most popular table grapes are seedless and easy to eat. Some seedless cultivars include 'Seedless Concord', 'Mars', 'Canadice', and 'Reliance'. You also can dry seedless grapes into raisins; 'Delight', 'Flame Seedless', and 'Lakemont' are a few that are especially good. If you have room for several plants, choose early-, midseason-, and late-ripening cultivars to extend your harvest season. Some early-ripening grapes include 'Baco Noir', 'Beta', 'Buffalo', and 'Cascade'. Midseason-maturing grapes include 'Chardonnay', 'Delaware', 'Niagara', 'Sauvignon Blanc', and 'Concord'. Late-ripening cultivars include 'Catawba', 'White Riesling', and 'Sheridan'.

Crowded clusters tend to ripen unevenly; prevent this by thinning in early summer, when fruits are small and hard.

## Choosing Your Plants

Start with 1-year-old plants that are virus-indexed and certified disease-free. For many American and hybrid grapes, it's fine to buy cuttings grown on their own roots. But for vinifera grapes, you'll probably need plants grafted on phylloxera-resistant rootstocks. Also look for cultivars that resist or tolerate the diseases that are most troublesome in your area. (For information on common grape diseases and resistant cultivars, see "Problem Prevention and Control.")

Be certain to read nursery catalog descriptions carefully to find out if a cultivar you're considering is self-fertile (meaning that you can get fruit from just one plant). Most cultivars are, but a few muscadines—including 'Scuppernong', 'Higgins', and 'Fry'—need cross-pollination with a second compatible cultivar to produce fruit.

## Planting and Care

Before planting, set up a support system, as explained in "Pruning and Training." Space American, hybrid, and vinifera grapes about 8 feet (2.4 m) apart along the support, with 5 feet (1.5 m) between rows. Space muscadines up to 20 feet (6 m) apart, with 12 feet (3.6 m) between rows.

On grafted grapes, set the graft union about 2 inches (5 cm) above the soil level. Set others at the same level they were growing before. After planting, you may want to let the grapevine grow untrained for a year to develop a stronger set of roots. Pinch off grape flowers during that year. You'll start training the vine early the following spring.

Keep the soil around young vines moist. After the first year or two, when vines are established, they usually don't need supplemental water. In fact, it's preferable to grow fruit-bearing wine grapes in dry conditions to encourage maximum flavor.

Mulch under the vines to control weeds. Feed with compost in spring. Vigorously growing muscadines may benefit from some nitrogen-rich fertilizer (such as alfalfa meal) at bloom time. If your vines are growing too vigorously, plant cool-season annual cover crops, such as rye or winter wheat, around them to use up some of the extra nutrients.

If your vine sets a heavy crop, thin out some of the clusters to minimize disease problems. While the fruits are still small and hard, remove some of the weakest clusters entirely. Snip off some of the fruits in the remaining clusters to open up the bunches. Reduce problems with Botrytis blight by pinching or cutting off some of the leaves around each ripening fruit cluster in mid- to late-summer.

Propagate grapes by cuttings, grafting, or—for muscadine grapes—layering.

## Pruning and Training

There are many different grape-training systems appropriate for different cultivars and needs. For example, in cold or disease-prone areas, you can start with two trunks per vine and train them on a V-shaped double trellis. That way, your plant will have another stem if one gets damaged. For vigorously growing vines, use a T-shaped trellis and let the longer side

Grapevines seldom need pruning in the summer, but you can thin dense growth as needed to improve air circulation.

branches cascade over the top to get the maximum amount of light. Most grapes adapt equally well to different training systems.

The simplest method for backyard grape growing is called the four-arm Kniffen system. Set two sturdy posts 20 feet (6 m) apart, and string two parallel wires between them at 36 inches (90 cm) and 60 inches (1.8 m) above the ground. (For hybrid grapes, use three wires at 30 inches [75 cm], 48 inches [1.2 m], and 66 inches [165 cm].) Plant your young grapevines under the wire at the spacing noted here.

Start the actual training the first year after planting. In late winter, cut the vine back to a stump with two buds. When the buds start growing, leave the stronger shoot and remove the other one. Train the remaining shoot upward on a wooden stake to form the trunk.

Besides producing a useful crop, grapevines can quickly cover a trellis, arbor, or pergola, screening out unpleasant views and providing welcome summer shade.

When the trunk reaches the lower wire, choose a sideshoot to creep in each direction on the wires. Tie the side branches carefully to the wires with soft, biodegradable twine. Pick two more arms for each of the higher wires. Remove the growing tip of the trunk about 6 inches (15 cm) below the highest wire and stretch the top two arms up to the wire.

Early each spring before growth resumes, remove unwanted shoots coming off the trunk or roots. (In areas where vines are likely to suffer winter damage, leave a short two-bud "spur" near the base of the trunk and beside each of the main lateral branches. They will be ready to replace the lost stems if necessary.) On the main arms of the vine, thin out the side branches so there's one every 4 inches (10 cm). Shorten the remaining side branches to 8 to 15 buds each.

## Harvesting

Grapes are ready to harvest when they develop ripe color and sweet flavor. On most grapes, entire bunches will ripen simultaneously; harvest the clusters by clipping them off the vine. On muscadines, pick individual grapes as they ripen.

Store muscadine grapes for a week or two in the refrigerator. Other grapes may last about 4 weeks. Freeze, dry, can, or make wine out of what you can't eat fresh.

## Problem Prevention and Control

Plant cultivars that resist diseases common in your area. Unless you live in arid areas with ideal conditions,

### Three Types of Trellises

A T-shaped trellis is ideal for very vigorous grapevines.

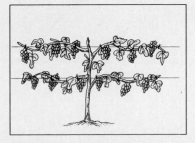

For Kniffen training, use a post-and-wire trellis system.

A V-shaped double trellis allows you to keep two trunks per vine.

you'll probably have to avoid highly disease-susceptible vinifera cultivars such as 'Cabernet Sauvignon', 'Chardonnay', 'Merlot', 'Pinot Noir', 'Riesling', and 'Sauvignon Blanc'.

Black rot can cause reddish brown leaf spots and hard, shriveled fruit (called mummies). Remove and destroy any mummies and diseased leaves you find. Also rake up and destroy fallen leaves. If black rot has been a problem in the past, spray copper fungicides in spring when the buds begin to turn green. Continue to spray with flowable sulfur about every 14 days (or as often as every 7 days when the weather is wet or over 40 percent relative humidity and the temperature is 50° to 80°F [10° to 27°C]). Do not spray sulfur when the temperature is over 80°F (27°C). Also avoid spraying sulfur-sensitive cultivars, including 'Concord', 'Concord Seedless', 'Chancellor', 'De Chaunac', 'Ives', 'Marechal Foch', 'Price', and 'Seneca'. Minimize black rot problems by planting resistant or tolerant cultivars, such as 'Alwood', 'Cascade', 'Delaware', 'Fredonia', 'Mars', 'Steuben', and 'Worden'.

Botrytis bunch rot causes a fluffy gray-brown coating on the fruit. Destroy infected fruit. Choosing resistant and tolerant cultivars and thinning out crowded fruit clusters will minimize this problem. Resistant and tolerant cultivars include 'Cascade', 'Catawba', 'Cayuga White', 'Concord', 'De Chaunac', 'Delaware', 'Einset', 'Fredonia', 'Mars', 'Niagara', and 'Steuben'.

Anthracnose infection produces sunken, dark-ringed spots on leaves and fruit. Remove and destroy infected plant parts. Prevent by spraying with lime-sulfur in spring as buds swell. Or plant resistant or tolerant cultivars, such as 'Alwood', 'Concord', 'Delaware', 'Mars', and 'Niagara'.

Powdery mildew produces a white powdery coating on the upper surfaces of leaves and dusty-looking or discolored fruit. It may also cause leaves to turn brown and drop early and dark patches on the canes. Prevent problems in future years by spraying lime-sulfur as the buds swell in spring. Or plant resistant or tolerant cultivars

Pick grapes when they are sweet and well colored; they won't ripen off the vine. Taste a few before harvesting.

such as 'Alwood', 'Canadice', 'Ives', 'Mars', and 'Steuben'.

Downy mildew causes cottony white growth on the undersides of leaves, as well as yellow leaf spots, leaf browning, and/or early leaf drop. Affected fruit clusters may have some healthy grapes and some that are hard and discolored. Remove and destroy all infected parts. Prevent by spraying lime-sulfur as the buds swell in spring. Resistant or tolerant cultivars include 'Alwood', 'Canadice', 'Cascade', 'Concord', 'Mars', 'Steuben', and 'Stover'.

Grape berry moth caterpillars produce webbing on fruit and chew holes in leaves and fruit. Prevent damage by hanging one grape berry moth pheromone trap by each trellis when fruit buds appear. Spray plants with BTK a week after you catch any grayish purple moths.

If birds are a problem, see "Coping with Animal Pests" on page 76 for control suggestions.

Botrytis bunch rot produces fluffy mold on the fruit.

Black rot produces leaf spots and hard, shriveled fruit.

Downy mildew causes spots on leaves and a white coating on fruit.

# Kiwis

Kiwis are interesting little oddities that have oval berries and a sweet, citrus flavor. They are produced on attractive, fast-growing vines that can cover a trellis or arbor in a single season. In Southern climates, you can grow fuzzy-skinned, emerald-fleshed kiwis. In Northern areas, try the smaller, smooth-skinned hardy kiwis.

## Best Climate and Site

Fuzzy kiwi (*Actinidia deliciosa*) is hardy in Zones 7 to 9. In northern parts of this range, protect plants from late-spring frosts, and use plants grown on their own roots, which survive cool weather better than grafted plants. For the Deep South, look for low-chill cultivars such as 'Vincent' and 'Allison'.

Hardy kiwi (*A. arguta*) can be hardy as far north as Zone 4. An even-hardier hardy kiwi (*Actinidia kolomikta*) can grow into Zone 3.

Provide well-drained, rich soil and full sun or—for *A. kolomikta*—light shade. Avoid planting kiwi vines on sites blasted by strong winds or low spots and other sites prone to late-spring frosts.

## Choosing Your Plants

With the exception of a few self-fertile cultivars such as 'Issai' and 'Blake', kiwi vines have either male or female flowers. For pollination, plant a male vine within about 40 feet (12 m) of the females—closer if possible. One male will pollinate up to eight female vines. If you have the room, plant several different male cultivars, so you'll be sure to have at least one male in bloom when your female plants are flowering.

## Planting and Care

Space kiwi vines about 15 feet (4.5 m) apart. Keep the soil moist up to harvest time to avoid premature leaf drop, but water less as winter approaches to help the vines adapt to colder temperatures. Mulch to conserve moisture and reduce weeds. Fertilize young vines lightly, if at all; give mature vines a healthy dose of compost in early spring. Kiwi trunks—even on the hardiest cultivars—are prone to winter injury unless you wrap them in burlap in the fall. Propagate kiwi vines using cuttings or grafting.

## Pruning and Training

You'll need to control enthusiastic kiwi growth so the vine won't tangle or shade itself out. Before planting, install a sturdy post-and-wire trellis (as you would for grapes). Insert a stake next to the vine at planting time, and cut out all

Kiwi vines are excellent for covering trellises and arbors. You can enjoy the shade and pick the fruit easily.

but one stem. Remove any sideshoots from the remaining stem and train it up the stake. When the stem reaches the height where you want the horizontal arms to be, pinch out the tip to promote sideshoots. Train one shoot in each direction; remove the others. For the first few years, trim these arms back each winter, leaving about 2 feet (60 cm) of the previous season's growth. Thin the fruiting canes (the shoots coming off the arms) to 1 foot (30 cm) apart.

On mature plants, cut the arms back to about 7 feet (2.1 m) each winter. Cut out 3-year-old fruiting canes. Head the sideshoots on remaining canes back to seven or eight buds. Several times through the growing season, remove any shoots that grow from the main trunk, and cut back any especially vigorous canes to four or five buds.

## Harvesting

Pick kiwi fruit in fall, when the seeds are black but most of the fruit is still quite firm. Cut the fruit off with a small piece of stem so it will keep longer. You can keep kiwis in cold storage up to 6 months or let them ripen at room temperature. Peel the fuzzy kiwi before eating. Eat kiwis fresh or preserve them by canning or drying.

## Problem Prevention and Control

Plant kiwi vines in well-drained soil to discourage root diseases. Surround young plants with a circle of wire mesh fencing to prevent cats from chewing or rolling on the leaves and stems.

# Raspberries

Raspberries, plucked soft and sweet, are the most delicate of fruits. This makes them perfect for home gardens—you can give them all the tender handling they need and enjoy them at their best.

Raspberries ripen through much of the summer and fall. Summer-bearing plants such as 'Boyne' fruit on 2-year old canes. Ever-bearing plants such as 'Heritage' and 'Redwing' can produce both a summer crop (on second-year canes) and a fall crop (on new canes). However, ever-bearers produce their best crops when only allowed to fruit in the fall, as explained in "Pruning and Training."

---

## Trellising Brambles

One way to make harvesting easy and keep your raspberries and trailing blackberries under control is to train them to a trellis. Install the trellis before planting your crop if possible. Start by setting sturdy 6-foot (1.8 m) posts every 20 feet (6 m) along the planting row. Then construct the trellis in one of the configurations described here.

**T-trellis:** This system makes picking easy for summer-bearing red, black, and purple raspberries, as well as blackberries. Add a cross arm to the top of each post and another arm about halfway down the post. Run wires between the ends of opposite arms. After cutting out the fruited canes after harvest, tie the remaining shoots to the bottom wires. When the shoots are tall enough, tie them to the top wire, too.

**Hedgerow Trellis:** A hedgerow trellis merely holds up bramble canes without spreading them apart. It works especially well for ever-bearing raspberries that you manage for one fall crop, since you don't need to think about separating the fruiting and nonfruiting canes. Put one cross arm about three-quarters of the way up each post so it resembles a T. Run wire along the end of each cross arm to support both sides of the planting.

---

## Best Climate and Site

Raspberries generally grow from Zones 3 to 9, but you'll need to find a cultivar that's appropriate for your climate. In Northern areas, try extra-hardy cultivars such as 'Boyne', 'Nova', and 'Nordic'. In the South, try heat-tolerant 'Dorman Red', 'Bababerry', and 'Southland'.

Find a site with full sun and good air circulation. Avoid places where high winds can whip the canes around and damage the plants. The site should be at least 1,000 feet (300 m) from any wild blackberries or similar bramble berries that could share problems. Provide fertile, well-drained soil that hasn't been used to grow bramble berries, tomatoes, potatoes, peppers, eggplants, or roses, which can leave behind diseases that attack raspberries.

## Choosing Your Plants

Buy only certified disease-free plants. You can get them bareroot, in containers, or as tissue-cultured plantlets. Your best option is probably vigorous, year-old, bareroot plants that have been propagated from virus-indexed stock.

Raspberries come in several colors. Yellow and red raspberries are the hardiest and are very sweet. Black raspberries are delicious but the least hardy and the most susceptible to diseases. Purple raspberries fall somewhere in between red and black.

Select raspberry cultivars that ripen at different times to spread out your harvest. For example, you could plant early-ripening, red summer raspberries such as 'Algonquin' and 'Chilliwack', then black raspberries such as 'Bristol', then ever-bearers such as 'Autumn Bliss' and 'Heritage'.

## Planting and Care

Plant red and yellow raspberries 2 feet (60 cm) apart in a row, and they'll fill in solid in a year or two. Space black and purple raspberries 3 feet (90 cm) apart. Keep the row width fairly narrow—6 to 24 inches (15 to 60 cm) wide—to allow every cane to get plenty of sun and be

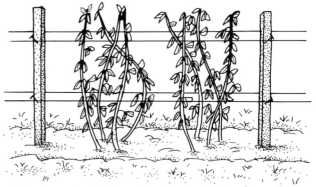

A basic post-and-wire trellis can serve to keep raspberries from sprawling out of bounds and make picking simple.

fully productive. Mow or till along the edge of the row as needed to keep the raspberries from creeping out.

Apply compost and a little balanced organic fertilizer in late winter, if needed, for good growth. Mulch to discourage weeds and keep the soil evenly moist; water during dry spells. Propagate by division or layering, but only if you are sure your plants are healthy. In many cases, you're best off buying new, certified disease-free plants.

## Pruning and Training

Regular pruning will encourage your plants to produce high yields of top-quality berries. For a single fall crop on ever-bearers, simply cut off all the old canes at ground level when they are done fruiting.

Summer-bearing red raspberries produce fruit on 2-year-old canes. Cut down the old, grayish brown fruit-producing canes after you harvest, but leave the new, current-season canes to produce berries next year. In late winter, remove the smallest canes to leave three to six sturdy canes per 1 foot (30 cm) of row.

Black and purple raspberries produce fruit on side branches that grow off the older canes. During summer, cut off the fruit-producing canes after you harvest, and snip off the tips of new canes when they're 3 to 4 feet (0.9 to 1.2 m) tall to make them branch. During the dormant season, remove the smallest canes to leave four to six sturdy canes per 1 foot (30 cm) of row. On the remaining canes, cut out any spindly side branches and trim the remaining side branches back to 8 to 10 inches (20 to 25 cm) long.

## Harvesting

Harvest berries when they're sweet and ripe. Eat them promptly or freeze them.

## Problem Prevention and Control

Several fungal diseases may attack raspberries. Powdery mildew can cause a white coating on fruit, leaves, and shoots. Anthracnose produces dark blotches on canes and possibly sideshoot dieback. Cane blight causes wilted shoot tips and dark spots on the canes.

Rust produces orange spots that later turn black.

Fruit rot produces gray mold on berries.

If birds are beating you to your berries, cover the plants with netting. Roll back the cover as needed to harvest.

Proper pruning, as previously described, should prevent many of the problems. If these diseases were a problem the previous year, spray with lime-sulfur when the buds begin to turn green. Check catalogs for resistant cultivars.

Viruses may produce stunted growth, curled, yellow-marked leaves, and/or crumbly, malformed berries. There is no cure; dig and destroy infected plants. Start a new patch in a different site with certified virus-free plants.

Crown gall can cause lumpy swellings on the roots and the base of shoots. Dig up and destroy infected plants. Replant new stock in a different site. Avoid wounding stems.

Bright orange spots on the undersides of leaves in spring indicates orange rust. This incurable disease attacks black and purple raspberries, as well as blackberries. Remove and destroy infected plants.

Gray fuzz on fruit indicates fruit rot. Pick and destroy infected berries. Gather ripe fruit daily.

Borers are insect pests that damage canes, causing wilted shoot tips. Look for a small entry hole near the base of the wilted area. Prune off damaged tips or canes, borer and all. If the shoot tip is wilted but you don't see an entry hole and if the inside of the cane is discolored, a disease may be the culprit; cut off the cane at the base and destroy it.

# Strawberries

Once you start to grow your own strawberries, you'll never want to be without them. You can pick your fill of the sweet, juicy fruits and still have some left over for freezing and making jam. For a large, early harvest, grow June-bearing strawberries. For smaller harvests in early summer and fall, try ever-bearing strawberries. Or, for strawberries any time during the growing season, grow day-neutral cultivars. (For an extraspecial taste sensation, try tiny-fruited alpine strawberries, too; you'll learn about them in the Strawberry, alpine entry on page 153.)

## Best Climate and Site

Strawberries can grow in Zones 3 to 10, but you need to choose cultivars appropriate for your climate. For Southern areas, try 'Apollo', 'Arking', 'Chandler', and 'Sequoia'. In the North, try 'Crimson King' or 'Fort Laramie'. Of the day-neutral types, 'Tristar', 'Tribute', 'Fern', and 'Selva' can grow well in a fairly wide range of climates; 'Brighton' and 'Heckler' are best in cooler areas of California.

Choose a site that's in full sun (or light afternoon shade for day-neutral strawberries) and free from late-spring frosts. The soil should be fertile and well drained. If possible, avoid garden areas previously used to grow peppers, tomatoes, potatoes, eggplant, melons, okra, mints, raspberries or blackberries, mums, or roses—crops that may leave behind problems that can attack strawberries. Add extra organic matter before planting to make the soil rich and moist.

Compact but prolific, strawberries are great for growing in pots and planters; see "Fruits for Containers" on page 22 for tips. Propagate strawberries at home by transplanting rooted runners. Commercially produced plants are often propagated by tissue culture.

## Choosing Your Plants

Always start with certified disease-free plants. In areas where diseases are a problem, grow disease-resistant cultivars (as suggested in "Problem Prevention and Control"). Strawberries are self-fruitful, so you can get fruit from just one plant. But to have the longest possible harvest, grow some of each type (June-bearers, ever-bearers, and day-neutrals).

## Planting and Care

For an easy-care strawberry bed, mound your garden soil in a bed about 6 inches (15 cm) tall and 2 feet (60 cm) wide, install drip irrigation, and cover it all

Ever-bearing and day-neutral types produce a harvest within months after planting; June-bearers fruit the next year.

with plastic mulch before planting. Cut X-shaped slits in the plastic, and plant through the slits into the soil.

In cold-winter areas (Zones 3 to 6), plant strawberries in early spring. In Zones 7 to 10, plant in fall or late winter. Space plants 1 to 2 feet (30 to 60 cm) apart, depending on the training system you want to use (see "Pruning and Training" for details). To help new plants get established, pinch off the flowers on all newly planted strawberries until June.

Keep the soil evenly moist from the time the plants are young until the berries are almost ripe. Apply compost tea to June- and ever-bearers once in early summer; apply it to day-neutral plants once a month during warm weather. Mulch with straw to reduce the spread of disease spores in splashing drops of rain.

At the end of the season, mow (with a mower set on high) or cut off all the leaves. Rake up and remove the leaves (destroy them if they are diseased). Dig out any weeds and unwanted strawberry plants. Then coat the bed with a 1-inch (2.5 cm) layer of compost and remulch with straw. In early winter, cover the plants with a couple of inches of straw to prevent cold damage. Pull back the mulch as soon as plants begin to grow again in spring. If frost threatens new growth, cover the plants overnight with a floating row cover.

Set strawberry plants so the crown is even with the soil surface.

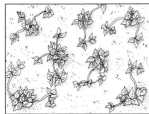 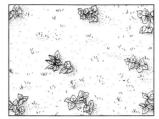

The matted row system is good for June-bearing types.

Use the hill system for plants with few runners.

## Pruning and Training

To get the most out of your strawberry patch, choose one of the systems below to manage the plants.

**Hill System** This system is especially good for ever-bearing or day-neutral strawberries. Set plants out in double, staggered rows. Space ever-bearers 12 inches (30 cm) apart and day-neutral types 7 inches (17.5 cm) apart. Regularly pinch out any runners that form.

**Matted Row System** June-bearing strawberries, which produce lots of runners, can fill up space fast with this system. Space plants 2 feet (60 cm) apart and leave 4 feet (1.2 m) between rows. Then let the runners spread out to fill in the open space. Mow along the edges of the beds as needed to keep the walkways between them at least 18 inches (45 cm) wide.

## Harvesting

Pick the berries when they are fully colored, tender, and sweet. Leave the stem on for better storage. Eat the fruit fresh, refrigerate it for a few days, or can or freeze just after picking for longer storage.

## Problem Prevention and Control

Gray mold (Botrytis blight) can produce a fuzzy gray coating on blossoms and berries. Pick ripe fruit

Starting over with new plants in a new site every 4 years can prevent diseases from getting established.

You'll avoid most problems by starting with certified disease-free plants of disease-resistant cultivars.

frequently. Remove and destroy damaged flowers and fruits as you spot them.

Several problems can cause wilted plants. To determine the cause, dig up a few plants. If there are few or no side roots and the roots are reddish inside when cut lengthwise, red stele is the problem. If the roots are black and rotting, root rot is the problem. Remove and destroy infected plants. Replant in a new site with red stele-resistant cultivars, such as 'Allstar', 'Delite', 'Guardian', 'Surecrop', and 'Tristar'.

If the roots are not damaged, cut the crown of the plant (the point where the leaves meet the roots) in half. If the center of the crown is hollowed out and has white grubs inside, crown moth larvae or crown borers are the problem. Dig and destroy infected plants. Replant in a new site at least 300 feet (90 m) away.

If there is no visible damage to the crown or roots, Verticillium wilt may be the problem. Dig and destroy plants. Replant in a new site with resistant cultivars, such as 'Allstar', 'Blakemore', 'Delight', 'Robinson', 'Surecrop', and 'Tristar'.

Fungal leaf spots are common problems. Removing all the leaves when you renovate the bed each year should control most problems. When establishing a new bed, use resistant cultivars, such as 'Blakemore', 'Delite', 'Earlibelle', and 'Surecrop'.

Keep an eye out for tarnished plant bugs, small green to brown bugs that can cause distorted fruits. Covering plants with floating row covers while the fruit is developing can keep these pests off plants.

If birds are a problem, see "Coping with Animal Pests" on page 76 for control suggestions.

# NUT-BEARING PLANTS

Nut trees are attractive and productive additions to any landscape. You'll enjoy the beautiful pink flowers on almonds and the creamy-colored flower clusters on chestnuts. For great fall foliage color, try hazelnuts, which change to burgundy before the leaves drop. As a bonus, you'll get a crop of tasty nuts from any of these easy-care plants.

In this chapter, you'll learn about several of the most popular nut-bearing plants, including almonds, chestnuts, hazelnuts, hickories, pecans, and walnuts. In "Uncommon Fruits, Berries, and Nuts," starting on page 124, you'll learn about other excellent nut producers, including beeches, butternuts, heartnuts, oaks, and pines.

As with any crop, the key to success with nut growing depends on choosing the right plants for your site and needs. First, decide what role you want the plant to play in your landscape. For a tall, regal shade tree, consider plants such as chestnuts, hickories, oaks, pecans, and walnuts. If space is limited, smaller plants are probably more in line with your needs. Almonds make good small ornamental trees, while bushy hazelnuts look great in shrub borders or informal hedges.

Once you have an idea of the kind of plant you want, take a look at your growing conditions—especially the soil. Greg Miller of the Empire Chestnut Company in Carrollton, Ohio, offers the following guidelines for good luck with nut trees:

- Pecans and shellbark hickories grow in rich, moist bottomlands. Pecans tend to grow in more Southern areas, while shellbark hickories are naturally more common in Northern areas.

- Shagbark hickories thrive on slightly higher land that's better drained.
- Black and English walnuts grow in deep, rich but well-drained soil. They will thrive on slight slopes or in sandy soil along rivers.
- Chestnuts are native to sandy mountainsides with acidic soil; good drainage is critical.

It's also important to choose a spot with good air circulation and lots of sunlight. The entries in this chapter offer further specifics for choosing just the right site for each particular nut crop.

Before finalizing your choice, make sure you have enough room for the plants to reach their mature size. Pecans, for instance, can reach 150 feet (45 m) tall and 50 feet (15 m) across. You'll actually need twice this space, however, since pecans and most other nut-bearing plants require a second compatible tree for pollination. Also keep in mind that big trees can drop their nuts quickly, so keep them away from patios, walkways, and other areas where the falling nuts could be a problem.

Most nut trees have long taproots, which make them hard to handle in the nursery and hard to get going when planted out. It's best to start with a young field-grown plant that's been specially handled several times to develop a bushy set of roots. Put the young plant in a broad, deep hole with loose soil. Then keep the planting site moist until the tree begins growing strongly. To learn more about the basics of establishing and caring for your carefully chosen nut crops, read their entries in this chapter—then get ready to enjoy your handsome, low-maintenance nut trees!

Nut-bearing plants come in a range of sizes, from bushy filberts and apricots to tall beech, hickory, and walnut trees. Choose the size and type that is best suited for your site and climate to enjoy a generous harvest each year.

# Almonds

In the right climate, almonds are beautiful and rewarding plants. They grow best in the mild Sacramento and San Joaquin valleys of California, but they are worth trying elsewhere, too; you just have to be careful to choose the right cultivars for the conditions your site has to offer.

## Best Climate and Site

Almonds grow best in full sun and fertile, well-drained, sandy loam soil. Most almonds are hardy from Zones 6 to 9, but they have special needs even within those zones. They bloom even earlier in spring than peaches, so they need a climate and site that protects the flowers from cold damage. For pollinating bees to be active this early, the spring weather also has to be warm and dry. To improve the chances for good fruit set, try the later-blooming cultivar 'Titan'. Once the almonds are set successfully, they'll need 180 to 240 frost-free days to ripen.

While almonds appreciate mild conditions, a climate that's warm year-round isn't the answer; most almonds also require some winter chilling at 45°F (8°C) or lower to begin growing promptly in spring. Look at chill hour requirements when you're looking for the right cultivar. For example, 'Ne-Plus-Ultra' needs 250 chill hours; 'All-In-One', a home garden favorite, requires 500 chill hours; 'Hall's Hardy', which will grow in the Pacific Northwest to Zone 5, needs 600 to 800 chill hours.

## Choosing Your Plants

Full-sized almond trees reach 20 to 30 feet (6 to 9 m) tall. With the exception of self-pollinating 'All-In-One', you'll have to plant two cultivars that bloom at the same time for cross-pollination; check catalog descriptions for recommended pollinators. (If you grow late-blooming 'Titan', you can pollinate it with peach cultivars.) Keep almond trees fairly close together to encourage better pollination.

If you prefer to spread out your harvest, you can choose early- and later-maturing almonds. One of the earliest-producing cultivars is 'Nonpareil'; 'Monterey' and 'Fritz' bear a month or so later.

## Planting and Care

Plant full-sized trees 25 feet (7.5 m) apart in well-drained but fertile soil. Mulch with compost each

Most almonds need cross-pollination to set their crop; check catalog descriptions to get the right companions.

spring. Water plants regularly when the weather is hot and dry. Propagate almond trees by grafting.

## Pruning and Training

Train almonds into an open-center form similar to that used for peaches. (See "Peaches and Nectarines" on page 93 for details.) But as you prune each year, do more heading and less thinning to develop a much thicker network of branches and, consequently, more nuts. Five- to 7-year-old fruit-bearing spurs are most productive. Give them room by cutting out older branches every few years.

## Harvesting

Most almond trees begin to produce nuts in 3 to 4 years. When they mature in late summer or early fall, the nut hulls will split open. Use a padded stick to knock the nuts from the tree onto a cloth on the ground. Let them dry for 10 days, then separate the nuts from the hulls. Store them at cool temperatures for maximum shelf life.

## Problem Prevention and Control

Unfortunately, disease resistance is minimal in almonds so they're seldom grown outside a dry climate. Keep mulch away from the trunk to discourage rodent activity. Pick up all fallen nuts and destroy the bad ones to reduce problems with navel orangeworm—white, brown-headed caterpillars that feed on the nut meat. 'Mission' is resistant to navel orangeworm. Almonds share many pests and diseases with peaches; see "Peaches and Nectarines" on page 93 for more information.

# Chestnuts

Roasted over an open fire or stuffed into holiday turkeys, chestnuts are a rich treat for winter enjoyment. Unlike other nuts, chestnuts contain about 40 percent carbohydrates, 10 percent protein, and only 3 percent fat—somewhat more like wheat than a nut. As a plus, the trees have creamy strands of flowers that look as good as the nuts taste.

Unfortunately, the classic American chestnuts (*Castanea dentata*) have been destroyed by chestnut blight disease in most parts of the United States. But you can still grow these delicious nuts on blight-resistant Chinese chestnuts (*C. mollissima*) or American-Chinese hybrids. You also can grow chestnut trees for their prized wood, which can be as valuable as black walnut.

## Best Climate and Site

Chestnuts generally grow from Zones 4 to 9. Most are hardy to about −25°F (−32°C). To really stretch Northern limits, try 'Miller's Manchurian' chestnut, which is hardy to −28°F (−33°C). But even the most cold-hardy cultivars need a site that's not prone to late-spring frosts, which can damage the new growth and prevent or reduce flowering. Provide full sun and well-drained, loose, fertile, acid soil.

## Choosing Your Plants

You can plant grafted or seedling trees. Seedling trees are not as predictable as far as habit and yield, but they are generally hardier and best to use in Zones 4 and 5. Grafted trees produce more consistent results and tend to fail less in Zones 6 to 9, but they still may have graft problems there.

Chestnuts produce more reliable crops if cross-pollinated with another tree. Hybrid chestnuts require cross-pollination, ideally with a seedling tree; see the catalog description for suggested pollinators.

## Planting and Care

Chestnuts can be spaced up to 100 feet (30 m) apart—but no farther—to ensure good pollination. Commercial growers sometimes plant them 20 feet (6 m) apart and train them into a hedge when they begin to touch. You can set chestnut trees even closer if you want them to grow straight, upright trunks for timber. Smaller-growing Chinese chestnuts mature from 20 to 40 feet (6 to 12 m) tall. For

Chinese chestnuts produce glossy, smooth, meaty nuts enclosed within a densely spiny husk.

nut production, plant them 40 to 80 feet (12 to 24 m) apart. Mulch to eliminate weeds; apply compost or balanced fertilizer in late spring after the danger of frost has passed. Propagate by seed.

## Pruning and Training

Train chestnut trees to a central-leader system (as explained in "Apples" on page 80). Encourage broad branching angles for strong limbs. Remove dead or damaged limbs as you spot them, along with any low-hanging branches that interfere with mowing and harvesting.

## Harvesting

Chestnuts bear in 3 to 5 years and continue to produce larger and larger harvests for many years. In fall, the nuts mature and drop to the ground. Pick them up promptly. You can store them at 33°F (1°C) and 90 percent humidity for up to 6 months. Fresh kernels may be damaged by freezing.

## Problem Prevention and Control

Grow resistant chestnut species and cultivars to avoid the deadly chestnut blight disease. Chestnut weevil larvae may feed inside nuts and then enter the soil when nuts fall to the ground. Pick up all fallen nuts daily and place them in a bag or bucket so any larvae that are present can't get to the soil to complete their life cycle. Wait a few weeks, then pick out the good nuts and destroy the rest.

# Hazelnuts

Hazelnuts, also known as fil-berts, produce small but plump nuts on several species of tree- and shrub-form plants. European hazels (*Corylus avellana*) have delicious nuts and are a popular orchard crop in the North-west. American and beaked hazels (*C. americana* and *C. cornuta*) are growing in importance because they are less prone to eastern filbert blight, a fungal disease that causes branches and eventually whole plants to die back to the roots. Hybrids between European and American hazels, called filazels or hazelberts, combine the hardiness of American species with the nut quali-ties of European hazels. Trazels are hybrids between European and Turkish hazels (*C. colurna*). They com-bine the big, rich-flavored nuts of the latter with the disease resistance of the former.

## Best Climate and Site

American and beaked hazels are hardy in Zones 2 to 8. European hazels are hardy in Zones 4 to 8. Turkish fil-berts are hardy in Zones 4 to 9. They all do best in full sun (or light afternoon shade in hot climates) and well-drained, light to loamy soil.

Hazels bloom during late winter or very early spring, long before the foliage is ready to emerge. Unlike almonds, hazels don't depend on mild weather for insect pollinators, since they are wind-pollinated. Light frost usually doesn't hurt the flowers either; they are hardy to a little below freezing. But in climates with extremely erratic temperatures, the flowers may be lost in a severe cold snap.

## Choosing Your Plants

Most hazels need a compatible partner for cross-pollination; some need pollen from two other cultivars. If you have the space, grow an assortment of compat-ible plants to ensure good pollination. (Check catalog descriptions for suggestions of compatible cultivars.) If you only have room for one plant, try the self-fertile 'Winkler' American hazel.

## Planting and Care

American hazels reach 6 to 10 feet (1.8 to 3 m) tall; beaked hazels grow 15 feet (4.5 m) tall; European hazels reach 15 to 25 feet (4.5 to 7.5 m) tall; Turkish hazels reach 70 feet (21 m) tall. You can plant shrubby American, beaked, and European hazels as an informal hedge or in a cluster by spacing them 3 to 5 feet (0.9 to 1.5 m) apart. Space Turkish filberts 30 feet (9 m) apart.

Besides yielding a tasty crop of nuts, filberts also produce a show of ornamental, dangling catkins in spring.

Water mature trees during drought or grow drought-tolerant beaked hazels. Mulch to reduce weeds. Propagate by seed, layering, or grafting.

## Pruning and Training

European, beaked, and American hazels naturally grow into dense bushes that make good hedges; thin out some of the older wood each winter to encourage new growth to sprout. Or grow them as small, multi-stemmed, vase-shaped trees by removing the root sprouts regularly. Turkish hazels grow into taller trees that need pruning only to maintain wide branch angles and to remove damaged or diseased wood.

## Harvesting

Hazels begin producing nuts in 2 to 3 years. They ripen in fall and are ready to pick when the nut comes free from the husk easily. Pluck them off the plant or tap the limbs with a padded stick to make the nuts drop onto a cloth. The European cultivar 'Barcelona' can drop its nuts without tapping. Let the nuts dry until they are crunchy. Store in a cool place for up to a year.

## Problem Prevention and Control

Where eastern filbert blight is a problem, plant less susceptible American hazels, resistant beaked hazels, or moderately resistant European cultivars such as 'Hall's Giant' and 'Barcelona'. Turkish hazels are quite resis-tant when mature and moderately resistant when young. Net shrubs to keep squirrels away from the nuts. Destroy damaged nuts to eliminate filbertworms.

# Hickories

Two of the most impressive trees of American woodlands are shagbark and shellbark hickories (*Carya ovata* and *C. laciniosa*). Both species are easy to identify by their shaggy, peeling bark. Shagbark hickories produce a sweet, white nut that's easy to pop out of its thin shell. Shellbark hickory nuts are light brown and larger but have a thicker shell. Both hickories have valuable, strong, dense wood.

## Best Climate and Site

Shagbark and shellbark hickories grow in Zones 3 to 8. They both appreciate fertile soil, but shagbark hickory thrives in drier sites while shellbark hickory excels in moist floodplains. Start young trees in sunny, open areas.

## Choosing Your Plants

Shellbark and shagbark hickories can be self-pollinating, so you may get a crop with only one tree. But there are some hickory cultivars, including 'Missouri Mammoth', that demand a second compatible tree for good pollination. To be sure of a bountiful harvest, it's smart to plant two compatible trees.

Seed-grown trees can produce good crops, but grafted plants will give you a harvest sooner. You can buy grafted cultivars with larger or more easily extracted nuts. Among shellbark hickories, for instance, 'Eureka' and 'Harold' are easier to crack, and 'Missouri Mammoth' has extra-large nuts. Among the shagbarks, 'Grainger', 'Yoder #1', 'Porter', and 'Weschcke' have especially thin shells and large kernels.

## Planting and Care

Hickories, which can get to be over 100 feet (30 m) tall with a 40- to 60-foot (12 to 18 m) spread, are appropriate for a fairly large yard. Because they tend to be deep rooted and have high branches, you can easily grow other plants in

To gather your hickory harvest, simply rake up the dropped nuts and separate them from the hulls.

Hickory trees grow quite large, and their dropped leaves, fruits, and stems can look messy, so give them a spot somewhat away from the house.

the light shade beneath them. If you buy a plant with a long taproot, give it a deep planting hole to accommodate the entire length of the root.

Mulch hickories with compost and irrigate young trees during dry weather. If the foliage becomes discolored or begins to emerge in bunched-up rosettes, have the foliage tested for nutrient shortages. If you start a tree in the lawn, keep the turf away from the root zone for several years after planting.

## Pruning and Training

Your hickory trees will naturally assume a central-leader shape. Prune occasionally to remove a branch that's competing with the main trunk or that emerges at a narrow angle. Call an arborist to remove large dead or damaged limbs. If you want to sell the wood, remove lower limbs to develop a long, straight trunk.

## Harvesting

Seed-grown hickories can take up to 15 years to produce nuts. But grafted trees such as shellbark hickory cultivars 'Harold', 'Keystone', and 'Kaskaskia' begin to produce nuts in 5 to 7 years. To harvest, rake up dropped nuts and hulls and pick out the nuts. Store the nuts in a cool, dry spot.

## Problem Prevention and Control

Hickories share many of the same pests and diseases as pecans. To prevent problems with nut-boring insects, pick up all fallen nuts promptly and destroy any bad ones. Hickories are less susceptible to scab than pecans.

# Pecans

In the South, the pecan is king. The large, rich-flavored nuts emerge easily from their shells—a big timesaver. They're handy to use for baking, stuffing, or sprinkling on desserts or vegetables. Pecan trees mature to be tall and stately, with a spreading oval canopy and dark green foliage.

## Best Climate and Site

Pecans generally grow best in Zones 6 to 9. They thrive in full sun and moist, rich soils. For the nuts to mature, they need growing-season temperatures that hover around 75°F (24°C) or higher—without much of a temperature drop at night. Many cultivars also need a long, frost-free growing season—from 150 to 210 days. If your growing season is closer to the 150-day range, choose extra-hardy and early-maturing cultivars such as 'Major' or 'Giles'. Plant them in a site not prone to late-spring or early-fall frosts.

## Choosing Your Plants

The male (pollen-providing) and female (nut-producing) flowers on pecan trees usually don't open at the same time. For this reason, you usually need to plant another tree that can provide pollen when the main crop tree is ready. Check with your county Cooperative Extension Service to find out which pecan pollinators work best in your region. A few cultivars, including 'Starking Hardy Giant', 'Hastings', 'Jackson', and 'Giles', may have some male and female flowers that bloom at the same time. They may produce nuts when planted alone but will be more productive if cross-pollinated.

## Planting and Care

Pecans grow to 150 feet (45 m) tall. Space them 35 to 50 feet (10.5 to 15 m) apart. Plant them in soil that's fertile, loose, deep, and light. Like hickories, pecan trees can be difficult to transplant because of their deep taproot. If you can't find bushy-rooted trees, buy small plants with most of the taproot intact, and plant them in a hole deep enough to accommodate the entire root. Mulch with compost as needed for good fertility and irrigate during drought. If growth becomes stunted and nuts are misshapen, have the foliage tested for nutrient deficiencies, particularly zinc. Propagate by grafting.

## Pruning and Training

Pecans naturally take on a central-leader shape. Prune as needed to remove a branch that's competing with

Established pecans seldom need much pruning; just trim out dead or damaged branches as you spot them.

the main trunk or that emerges with a narrow angle. Call an arborist to remove large dead or damaged limbs. If you want to sell the wood, remove lower limbs to develop a long straight trunk.

## Harvesting

Grafted trees will begin bearing nuts in 4 to 7 years. Tap limbs with a padded stick or pick up fallen nuts to gather the harvest. Remove the husks and dry the nuts for several weeks. Store in a cool place for a few months or freeze for longer storage.

## Problem Prevention and Control

Pecan weevils lay their eggs in almost-mature nuts, and their larvae feed inside the nuts. Rake up and destroy damaged nuts. Catch adults weevils with a Tedder's trap, as explained for plum curculio in "Apples" on page 80. Whitewash the trunks of your trees and set two of these dark, tall, pyramidal traps beside each tree. The weevils will climb up and fall into a trap inside.

You also can barricade weevils away from the tree. In late July, mow any vegetation under the tree as short as you can, then cover the soil from the trunk out to the branch tips with a floating row cover. Leave the row cover in place until you're done harvesting. Pick up any nuts that have fallen early and destroy them.

Diseases such as scab can be a problem in moist, humid areas, causing olive-brown spots on leaves and shucks, as well as early nut drop. Try disease-resistant cultivars such as 'Cape Fear', 'Caddo', 'Desirable', 'Elliott', 'Jackson', and 'Stuart'.

# Walnuts

Walnut trees combine a big, bold shape with feathery—almost delicate—foliage that allows some filtered sun to peek through. Because they're deep-rooted, walnuts make great shade trees for lawn or garden areas. The main nut-producing species are English (also called Persian) walnuts (*Juglans regia*) and black walnuts (*J. nigra*). English walnuts fall free of their husk when mature—a very handy trait. English walnut trees also stay smaller than black walnuts and begin to produce nuts at a younger age. Black walnuts are hardier and taller growing, but the nuts fall sealed in a tough husk that you'll have to remove.

## Best Climate and Site

English walnuts generally grow best in Zones 6 to 9. Most cultivars require a relatively long, warm growing season for the nuts to mature. In cooler areas, try early maturing 'Hansen'.

Black walnuts, hardy in Zones 4 to 8, grow best in moist, rich soil. They will tolerate drought once established. Be careful when you grow other plants near walnut trees. Black walnuts, in particular, but also English walnuts, give off a compound called juglone that will kill tomatoes, blueberries, potatoes, rhododendrons, blackberries, pines, apples, and some other plants growing nearby.

## Choosing Your Plants

Like pecans, walnut trees have separate male and female flowers that usually open at different times. This means you need to plant another compatible cultivar to provide pollination. Check with your county Cooperative Extension Service for recommended pollinators.

You can buy inexpensive seedling walnuts to grow for timber. But for nut crops, start with earlier-producing grafted cultivars. In the western United States, avoid English walnuts grafted on black walnuts; they can develop a fatal graft incompatibility problem.

## Planting and Care

English walnuts can grow 30 to 50 feet (9 to 15 m) tall; black walnuts can grow 100 feet (30 m) tall. Space both kinds 25 to 30 feet (7.5 to 9 m) apart. Keep the young trees free of weeds and well watered. Propagate by seed or grafting.

Walnuts have deep roots, so it's easy to plant under them. However, they also release a substance that is harmful to some plants.

## Pruning and Training

Walnuts naturally grow into a central-leader shape. Prune occasionally to remove a branch that's competing with the main trunk or that emerges with a narrow angle. Call an arborist to remove large dead or damaged limbs.

## Harvesting

Seedlings can take 10 years to produce nuts; most grafted trees begin to bear in 3 to 5 years. English walnuts drop mature nuts after they split out of their husk; black walnuts drop them enclosed in the husk. The husk on black walnuts releases a dark stain, so wear rubber gloves when you handle them. Place the nuts on your driveway or on some flat rocks, and drive over them, hit them, or step on them until the husks come loose. Wash the nuts off, let them dry for a couple of weeks, and store them for a few months in a cool place or longer in the freezer.

## Problem Prevention and Control

Pick up fallen leaves and nuts and destroy the ones that are damaged or diseased. Where anthracnose is a problem, causing brown-spotted leaves, grow resistant black walnuts such as 'Clermont', 'Ridgeway', and 'Farrington'. If you notice nuts drying up and dropping early, codling moth larvae may be at work; see "Apples" on page 80 for control information.

# Uncommon Fruits, Berries, and Nuts

When you decide to raise your own fruits, berries, and nuts, you have the luxury of choosing from among the many cultivars of familiar fruits, berries, and nuts, as well as from among the less familiar ones which are the subject of this section. These uncommon fruits, berries, and nuts are not all exotic, tropical plants. For example, service-berry is native throughout much of the USA, lingon-berry is native into the northern reaches of Canada and Scandinavia, and sea grape is a tropical fruit that grows wild in the sands of our south Florida coastline.

Uncommon fruits, berries, and nuts are easy to grow. Give them nothing more than a site to their liking as well as timely weeding and watering, at least in their infancy, and you will be rewarded with regular and abundant harvests. Pest or disease problems are rare, and many of the plants do not even need regular pruning.

A real plus for some uncommon fruits, berries, and nuts is the beauty of the plants themselves. Feast your eyes on the stunning flowers of maypop or pomegran-ate, the silvery leaves of feijoa, the majestic form of beech. As testimony to their beauty, some of the plants we are calling "uncommon fruits, berries, and nuts"—highbush cranberry, Nanking cherry, and barberry, for example—are actually familiar ornamental shrubs. Ironically, many people appreciate the way the bright red fruits adorn these plants without realizing that they also are edible. You will find every category of landscape plant—tree, shrub, vine, groundcover—among uncommon fruits, berries, and nuts, making them perfect for edible landscaping.

A few uncommon fruits, berries, and nuts do hail from tropical or subtropical climates. But even if you live where winters are frigid, don't let that deter you from growing some of these warm-weather plants. Many can be grown in pots and wintered indoors. A kumquat, for example, can happily live its whole life in a 2-gallon (9 l) pot. This handsome evergreen tree will fill a sunny room with the wonderful aroma of its blossoms, as well as providing you with fruit.

Growing uncommon fruits, berries, and nuts is a nice way to round out your fruit larder. And if you ever had occasion to taste one of these uncommon fruits, berries, or nuts and got hooked on its flavor, growing your own may be the only way to reliably have the delicacy on hand.

You may be surprised by how many ornamental plants also have edible parts. Prickly pears (*Opuntia* spp.), for instance, produce showy yellow flowers followed by mild-flavored, egg-shaped fruits. The fleshy pads are also edible.

*Akebia quinata*                    Lardizabalaceae    *Persea americana*                    Lauraceae

# AKEBIA

# AVOCADO

*Akebia vines produce bluish or purple fruits. Numerous dark seeds are embedded in the edible, jelly-like flesh within. The fruit has a mild flavor reminiscent of watermelon.*

*Because of its rough skin and green, sometimes almost black, color, avocado was once called "alligator pear." Inside, the edible flesh is buttery smooth, with a rich, nutty flavor.*

BEST CLIMATE AND SITE: Zones 4–8. Akebia grows best in full sun but tolerates light shade. The plants are not finicky as to soil as long as it is well drained. The flowers appear early, so choose a site that's not prone to late-spring frosts.

HEIGHT AND SPREAD: Height 10–20 feet (3–6 m); spread 15–20 feet (4.5–6 m).

GROWING GUIDELINES: Plant container-grown vines any time the ground isn't frozen, or set out bareroot plants in spring or fall, while they are dormant. Space plants 10 feet (3 m) apart to spread out on a trellis or arbor. If fruit set is poor, try hand pollination: Transfer pollen with a paintbrush from the male flowers (the ones toward the end of each flower stalk) to the female flowers (near the base of each flower stalk).

PRUNING: Just before growth begins, thin out stems that are spindly or tangled.

PROPAGATION: Mix seed with moist peat moss and keep it at temperatures just above freezing for 1–2 months; then sow the seed in a warm, bright place. Akebia will also root from softwood cuttings.

PEST AND DISEASE CONTROL: Generally no significant problems.

HARVESTING AND STORAGE: When the fruit is ripe, the skin splits lengthwise; pick the fruit at this point for fresh eating. For storage, pick fruit just as it starts to split along its seam.

BEST CLIMATE AND SITE: Zones 9–10. Plant in full sun. Avocado grows best in well-drained soil with a pH between 5.5 and 6.5.

HEIGHT AND SPREAD: Height 20–60 feet (6–18 m); spread 25–35 feet (7.5–10.5 m).

GROWING GUIDELINES: Plant in spring, with the base of the trunk slightly higher out of the ground than it was in the nursery. Space plants 25–35 feet (7.5–10.5 m) apart. Avocados are self-fruitful (so you can get fruit from just one plant), although cross-pollination may improve yields.

PRUNING: Prune as needed after harvest, mostly to limit the size of the tree.

PROPAGATION: Graft onto seedling or cutting-grown rootstocks.

PEST AND DISEASE CONTROL: Avocado root rot can occur where drainage is poor. Avoid this problem by planting certified disease-free plants in a good site. There is no cure for infected trees. In humid areas, watch for leaf diseases. Minimize damage by keeping trees fertilized and watered as needed, pruning to promote air circulation among branches, and cleaning up infected leaves that fall.

HARVESTING AND STORAGE: When fruit is mature but still hard, clip it off with piece of stem attached. Dark-skinned cultivars turn dark when mature; green cultivars yellow slightly. Use fruits when they soften slightly.

*Musa* spp.                                    Musaceae

# BANANA

*Bananas are produced on large perennial plants that grow to tree-like proportions. The edible flesh of all bananas is yellow, with a creamy texture and a sweet, rich flavor.*

BEST CLIMATE AND SITE: Zone 10. Give bananas full sun and well-drained, slightly acid soil.

HEIGHT AND SPREAD: Height 8–30 feet (2.4–9 m); spread 8–20 feet (2.4–6 m).

GROWING GUIDELINES: Plant any time of year, spacing plants 10–20 feet (3–6 m) apart. Bananas do not need cross-pollination, so you can get fruit from just one plant. The "stem" is really a pseudostem, a tightly wound sheath of leaves. The pseudostem dies to the ground after fruiting but is replaced by others growing up from the rhizome (thickened underground stem). Cut off male flowers, which form at the far end of the fruit stalk. Plants are heavy feeders, so fertilize regularly, and provide abundant water in warm weather.

PRUNING: Remove all but three pseudostems—one fruiting, one ready to follow, and one just peeking up from below. Cut down the fruiting pseudostem after harvest.

PROPAGATION: Divide rhizomes or dig up suckers with some attached roots.

PEST AND DISEASE CONTROL: Generally no significant problems.

HARVESTING AND STORAGE: Cut off the entire stalk when some fruits just begin to turn color. Allow the fruits to ripen to their yellow or red color at room temperature. Bananas are best for fresh eating; you can also dry them for storage.

*Berberis* spp.                              Berberidaceae

# BARBERRY

*Barberries produce red, yellow, or black berries; both the flesh and skin of the berries are edible. The flavor is usually tart, but some species have enough sugar to be dried into "raisins."*

BEST CLIMATE AND SITE: Zones 3–9, depending on the species. (Evergreen species are generally less hardy than deciduous species.) Barberries prefer full sun and moist, well-drained soil.

HEIGHT AND SPREAD: Height 3–12 feet (90–360 cm); spread 3–12 feet (90–360 cm).

GROWING GUIDELINES: Set out container-grown plants any time the soil isn't frozen, or plant bareroot shrubs in spring or fall, while they are still dormant. Space plants 3–12 feet (90–360 cm) apart, depending on how big the species gets.

PRUNING: Cut a few of the oldest stems to the ground in winter. Also shorten spindly stems and thin out suckers if the stems are crowded.

PROPAGATION: Mix seed with moist peat moss and refrigerate it for 2–3 months before sowing in a warm, bright place. Or dig up and transplant suckers from the base of a bush.

PEST AND DISEASE CONTROL: Generally no significant problems.

HARVESTING AND STORAGE: Harvest the berries any time after they are fully colored. Make the fruit into conserves, jams, or pickles for storage, or dry them and store in airtight jars.

COMMENTS: Besides common barberry (*B. vulgaris*), other species that have been used for their fruits include Nepal barberry (*B. aristata*) and raisin barberry (*B. asiatica*).

| *Arctostaphylos uva-ursi* | Ericaceae | *Fagus* spp. | Fagaceae |

# BEARBERRY

# BEECH

*Low-growing bearberries have small, tart fruits with edible skin, flesh, and seeds. The shiny red berries are slightly smaller than cranberries and are used in much the same way.*

BEST CLIMATE AND SITE: Zones 2–6. Bearberry grows in full sun or partial shade. It prefers well-drained or even sandy soil that's on the acid side (pH 4.5–5.5), although it will grow even on limestone rock.

HEIGHT AND SPREAD: Height 6–12 inches (15–30 cm); unlimited spread.

GROWING GUIDELINES: Bearberry is difficult to transplant, so purchase plants growing in containers. Set them out any time the ground isn't frozen. To blanket the ground, space plants 1–3 feet (30–90 cm) apart and let them spread to fill in. Do not fertilize.

PRUNING: No pruning is necessary.

PROPAGATION: Nick seeds with a file, keep them warm and moist for 2–4 months, and then keep them cool and moist for 2–3 months. For stem cuttings, cut off young sideshoots in early fall or early spring, then put their bases in sand and maintain high humidity.

PEST AND DISEASE CONTROL: Generally no significant problems.

HARVESTING AND STORAGE: Pick berries that are fully red. Enjoy them fresh or dry them. Berries not harvested will hang on the plant through winter. Use the fruit in the same way as you would use cranberries (see the Cranberry entry on page 134).

COMMENTS: Bearberry adapts to many sites, so it is useful as an edible, evergreen groundcover.

*Beeches are large, deciduous trees that produce edible nuts encased in bur-like husks. The small, triangular nuts are especially rich in both fat and protein.*

BEST CLIMATE AND SITE: Zones 3–9 for American beech (*F. grandifolia*); Zones 5–7 for European beech (*F. sylvatica*). Both species prefer full sun and moist, well-drained soil.

HEIGHT AND SPREAD: Height 50–80 feet (15–24 m); spread 100–120 feet (30–36 m).

GROWING GUIDELINES: Set out plants in spring. Space them 15–30 feet (4.5–9 m) apart. Protect the thin bark of young beeches from sunscald either by painting it with a mix of equal parts of white latex paint and water or by wrapping it in protective paper made for this purpose. Otherwise, beeches need little or no care.

PRUNING: Little pruning is necessary.

PROPAGATION: Mix the seed with peat moss and keep it moist and cool for 3 months; then sow in a warm, bright place. Graft cultivars of European beech onto European beech seedlings.

PEST AND DISEASE CONTROL: Control beech bark canker disease, which causes dark, sunken cankers on bark and dead branches, by ridding the tree of the woolly beech scale insect. Scrub the pests off the bark or use a dormant spray of lime-sulfur.

HARVESTING AND STORAGE: Either knock the burs off the tree as they start to open or pick up the released and fallen nuts from the ground. Eat the nuts fresh (remove the thin shells from the kernels), or store them at a temperature just above freezing.

*Rubus* spp.                                    Rosaceae

# BOYSENBERRY

*Boysenberry fruits are large, maroon, and almost seedless. Completely ripe fruits have a delectable flavor and aroma. They are also very soft, so use them quickly.*

BEST CLIMATE AND SITE: Zones 8–9. Plant boysenberries in full sun and well-drained, humus-rich soil.

HEIGHT AND SPREAD: Height 8–12 feet (2.4–3.6 m); spread 8–12 feet (2.4–3.6 m).

GROWING GUIDELINES: Plant container-grown stock any time the ground isn't frozen, or set out bareroot plants in spring or fall, while they are dormant. Boysenberries are self-fruitful, so you can get fruit from just one plant. Space plants 3–6 feet (90–180 cm) apart. Set up a post next to each plant or erect a one- or two-wire trellis on which to train the canes. (Train as described for blackberries in "Pruning and Training" on page 102.) The canes are biennial, bearing fruit in their second season.

PRUNING: In winter, cut to the ground any canes that fruited the previous summer—they are dead anyway. Thin remaining canes to leave eight to ten of the most vigorous ones per plant. Shorten those canes to 7 feet (2.1 m), and cut back any sideshoots to 12–18 inches (30–45 cm).

PROPAGATION: Propagate by layering.

PEST AND DISEASE CONTROL: When you give them good growing conditions, boysenberries usually don't have any significant problems.

HARVESTING AND STORAGE: For full flavor, harvest when the fruit practically drops off into your hand. Even at cool temperatures and high humidity, fruit keeps only 2–3 days, so use it quickly.

*Shepherdia argentea*                    Elaeagnaceae

# BUFFALO BERRY

*Buffalo berry is a shrub that produces small, edible berries. The single-seeded, red or yellow berries have a tart flavor, although they sweeten a bit after being touched by frost.*

BEST CLIMATE AND SITE: Zones 2–6. Plant in full sun and well-drained soil. Buffalo berry blooms early, so avoid sites subject to late-spring frosts.

HEIGHT AND SPREAD: Height 6–20 feet (1.8–6 m); spread 4–15 feet (1.2–4.5 m).

GROWING GUIDELINES: Plant container-grown shrubs any time the ground isn't frozen, or set out bareroot plants in spring or fall, while they are dormant. Space plants 6 feet (1.8 m) apart. Plants are either male or female; plant at least one male to pollinate up to about eight females. Only females will produce fruit.

PRUNING: No pruning is necessary.

PROPAGATION: Grow new plants from hardwood cuttings or by sowing seed. Do not let seed dry out, and keep it cool and moist for 2–3 months before sowing to stimulate germination. Seedlings usually bloom by their third year.

PEST AND DISEASE CONTROL: Birds will eat some of the fruits, but otherwise buffalo berry has no significant pest or disease problems.

HARVESTING AND STORAGE: Harvest the fruits right after frost, or let them hang on the bushes into winter before harvesting them. Fresh berries store best at cool temperatures and high humidity. Eat the fruits fresh, dried, or cooked into conserves or jelly.

*Juglans cinerea*  Juglandaceae

# BUTTERNUT

*Butternuts are large trees that produce edible nuts encased in a husk and shell. The hard shell is somewhat elongated and ends in a point. The meat within is rich and buttery.*

BEST CLIMATE AND SITE: Zones 3–7. Full sun and deep, moist, rich soil is best, but plants will tolerate dry, rocky soil, especially on limestone.

HEIGHT AND SPREAD: Height 40–60 feet (12–18 m); spread 30–50 feet (9–15 m).

GROWING GUIDELINES: Transplant in spring, taking care to preserve as much of the taproot as possible if the plant is not growing in a container. Space plants 30–50 feet (9–15 m) apart.

PRUNING: Train young trees to form a sturdy framework of well-spaced, wide-angled branches. On mature trees, just prune out dead or diseased wood and the occasional misplaced branch.

PROPAGATION: Mix seed with damp peat moss and refrigerate for 3–4 months before sowing in a warm, bright place. Graft cultivars onto black walnut rootstocks.

PEST AND DISEASE CONTROL: Small, black pustules and dying limbs indicate butternut dieback disease. Fertilize and water trees to help them recover, and cut diseased branches back to healthy wood.

HARVESTING AND STORAGE: Harvest nuts when they have fallen to the ground. Allow the husks to dry, and they will crumble off when you are ready to crack the nut. Store the kernels at cool temperatures and high humidity.

COMMENTS: The spongy husks stain, so wear waterproof gloves when removing them.

*Citrofortunella mitis*  Rutaceae

# CALAMONDIN

*Calamondins grow as bushes or small trees. The fruits are small, round, and reddish orange. The sweet, edible rind easily peels away from the segmented flesh, which is juicy and tart.*

BEST CLIMATE AND SITE: Zones 9–10 for outdoor culture. Give calamondins full sun and slightly acid, well-drained soil.

HEIGHT AND SPREAD: Height 6–24 feet (1.8–7.2 m); spread 3–12 feet (90–360 cm).

GROWING GUIDELINES: Set out container-grown plants anytime. Space them 3–12 feet (90–360 cm) apart, depending on whether you want a hedge or individual plants. Calamondins are self-fruitful, so you only need one plant. They are easy to grow in containers. Water your tree regularly to keep the soil evenly moist, especially during bloom.

PRUNING: Calamondins don't need regular pruning, except when you want to keep a plant small. Plants can be sheared as hedges.

PROPAGATION: Propagate calamondins by sowing fresh seed, taking stem cuttings, or grafting. Trifoliate orange (*Poncirus trifoliata*) is a good disease-resistant, dwarfing rootstock.

PEST AND DISEASE CONTROL: Problems are usually minimal if soil drainage is good, but keep an eye out for scale, mealybugs, mites, and whiteflies.

HARVESTING AND STORAGE: Harvest when the fruits are fully colored, or let them hang on the tree until you are ready to use them. Store in a refrigerator crisper. The fruit is too tart to just pop into your mouth, but you can use it to flavor drinks, or use whole fruit to make marmalade.

*Physalis pruinosa*                    Solanaceae

# CAPE GOOSEBERRY

*The pale yellow berries of cape gooseberry ripen within a husk on a small, spreading bush. The husk is not edible, but it protects the sweet, juicy berry.*

BEST CLIMATE AND SITE: All Zones. Cape gooseberry is a perennial in the tropics, but you can grow it as an annual wherever you can grow tomatoes. It needs full sun and well-drained soil that is not overly rich in nitrogen.

HEIGHT AND SPREAD: Height 3–6 feet (90–180 cm); spread 3–6 feet (90–180 cm).

GROWING GUIDELINES: Start seed indoors about 8 weeks before the average date of your last killing spring frost. Transplant outdoors 1 week after that last frost date. Space plants 3 feet (90 cm) apart.

PRUNING: No pruning is necessary, but in year-round warm climates, cutting back plants severely after the first harvest reduces pest problems.

PROPAGATION: Grow from seed sown indoors in early spring. Even where cape gooseberries are perennial, yields are better if you start new plants every 2–3 years.

PEST AND DISEASE CONTROL: Plants usually have no significant problems in temperate climates.

HARVESTING AND STORAGE: Harvest fruits when the husks are dry and papery. Pick them individually, or shake the plant and gather those that drop. Fruits store for months if kept dry and intact in their husks.

COMMENTS: Pop the golden fruits out of their husks for fresh eating, cook them into jam, or dry them like raisins. Unripe fruits are poisonous.

*Averrhoa carambola*                    Oxalidaceae

# CARAMBOLA

*Carambola trees produce fruits that are star-shaped in cross section and enclosed within a waxy, yellow skin. Both the skin and the crisp flesh are edible.*

BEST CLIMATE AND SITE: Zone 10. Plant in full sun and well-drained, slightly acid soil with low salt content. Avoid sites with hot, dry winds.

HEIGHT AND SPREAD: Height 20–30 feet (6–9 m); spread 15–25 feet (4.5–7.5 m).

GROWING GUIDELINES: Set out container-grown plants anytime. Space trees 15–25 feet (4.5–7.5 m) apart. Yields are usually improved with cross-pollination.

PRUNING: Carambola needs little pruning beyond the removal of vigorous, upright shoots.

PROPAGATION: Seed germinates readily when fresh. However, grafted plants bear more quickly, and their fruit quality is more predictable.

PEST AND DISEASE CONTROL: Work compost into the soil before planting, and use it as a mulch to prevent nutrient deficiencies. Plants have no significant pest or disease problems.

HARVESTING AND STORAGE: Pick fruits when they are pale green with some yellow. Ripe fruits often fall to the ground. Fruits keep for a few weeks at 50°F (10°C).

COMMENTS: Carambolas come in either sweet or sour types. For jelly, use slightly underripe sweet types or fully ripe sour types. Ripe carambolas can be cooked in puddings, tarts, and curries; pickle underripe fruits or cook like a vegetable.

*Ceratonia siliqua*                    Leguminosae     *Annona cherimola*                    Annonaceae

# CAROB

# CHERIMOYA

*Carob trees yield flat, brown, edible pods that are filled with a row of seeds and soft, sweet, brown flesh. When roasted and ground, the pods have a somewhat chocolate-like flavor.*

*Inside the pale green skin, cherimoya flesh is white and custardy, with a combination of banana, pineapple, and papaya flavor. Eat the flesh but not the seeds or skin.*

BEST CLIMATE AND SITE: Zones 9–10. Carob prefers climates with a hot, dry summer; give it full sun and alkaline, well-drained soil.

HEIGHT AND SPREAD: Height 25–50 feet (7.5–15 m); spread 15–35 feet (4.5–10.5 m).

GROWING GUIDELINES: Transplant young plants carefully or set out container-grown stock. Plant potted plants anytime, or set out bareroot plants in spring or fall, while they are dormant. Space plants 15–35 feet (4.5–10.5 m) apart. Male trees are usually needed to pollinate female trees; either plant a male for every 25 to 30 females, or graft a single male branch onto a female tree.

PRUNING: No regular pruning is necessary.

PROPAGATION: Fresh seed germinates readily, but dry seed germinates slowly and at a low rate even when helped along by being nicked with a file. Propagate cultivars by budding or grafting scions onto seedling rootstocks.

PEST AND DISEASE CONTROL: Keep deer and rabbits from trees with traps and fences. Where scale insects become a problem, spray with horticultural oil.

HARVESTING AND STORAGE: Pods turn dark brown when they are ripe. Pick ripe pods before wet weather or even heavy dew. Shake or knock ripe pods from the branches, then dry the pods in the sun. Munch on raw pods, or remove the seeds and bake and grind the pods for use as a chocolate substitute.

BEST CLIMATE AND SITE: Zone 10, with a period of cool, but not cold, winter weather. Plant in a sheltered spot in full sun and well-drained, slightly acid soil.

HEIGHT AND SPREAD: Height 15–30 feet (4.5–9 m); spread 10–25 feet (3–7.5 m).

GROWING GUIDELINES: Plant container-grown stock anytime, or set out bareroot plants in spring or fall, while they are dormant. Space plants 10–25 feet (3–7.5 m) apart. Hand-pollinate flowers with a fine brush for best yields and large fruits. Water less in winter to encourage plants to go dormant.

PRUNING: Prune just before growth begins for the season, while the plant is leafless. Remove a moderate amount of wood each year to keep fruiting branches close to the main stems.

PROPAGATION: For the best-tasting fruits at an early age, graft cultivars to seedling rootstocks just as buds are swelling.

PEST AND DISEASE CONTROL: Generally no significant problems.

HARVESTING AND STORAGE: Clip firm fruits from the tree when their color changes to pale green or yellow, then let them soften at room temperature. For storage, keep harvested fruits at 50°F (10°C) before ripening them at room temperature.

COMMENTS: Cherimoya is a rich fruit, which, when frozen, can be eaten like ice cream.

*Cornus mas*                 Cornaceae

# CHERRY, CORNELIAN

*The red fruits of Cornelian cherry resemble true cherries. The flavor is tart—much like a sour cherry. You can eat the whole fruit, except for the seed.*

BEST CLIMATE AND SITE: Zones 4–8. Give plants full sun and average, well-drained soil.

HEIGHT AND SPREAD: Height 15–25 feet (4.5–7.5 m); spread 10–20 feet (3–6 m).

GROWING GUIDELINES: Set out container-grown plants any time the ground isn't frozen, or plant bareroot stock in spring or fall, while it is still dormant. Space plants 10–20 feet (3–6 m) apart. The flowers are partially self-fertile, so cross-pollination increases yields.

PRUNING: No regular pruning is required.

PROPAGATION: Cornelian cherry is easy to graft onto seedling rootstocks. To grow seedlings, either nick the seed with a file or keep it warm and moist for 4 months; move the seed to a cool, moist spot for 1–4 months, then put it in a warm, bright place to sprout.

PEST AND DISEASE CONTROL: Generally no significant problems.

HARVESTING AND STORAGE: Harvest fruits any time after they are fully colored. (Most turn red; a few kinds ripen yellow or white.) The longer they hang, the more they mellow in flavor. Harvested fruits also mellow if kept at room temperature.

COMMENTS: You can enjoy the fruits out of hand, although they are normally used to make a drink, preserves, or a thickened, sweet syrup called *rob de cornis.*

*Prunus tomentosa*              Rosaceae

# CHERRY, NANKING

*Nanking cherries grow as large bushes with small red or yellow fruit. Depending on the plant, the fruit may taste like sweet or sour cherries. You can eat the whole fruit, except for the seed.*

BEST CLIMATE AND SITE: Zones 3–6. Nanking cherries need full sun but tolerate a wide range of soil types as long as they have good drainage.

HEIGHT AND SPREAD: Height 9–15 feet (2.7–4.5 m); spread 9–15 feet (2.7–4.5 m).

GROWING GUIDELINES: Set new plants out in spring, spacing them 6–16 feet (1.8–4.8 m) apart. Nanking cherries generally need cross-pollination, so grow at least two plants. This shrub thrives with little or no care.

PRUNING: No pruning is needed, but you can keep the plants smaller or even train them as hedges with regular, late-winter pruning.

PROPAGATION: Keep the seed moist and cold for 3 months before sowing it in a warm, bright place. Seedlings typically begin bearing by their third season.

PEST AND DISEASE CONTROL: Twigs or stems occasionally die back; cut them back into healthy wood.

HARVESTING AND STORAGE: Harvest fruit as soon as it fully turns color. Harvested fruits store poorly, so just pick and eat them.

COMMENTS: Although it has a delicate beauty, Nanking cherry is a tough shrub: Its blossoms resist frost, and the plants tolerate drought, extremely cold winters, and hot summers.

*Malus* spp.                                    Rosaceae

# CRAB APPLE

*Some crab apples taste delicious out of hand, while others taste good only when cooked with sweetener into jellies. You can eat the whole fruit, except for the seeds.*

BEST CLIMATE AND SITE: Zones 3–9. Plant in full sun and well-drained soil.

HEIGHT AND SPREAD: Height 8–25 feet (2.4–7.5 m); spread 8–25 feet (2.4–7.5 m).

GROWING GUIDELINES: Plant container-grown stock any time the ground isn't frozen, or set out bareroot plants in spring or fall, while they are dormant. Space plants 8–25 feet (2.4–7.5 m) apart. The plants need cross-pollination, but the pollinator can be an apple or a crab apple.

PRUNING: Train young plants to a sturdy framework of wide-angled, well-spaced main limbs. Mature plants need little pruning beyond removing water-sprouts and thinning congested growth.

PROPAGATION: Graft or bud cultivars onto seedling apple or crab apple rootstocks. Seed, for seedling rootstocks, germinates readily once it has been kept cool and moist for 2–3 months.

PEST AND DISEASE CONTROL: Crab apples can have the same pest and disease problems as apples but are usually less troubled. (See "Problem Prevention and Control" on page 84 for descriptions and control suggestions.)

HARVESTING AND STORAGE: Pick fruits when they are fully colored and come off the plant easily. Store in the refrigerator in a plastic bag with a few holes in it.

COMMENTS: Fruits of most crab apples are used for cooking, but a few cultivars are excellent for eating fresh.

*Vaccinium macrocarpon*                          Ericaceae

# CRANBERRY

*Cranberries grow as low, creeping bushes. Their white flowers are followed by hard, red berries, each about the size of a thumbnail. The tart berries are completely edible.*

BEST CLIMATE AND SITE: Zones 2–6. Cranberries thrive in sun and moist, well-drained, humus-rich soil with a very acid pH (4.0–5.5). The plants do not tolerate dry soil, but they can withstand flooding in cold weather.

HEIGHT AND SPREAD: Height to 1 foot (30 cm); spread unlimited. (The sprawling stems root where they touch the ground and continue to grow outward.)

GROWING GUIDELINES: Plant in spring or fall where winters are mild or in spring where winters are severe. Space plants 1–2 feet (30–60 cm) apart. Mix plenty of acid peat into the soil before planting. Mulch with sawdust or sand; renew the mulch periodically.

PRUNING: Cut away some of the sprawling stems and some of the upright fruiting stems when they become overcrowded.

PROPAGATION: Summer stem cuttings root readily. Where winters are mild, set rooted cuttings outdoors in fall; otherwise, set them out as early as possible in spring.

PEST AND DISEASE CONTROL: Generally no significant problems.

HARVESTING AND STORAGE: Pick berries in fall, after they are fully colored. Cranberries will keep for 2–4 months at high humidity and temperatures just above freezing.

*Viburnum trilobum*          Caprifoliaceae

# CRANBERRY, HIGHBUSH

*The shiny, bright red berries of highbush cranberry ripen in drooping clusters. The tart fruits contain a single, large seed. Eat the whole fruit, except for the seed.*

BEST CLIMATE AND SITE: Zones 4–9. Plant in full sun or partial shade in moist, well-drained soil.

HEIGHT AND SPREAD: Height 8–12 feet (2.4–3.6 m); spread 8–12 feet (2.4–3.6 m).

GROWING GUIDELINES: Plant container-grown shrubs any time the ground isn't frozen, or set out bareroot plants in spring or fall, while they are dormant. Space plants 6–9 feet (1.8–2.7 m) apart. Plant several of them close together as an informal hedge, or grow just one as a specimen shrub.

PRUNING: In winter, cut old, nonproductive stems down to the ground.

PROPAGATION: Take hardwood or softwood cuttings. Seed does not germinate until it has been kept warm and moist for 4 months, then cool and moist for 3 months.

PEST AND DISEASE CONTROL: Generally no significant problems.

HARVESTING AND STORAGE: Harvest any time after the berries turn fully red. Fruits not harvested hang on the bush well into winter, shriveling with time. Store at cool temperatures and high humidity, such as in a covered container in the refrigerator.

COMMENTS: The fruit has a single, large seed that must be strained out when you use the fruit for jam or jelly. Don't be put off by the offensive aroma of the cooking fruit—it does not find its way into the finished product.

*Sambucus* spp.          Caprifoliaceae

# ELDERBERRY

*Elderberries produce clusters of small blue-black berries. The flavor is very mild, so elderberries taste best cooked with sweetener and another, more acidic fruit. The whole fruit is edible.*

BEST CLIMATE AND SITE: Zones 2–9. Plant in full sun or partial shade and evenly moist soil.

HEIGHT AND SPREAD: Height 6–10 feet (1.8–3 m); spread 3–6 feet (90–180 cm).

GROWING GUIDELINES: Plant container-grown shrubs anytime, or set out bareroot plants in spring or fall, while they are dormant. Space plants 6 feet (1.8 m) apart. Plant two seedlings or two different cultivars for best yields.

PRUNING: On established bushes, cut stems that are more than 3 years old to ground level each winter. Also prune away suckers to control the spread.

PROPAGATION: Dig up and transplant suckers from around the base of the plant. You also can take cuttings or sow seed.

PEST AND DISEASE CONTROL: If necessary, cover the bushes with netting to keep birds at bay.

HARVESTING AND STORAGE: Harvest the berries when they are fully colored. An easy way to pick fruit from the clusters is to pop it off with the tines of a dinner fork. Store it in a covered container in the refrigerator. The fruit is most often used in jams, pies, and preserves.

COMMENTS: Edible species include blueberry elder (*S. caerulea*), American elder (*S. canadensis*), and European elder (*S. nigra*). Some species (such as *S. ebulus*) have poisonous berries, so make sure you know what you're planting and harvesting!

*Feijoa sellowiana*  Myrtaceae

# FEIJOA

*The green fruit of feijoa forms on a large, bushy plant. The edible, greenish flesh, embedded with small, edible seeds, has a flavor combining the best of pineapple, strawberry, and mint.*

BEST CLIMATE AND SITE: Zones 9–10; possibly Zone 8. Feijoa needs some winter chilling to flower and fruit. Plant in well-drained soil and full sun, except in desert areas, where some midday shade is needed.

HEIGHT AND SPREAD: Height 15–20 feet (4.5–6 m); spread 15–20 feet (4.5–6 m).

GROWING GUIDELINES: Set out container-grown plants anytime. Space them 3–15 feet (90–450 cm) apart. Most feijoas need cross-pollination, but a number of cultivars are self-fertile. In cool climates, you can grow feijoas in pots; give them a cool, bright location indoors in winter.

PRUNING: Train as a shrub, small tree, or sheared hedge. Train grafted plants as single-trunked trees, removing all sprouts that come off the base of the stem. Feijoas don't require much pruning; do what little is needed after harvest.

PROPAGATION: Propagate cultivars by taking cuttings or by grafting them onto seedling rootstocks.

PEST AND DISEASE CONTROL: Generally no significant problems.

HARVESTING AND STORAGE: Ripe fruits drop to the ground; gather them every few days. Nearly ripe fruits will ripen indoors. Fruits keep well with high humidity and temperatures near freezing.

COMMENTS: The fleshy flower petals, white with a tinge of purple, are sweet and edible.

*Psidium* spp.  Myrtaceae

# GUAVA

*When ripe, the tropical guava gives off a musky aroma but is somewhat insipid in flavor; the strawberry guava has a spicy flavor. The flesh of both kinds is edible.*

BEST CLIMATE AND SITE: Zone 10. Plant in full sun. Well-drained, slightly acid soil rich in organic matter is ideal.

HEIGHT AND SPREAD: Height 10–25 feet (3–7.5 m); spread 7–15 feet (2.1–4.5 m).

GROWING GUIDELINES: Set out container-grown plants anytime. Space them 9–15 feet (2.7–4.5 m) apart. Plants are partially self-fruitful; growing two or more seedlings or cultivars may increase yields. Fertilize often to keep plants vigorous.

PRUNING: Prune heavily to stimulate new growth and keep fruits close to the center of the plant.

PROPAGATION: Dig suckers from around the base of an established bush, or take stem cuttings. Seed germinates fairly easily.

PEST AND DISEASE CONTROL: Generally not a problem in home plantings.

HARVESTING AND STORAGE: The aroma and color change tell you when the fruits are ripe. Tropical guava turns yellow when ripe. It is usually stored just below 50°F (10°C). Strawberry guava turns yellow or red when ripe and is best stored at temperatures just above freezing. Slightly underripe fruit will keep for a few weeks at cool temperatures and high humidity.

COMMENTS: Tropical guava (*P. guajava*) has larger fruits than strawberry, or Cattley, guava (*P. littorale*). Both kinds make excellent jelly, jam, or juice.

*Juglans ailantifolia* var. *cordiformis*    Juglandaceae

# HEARTNUT

*Heartnut trees are closely related to walnuts. They produce edible, heart-shaped nuts with a sweet flavor and no trace of bitterness.*

BEST CLIMATE AND SITE: Zones 5–9. Plant heartnuts in moist, well-drained soil and full sun.

HEIGHT AND SPREAD: Height to 60 feet (18 m); spread to 60 feet (18 m).

GROWING GUIDELINES: Plant in spring. Space plants 60 feet (18 m) apart. Established trees need virtually no care.

PRUNING: Train the young tree to a sturdy framework of well-spaced, wide-angled branches. Mature trees require little pruning beyond the removal of dead, diseased, and poorly placed limbs.

PROPAGATION: Nuts germinate following a period of cool, moist storage. Graft cultivars onto black walnut rootstocks, or layer low branches for two seasons.

PEST AND DISEASE CONTROL: Walnut bunch disease results in a broom-like clustering of stems. There is no cure for this viral disease, so remove infected trees to prevent the disease from spreading to healthy trees.

HARVESTING AND STORAGE: Harvest as nuts begin to fall. Nuts or shelled kernels store for many months if kept where temperatures are just above freezing and humidity is high.

COMMENTS: Heartnuts have been hybridized with butternuts to produce a number of cultivars of "buartnuts."

*Gaylussacia* spp.                              Ericaceae

# HUCKLEBERRY

*Huckleberry fruit looks and tastes like blueberries, but huckleberries have small, crunchy seeds. You'll enjoy the plant's beautiful fall color, too.*

BEST CLIMATE AND SITE: Generally Zones 5 to 8, but plants vary in adaptability, depending on their origin. *G. frondosa* and *G. dumosa* enjoy wet sites; *G. baccata* prefers drier sites. All huckleberries like full sun and very acid soil (pH 4.5–5.5).

HEIGHT AND SPREAD: Height 1–6 feet (30–180 cm); spread to 3 feet (90 cm) or more (some creep with underground stems).

GROWING GUIDELINES: Plant container-grown shrubs any time the ground isn't frozen, or set out bareroot plants in spring or fall, while they are dormant. Space plants 3 feet (90 cm) apart. Before planting, make sure the soil is very acid and rich in humus. Digging acid peat moss into the soil is one way to fulfill both of these needs.

PRUNING: No regular pruning is necessary.

PROPAGATION: Fresh seed germinates fairly well, but for best results, keep the seed warm and moist for 1 month, then cool and moist for 1–2 months. Cuttings taken from late summer through fall root well in a mix of peat and either sand or perlite.

PEST AND DISEASE CONTROL: Generally no significant problems.

HARVESTING AND STORAGE: Pick fruits when fully colored. To harvest a large quantity, spread a clean cloth on the ground and shake the plant; ripe fruits will drop onto the cloth. Store at temperatures just above freezing with high humidity.

*Ribes nidigrolaria*                    Saxifragaceae

# JOSTABERRY

*Jostaberry bushes produce dark, almost black, blueberry-sized fruits with a flavor that reflects their gooseberry and black currant parentage. The whole fruit is edible.*

BEST CLIMATE AND SITE: Zones 4–8. Plant in well-drained soil with full sun or partial shade. Choose a site free from late-spring frosts.

HEIGHT AND SPREAD: Height to 8 feet (2.4 m); spread to 6 feet (1.8 m).

GROWING GUIDELINES: Set out container-grown plants any time the ground isn't frozen, or plant bareroot stock in spring or fall, while it is dormant. Space plants about 6 feet (1.8 m) apart or closer if you want to make a hedge. Plants enjoy cool soil, so give them a deep, organic mulch.

PRUNING: Each winter, cut one or two of the oldest stems to ground level.

PROPAGATION: Propagate jostaberries by hardwood cuttings, softwood cuttings, or layering.

PEST AND DISEASE CONTROL: Jostaberry is less subject to diseases than its parents. Imported currant-worm sometimes strips leaves early in the season. Spray with a mixture of rotenone and pyrethrin as soon as you notice damage, which begins down within the bush. Sometimes a second spray is needed right after harvest.

HARVESTING AND STORAGE: Harvest clusters of fruits as they ripen (when their skin turns dark). Store ripe fruit at high humidity with temperatures just above freezing.

COMMENTS: Harvest slightly underripe fruit for jams and preserves. The fruit is very high in vitamin C.

*Ziziphus jujuba*                    Rhamnaceae

# JUJUBE

*Fresh jujube fruits have pale green skin that's mottled with brown and a crunchy texture and flavor similar to apples. You can eat the skin and flesh but not the seed.*

BEST CLIMATE AND SITE: Zones 5–8. Jujube needs full sun and abundant summer heat but grows in almost any soil, even very wet or dry types.

HEIGHT AND SPREAD: Height to 30 feet (9 m); spread to 20 feet (6 m).

GROWING GUIDELINES: Plant container-grown trees any time the ground isn't frozen, or set out bareroot plants in spring or fall, while they are dormant. Space plants 20 feet (6 m) apart. Pollination needs are not well defined, but cross-pollination generally increases fruit size and yield. The trees tend to sucker, especially when young.

PRUNING: No regular pruning is necessary.

PROPAGATION: Increase cultivars by grafting or, if the mother tree is not grafted, by digging suckers. To grow a seedling for a rootstock, open the seed lengthwise to extract the two kernels, then keep the kernels cool and barely moist for 2 months to enhance germination.

PEST AND DISEASE CONTROL: Generally no significant pest or disease problems.

HARVESTING AND STORAGE: Harvest fruits for fresh eating just as they become mottled with brown. Store for a month or more at 50°F (10°C). Fruits left hanging on the tree turn completely brown, then shrivel and lose moisture. Dried fruits keep for over a year at cool temperatures; they taste much like dates.

*Fortunella* spp.                    Rutaceae    *Vaccinium vitis-ideae*                    Ericaceae

# KUMQUAT

# LINGONBERRY

*Kumquat fruit looks like a miniature orange—about the size of a cherry and either round or elongated. The skin is edible and sweet, and the juicy flesh ranges from tart to sweet.*

BEST CLIMATE AND SITE: Zones 9–10. Plant in full sun and well-drained, slightly acid soil. Kumquat tolerates winter weather as cold as 18°F (–7.7°C), but without sufficient heat in summer, the fruits are few and of poor quality.

HEIGHT AND SPREAD: Height 8–15 feet (2.4–4.5 m); spread 6–12 feet (1.8–3.6 m).

GROWING GUIDELINES: Plant container-grown stock anytime, or set out bareroot plants in spring or fall, while they are dormant. Space plants 6–12 feet (1.8–3.6 m) apart. Kumquats make beautiful potted plants that also fruit reliably. Provide a cool, sunny room in winter and repot every year.

PRUNING: Kumquat needs no pruning other than to shape the plant and thin out crowded branches.

PROPAGATION: Kumquats are usually grafted onto trifoliate orange (*Poncirus trifoliata*), which also dwarfs the tree, or onto sour orange (*Citrus aurantium*) or grapefruit rootstock.

PEST AND DISEASE CONTROL: Problems are usually minimal if soil drainage is good, but keep an eye out for scale, mealybugs, mites, and whiteflies.

HARVESTING AND STORAGE: Harvest fruits when they are fully colored. They keep well in the refrigerator.

COMMENTS: Fruits are tasty fresh, candied, or cooked into marmalade or a sauce.

*Lingonberry is a low, creeping bush that produces wholly edible fruit. The round, red berries are a little larger than peas and have a flavor similar to, but less sharp than, the true cranberry.*

BEST CLIMATE AND SITE: Zones 2–6. Give lingonberries full sun or partial shade and humus-rich, well-drained, very acid (pH 4.5–5.5) soil.

HEIGHT AND SPREAD: Height 6–24 inches (15–60 cm); spread unlimited (plants send up shoots from creeping underground stems).

GROWING GUIDELINES: Set out container-grown plants any time the ground isn't frozen, or plant bareroot stock in spring or fall, while it is dormant. Space plants of the variety *vitis-ideae* 1½ feet (45 cm) apart and those of the variety *minus* 10 inches (25 cm) apart. Lingonberries compete poorly with weeds, so weed thoroughly before planting. Also dig in plenty of acid peat moss. Mulch with sand or sawdust to further suppress weeds and to keep the shallow roots cool and moist. Plants are partially self-fertile, but planting at least 2 seedlings or cultivars increases yields.

PRUNING: Once plants are a few years old, mow a different third or quarter of the planting in late fall each year (so each part gets mowed every 3–4 years) to about 1 inch (2.5 cm) high.

PROPAGATION: Take cuttings in spring.

PEST AND DISEASE CONTROL: Generally no significant problems.

HARVESTING AND STORAGE: Wait to harvest until fruit is thoroughly red and ripe. Store fruit at temperatures just above freezing with high humidity.

*Eriobotrya japonica*                    Rosaceae

# LOQUAT

*Mangifera indica*                    Anacardiaceae

# MANGO

*Loquat trees produce yellow, plum-sized, round, oval, or pear-shaped fruit. Inside is an aromatic white pulp that is sweet with a bit of tang. Remove the skin and seeds before eating loquats.*

BEST CLIMATE AND SITE: Zones 8–10. Loquats need full sun or partial shade and well-drained soil. They are somewhat drought-resistant.

HEIGHT AND SPREAD: Height 20–30 feet (6–9 m); spread 25–35 feet (7.5–10.5 m).

GROWING GUIDELINES: Set out container-grown plants anytime, spacing them 20–30 feet (6–9 m) apart. Most cultivars are self-fruitful. Thin fruits in winter by clipping off some of the clusters or individual fruitlets. Mulch to protect the shallow roots. Fertilize regularly. To grow loquats in containers, plant a dwarf cultivar and repot annually.

PRUNING: When you thin fruits by removing clusters, you already have taken care of much of the pruning. Shorten additional stems to let in light.

PROPAGATION: Graft cultivars onto seedling loquat rootstocks. Quince or pyracantha have been used as dwarfing rootstocks.

PEST AND DISEASE CONTROL: Watch for blackened leaves and curled shoots—signs of fire blight. For controls, see "Fighting Fire Blight" on page 73. Enclose fruits in paper bags to protect them from sunburn if plants are growing in full sun.

HARVESTING AND STORAGE: Clip off fruits when they are fully colored and slightly soft. They will keep in the refrigerator for 1–2 weeks.

COMMENTS: Eat loquats fresh, cook them into a sauce, or cut them in half and dry them.

*The ripe fruit of mango trees resembles a large, elongated peach with skin in shades of red, yellow, and green. Inside, the juicy, orange pulp has a sweet, rich flavor.*

BEST CLIMATE AND SITE: Zone 10. Mangos need full sun and well-drained soil that is not overly fertile.

HEIGHT AND SPREAD: Height 50–90 feet (15–27 m); spread 30–125 feet (9–37.5 m).

GROWING GUIDELINES: Set out container-grown plants anytime, spacing them 30–60 feet (9–18 m) apart. Plants are self-fruitful, so you only need one to get a harvest. Thin fruits and fertilize during years of good production; otherwise, the tree tends to bear only every other year.

PRUNING: Prune to remove dead and crowded wood and to keep the tree within bounds. In late summer, shorten some of the stems and remove any vigorous, upright ones.

PROPAGATION: Some cultivars come true from seed, which should be sown fresh, with the top of the seed at soil level. A more reliable way to propagate any cultivar is to graft or bud it onto a mango seedling while the tree is actively growing.

PEST AND DISEASE CONTROL: Where anthracnose disease is a problem, rake up and dispose of infected leaves and fruit.

HARVESTING AND STORAGE: Pick fruits when they soften slightly and change color. For storage, pick them firm to ripen at room temperature.

COMMENTS: Remove the seed and skin before eating the pulp. The fruits are good fresh or when used for chutney, ice cream, and sauces.

*Passiflora incarnata*        Passifloraceae

# MAYPOP

*Maypop fruits are yellow to yellow-green with many seeds, each surrounded by a gelatinous pulp that has a tropical flavor. Eat the fleshy seed covering with or without the seeds.*

BEST CLIMATE AND SITE: Zones 4–10. Plant in full sun and well-drained soil.

HEIGHT AND SPREAD: Height to 20 feet (6 m); spread to 20 feet (6 m) or more, if allowed.

GROWING GUIDELINES: Plant container-grown vines any time the ground isn't frozen, or set out bareroot plants in spring or fall, while they are dormant. Space plants 6–18 feet (1.8–5.4 m) apart, depending on whether you plan to train the vines upward or outward. This vine likes to have a fence, arbor, or deciduous shrub to climb on. The roots spread fast and far, so contain them with a barrier strip or with mowed lawn. Maypops need cross-pollination; hand-pollination sometimes helps with fruit set.

PRUNING: Cut the whole plant to the ground each year at the end of the growing season.

PROPAGATION: Suckers root readily if dug from the mother plant when a few inches high. To grow maypops from seed, first soak the seed in water for 24 hours. After sowing, provide a warm, dark environment until sprouts appear.

PEST AND DISEASE CONTROL: No significant pest or disease problems.

HARVESTING AND STORAGE: Ripe fruit drops to the ground; gather it as soon as possible. Store the fruit at high humidity, such as in a plastic bag, with cool but not cold temperatures.

*Mespilus germanica*        Rosaceae

# MEDLAR

*Medlar fruit looks like a small, russeted apple, tinged with dull yellow or red. The flesh is soft and brown and tastes like thick applesauce. Eat the flesh but not the seeds or skin.*

BEST CLIMATE AND SITE: Zones 4–8. Give medlars full sun and moderately rich, well-drained soil.

HEIGHT AND SPREAD: Height 9–20 feet (2.7–6 m); spread 9–20 feet (2.7–6 m).

GROWING GUIDELINES: Plant container-grown stock any time the ground isn't frozen, or set out bareroot plants in spring or fall, while they are dormant. Space plants 12–25 feet (3.6–7.5 m) apart. Plant with the graft union below ground level so the scion also takes root. Medlars are self-fertile, and virtually every blossom sets fruit. On young trees, pinch off some blossoms to channel more energy into shoot growth.

PRUNING: This small tree needs almost no pruning; simply trim as needed to shape it and to remove the occasional dead or diseased branches.

PROPAGATION: Graft medlar onto a seedling pear, hawthorn, quince, or medlar.

PEST AND DISEASE CONTROL: No pest or disease problems worth noting.

HARVESTING AND STORAGE: Harvest the fruits as the leaves begin to drop in fall. Although the fruits may feel rock hard, handle them carefully to avoid bruising. Place them on a shelf in a cool room to "blet," or soften. Fruits will be soft and ready to eat in 2 weeks or more. (The process goes more slowly in cool temperatures.)

*Morus* spp.                    Moraceae

# MULBERRY

*Mulberry trees produce black, red, or white blackberry-shaped fruits. Flavor ranges from sweet with a refreshing tang to purely sweet. The whole fruit is edible.*

BEST CLIMATE AND SITE: Zones 5–10. Plant in full sun and average, well-drained soil.

HEIGHT AND SPREAD: Height 15–30 feet (4.5–9 m); spread 10–20 feet (3–6 m).

GROWING GUIDELINES: Plant container-grown stock any time the ground isn't frozen, or set out bareroot plants in spring or fall, while they are dormant. Space plants 10–30 feet (3–9 m) apart. Do not plant mulberries where falling fruits will cause problems with staining. Cultivars selected for fruit production generally do not need cross-pollination.

PRUNING: No regular pruning is necessary.

PROPAGATION: Russian mulberry (*M. alba* 'Tartarica') makes a good rootstock for most other mulberries. Softwood or hardwood cuttings of most species usually root readily. With hardwood cuttings, either split the lower end or take a small "heel" of 2-year-old wood along with the 1-year-old wood used for the cutting.

PEST AND DISEASE CONTROL: Control scale insects with dormant oil, and handle dieback by cutting off infected portions.

HARVESTING AND STORAGE: To harvest in quantity, spread a clean sheet under the tree and shake the branches. Ripe fruits do not keep well fresh but can be dried.

COMMENTS: For cooking, pick the fruit when it is slightly underripe.

---

*Carissa grandiflora*          Apocynaceae

# NATAL PLUM

*The roundish fruit of Natal plum is the size of a Ping-Pong ball, with a crimson skin and strawberry red flesh. The whole fruit is edible; some people prefer to remove the small seeds.*

BEST CLIMATE AND SITE: Zone 10. Plant in full sun or partial shade in well-drained soil. Natal plum withstands salt spray and is moderately drought-tolerant.

HEIGHT AND SPREAD: Height range of the species is 2–18 feet (60–540 cm), but cultivars vary in their eventual height and spread.

GROWING GUIDELINES: Set out container-grown plants anytime, spacing them roughly 10 feet (3 m) apart, depending on the eventual size of particular cultivars. Natal plum generally needs cross-pollination, so plant at least two seedlings or cultivars. Hand-pollination often helps when fruiting is poor. In areas where Natal plum is not hardy, grow it indoors in a container.

PRUNING: Prune only as needed to shape the plant and to remove dead or crossing branches. You can even shear this plant as a hedge.

PROPAGATION: Take cuttings of semi-woody shoots, or layer a branch from an established plant.

PEST AND DISEASE CONTROL: Generally no significant problems.

HARVESTING AND STORAGE: For fresh eating, pick fruit when fully ripe (fully colored); pick slightly underripe for cooking. Plants produce fruit almost year-round, so pick fruit as you need it.

COMMENTS: Natal plum fruit is usually cooked into jellies, sauces, and pies.

# OAK

*Each nut, or acorn, has a round bottom and a cap. The nutty flavor of the edible interior may be sweet or sweet with some degree of bitterness.*

BEST CLIMATE AND SITE: Zones 2–10, depending on the species. Oaks grow well in full sun; optimum soil conditions, especially with respect to soil moisture, vary with the species.

HEIGHT AND SPREAD: Height 30–150 feet (9–45 m), depending on the species; spread is similar.

GROWING GUIDELINES: Plant in spring. Established oaks need little or no care.

PRUNING: Train young trees to a sturdy framework of well-spaced, wide-angled branches. Mature trees require little pruning beyond removal of the occasional dead, diseased, or poorly placed limb.

PROPAGATION: Acorns of species with edible nuts generally germinate readily.

PEST AND DISEASE CONTROL: Generally no significant problems.

HARVESTING AND STORAGE: Pick up fallen nuts from the ground. Store them at cool temperatures and high humidity.

COMMENTS: The white oak group, which includes the white oak (*Q. alba*) itself, is the one with sweet, edible acorns. However, even some of the "sweet" acorns must be processed to make them edible. To process acorns, boil whole, hulled acorns in several changes of water. Or grind the nut meat into a meal, and mix it with several changes of hot water to wash out any bitter tannins. Use the resulting slurry in breads and to thicken soups.

# OLIVE

*Olive trees produce grape-sized fruit with edible flesh and skin (don't eat the seeds). The fruits have a rich, oily taste, especially when they are ripe.*

BEST CLIMATE AND SITE: Zones 9–10. Give olives full sun and well-drained soil. They bear best where summers are long and hot, with low humidity.

HEIGHT AND SPREAD: Height to 30 feet (9 m); spread to 30 feet (9 m).

GROWING GUIDELINES: Plant container-grown stock anytime, or set out bareroot plants in spring or fall, while they are dormant. Space plants 20–80 feet (6–24 m) apart, with the greater distances reserved for drier climates where the trees will not be irrigated. Cross-pollination usually increases yield. Do not plant olives along patios, walkways, or driveways, where fallen fruit will be a nuisance. Where many fruits are close together on a stem, thin by just cutting back the stem; otherwise, remove excess fruits individually.

PRUNING: Keep pruning to a minimum on young trees. Prune mature trees as needed to keep them from growing too large.

PROPAGATION: Propagate olives by hardwood or softwood cuttings.

PEST AND DISEASE CONTROL: Where olive knot disease is a threat, prune in summer to prevent problems. Cut away galls produced by this disease.

HARVESTING AND STORAGE: Harvest the fruit when it is green (unripe) or black (ripe). Do not expose olives reserved for eating to cool temperatures. Olives are usually brined or canned for storage.

*Passiflora* spp.                    Passifloraceae

# PASSIONFRUIT

*Passionfruits are filled with many seeds, each of which is enclosed in a membrane that has a sweet-tart, musky flavor. You can eat the fleshy covering around the seeds, as well as the seeds.*

BEST CLIMATE AND SITE: Zone 10. Grow in full sun or, in very hot areas, partial shade. The vines need well-drained soil rich in humus and low in salts.

HEIGHT AND SPREAD: A sprawling vine, spreading 20 feet (6 m) or more in a season, unless pruned.

GROWING GUIDELINES: Set out container-grown plants anytime, spacing them 9–18 feet (2.7–5.4 m) apart. Some need cross-pollination; it's smart to plant at least two seedlings or cultivars to be on the safe side. The vines need some support, such as a fence or a three-wire trellis, on which to climb. Where they are not cold-hardy, grow passionfruit vines in containers with a well-drained mix. In a cool room, the plants can wait out winter without full sun; in spring, cut back branches and give them full sunlight.

PRUNING: Regular pruning is not a necessity, but it will help to keep the vine untangled. For the neatest growth, train one or two permanent "arms" along the top of the support. Each winter, cut all sideshoots to within a few inches of these arms.

PROPAGATION: Sow fresh seed or take cuttings.

PEST AND DISEASE CONTROL: Generally no significant problems.

HARVESTING AND STORAGE: Pick up ripe fruits from the ground. To store them for a few weeks, put the fruit in a plastic bag and keep at around 50°F (10°C).

*Asimina triloba*                    Annonaceae

# PAWPAW

*Ripe pawpaw fruit has greenish yellow skin speckled with brown. The white, custardy flesh tastes like banana, with hints of pineapple, mango, and vanilla. Eat the flesh only.*

BEST CLIMATE AND SITE: Zones 4–8. Pawpaws prefer full sunlight but aren't finicky about soil, as long as it is well drained.

HEIGHT AND SPREAD: Height 10–25 feet (3–7.5 m); spread 5–15 feet (1.5–4.5 m).

GROWING GUIDELINES: Plant young trees in spring, 15 feet (4.5 m) apart. Pawpaws need cross-pollination, so plant at least two seedlings, a seedling and a named cultivar, or two different cultivars. Pawpaws sometimes need hand-pollination for good fruit set.

PRUNING: Little or no pruning is necessary.

PROPAGATION: Seed germinates easily after you keep it cool and moist for 2–3 months. Growth is very slow for the first 3 years; it takes 6 years or more for fruits to appear. For quicker fruit of more reliable quality, graft selected cultivars onto seedling pawpaws just as the buds are swelling in spring.

PEST AND DISEASE CONTROL: Generally no significant problems.

HARVESTING AND STORAGE: Ripe pawpaws are slightly soft and have black specks on their skin. Either let the fruits ripen on the tree, or pick them slightly underripe for refrigerated storage followed by ripening at room temperature.

COMMENTS: Pawpaws are delicious raw or cooked into puddings and pies. Use only slight heat while cooking to preserve the delicate flavor.

Diospyros spp.                                    Ebenaceae

# PERSIMMON

*Persimmon flesh has a honey-like sweetness: smooth as silk in oriental persimmon* (D. kaki) *but drier and richer in the case of the American persimmon* (D. virginiana).

BEST CLIMATE AND SITE: Zones 7–10 for most oriental persimmons; Zones 4–9 for American persimmons. Give persimmons full sun and well-drained soil.

HEIGHT AND SPREAD: Height 25–60 feet (7.5–18 m); spread 20–35 feet (6–10.5 m).

GROWING GUIDELINES: Plant in spring, preserving as much of the taproot as possible. Space plants 20–35 feet (6–10.5 m) apart. Pollination needs vary with the cultivar. Hand-thin oriental persimmon fruits when they appear crowded.

PRUNING: Shorten long, willowy growth on young trees to stimulate branching. Prune mature trees only enough to stimulate some new growth for regular fruiting and to keep bearing wood near the main branches.

PROPAGATION: Graft selected cultivars onto *D. virginiana, D. kaki,* or *D. lotus* rootstocks in spring, just as buds are swelling.

PEST AND DISEASE CONTROL: Where persimmon girdler is a problem, regularly pick up and burn fallen twigs in fall.

HARVESTING AND STORAGE: Clip ripe persimmons from trees. Harvest non-astringent oriental types when they are fully colored and firm. Astringent oriental types and American persimmons are not edible until very soft. Fresh persimmons keep for about 2 months in the refrigerator. Besides eating persimmons fresh, you also can freeze or dry them.

---

*Pinus* spp.                                       Pinaceae

# PINE

*Many pine species yield edible nuts. The elongated, white nuts are usually about ¹/₂ inch (1 cm) long, with a dry texture and delicate flavor. They are held within the cones.*

BEST CLIMATE AND SITE: Zones 3–8, depending on the species. Plant pines in full sun and well-drained soil. They tolerate infertile conditions but grow better in rich soil.

HEIGHT AND SPREAD: Height 25–150 feet (7.5–45 m); spread 10–75 feet (3–22.5 m). Eventual size varies with species.

GROWING GUIDELINES: Plant container-grown stock any time the ground isn't frozen; or set out small bareroot plants between spring and fall where winters are mild or in spring where winters are severe. Space plants 10–75 feet (3–22.5 m) apart, depending on the eventual size of the plant.

PRUNING: Pines need little pruning. If desired, pinch shoot tips in spring for bushier growth.

PROPAGATION: Enhance germination by keeping sown seed warm for 2–3 months, then cool for a few months. Graft pines using a side graft indoors in winter or, where winters are mild, outdoors in late summer or early fall.

PEST AND DISEASE CONTROL: Generally no significant problems.

HARVESTING AND STORAGE: Gather cones of pines that drop ripe seed just before the cones open. To get seed out of other pines, open the fallen cones either by heating them in the oven or smashing them with a hammer. Store in cool, dry conditions.

*Ananas comosus*                    Bromeliaceae

# PINEAPPLE

*Individual pineapple flowers fuse together to form the warty, green-and-yellow covering of the fruit. Inside, the edible flesh is yellow or almost white, with a tangy and sweet flavor.*

BEST CLIMATE AND SITE: Zone 10. Pineapples need full sun and well-drained, acid (pH 4.5–6.5) soil. They are somewhat drought-tolerant.

HEIGHT AND SPREAD: Height 3–6 feet (90–180 cm); spread 3–6 feet (90–180 cm).

GROWING GUIDELINES: Plant anytime, setting plants 1 foot (30 cm) apart in double rows 2 feet (60 cm) apart. No pollination needed. In areas cooler than Zone 10, grow pineapple plants in containers, with a growing mix that contains extra sand or perlite for drainage. Avoid overwatering. When the plant is about 2 years old, you can induce flowering by covering the crown, along with a slice of apple, with a paper bag for a few days.

PRUNING: Prune 1–2 months after harvest, cutting off sideshoots arising near ground level as well as those originating at the base of or along the fruit stalk. If the remaining sideshoots along the stem are crowded, thin them out.

PROPAGATION: Pull off and plant sideshoots. Or twist the crown of leaves off the top of the fruit, and let it dry for a few days before planting.

PEST AND DISEASE CONTROL: If mealybugs are a problem, control them with oil sprays.

HARVESTING AND STORAGE: Cut or snap fruit from the stem when the color change, slight softening, and aroma indicate ripeness. Store fruit above 50°F (10°C).

*Pistacia vera*                    Anacardiaceae

# PISTACHIO

*Pistachio plants grow as shrubs or trees and produce edible nuts. At maturity, the nut shell is pale (perhaps blushed with pink) and the nut loosens within.*

BEST CLIMATE AND SITE: Zones 8–10. Pistachios prefer full sun and average, well-drained soil, although they can tolerate aikaline and saline conditions. They need some winter cold (about 1,000 total hours below 45°F [7.2°C]), as well as summers that are long and hot with low humidity.

HEIGHT AND SPREAD: Height 20–25 feet (6–7.5 m); spread 25–30 feet (7.5–9 m).

GROWING GUIDELINES: Set out container-grown plants anytime, spacing them at least 25 feet (7.5 m) apart. Trees are male (nonfruiting) or female (fruiting); you'll need both to get a harvest. One male can pollinate eight to twelve female trees.

PRUNING: Prune young plants to make them bushy, shortening stems by about one-quarter as soon as they are 3 feet (90 cm) long. Prune mature plants lightly, shortening some of the branches in winter.

PROPAGATION: Propagate by grafting onto a selected rootstock. The best rootstock depends on your climate and soil conditions. *P. terebinthus* is the most cold-resistant; *P. integerrima* is resistant to Verticillium fungi; and *P. terebinthus* and *P. atlantica* resist nematodes.

PEST AND DISEASE CONTROL: Avoid root diseases by selecting a good site and rootstock.

HARVESTING AND STORAGE: Shake the branches to dislodge ripe nuts. Rub off the hulls and dry the nuts at 150°F (65.5°C) for 8–10 hours.

# PLUMCOT

*In both appearance and flavor, plumcots resemble their parents: apricots and plums. The flesh and skin of the fruit is edible, but not the seed.*

BEST CLIMATE AND SITE: Zones 6–9. Plant in full sun and well-drained soil. Avoid sites subject to late frost early in the season.

HEIGHT AND SPREAD: Height 8–20 feet (2.4–6 m); spread 8–20 feet (2.4–6 m).

GROWING GUIDELINES: In colder regions, plant only in spring; elsewhere, plant in either spring or fall. Train young plants to an open-center form, with branches well spaced and open to light and air. Plumcots need cross-pollination, although the pollinator can vary, depending on the cultivar. (Ask the nursery or check catalog descriptions to get the right pollinator for your plant.) Dwarf cultivars can grow in containers.

PRUNING: Prune out a moderate amount of wood each year, just before blossoms open, to keep the center of the plant open to light and air.

PROPAGATION: Graft cultivars onto either seedling or cutting-grown apricot or plum rootstocks.

PEST AND DISEASE CONTROL: Brown rot may damage the fruit; see "Problem Prevention and Control" on page 99 for details on dealing with this disease. Also remove and destroy any shriveled fruit hanging on the tree at the end of the season.

HARVESTING AND STORAGE: Pick fruits when they are fully colored and slightly soft. Store for up to a couple of weeks at high humidity and temperatures just above freezing.

# POMEGRANATE

*Pomegranate fruit is usually red and the size of a softball. Inside, the seeds are embedded within supporting membranes. You can eat the fleshy seed covering with or without the seeds.*

BEST CLIMATE AND SITE: Pomegranates prefer a hot, dry climate; they will grow in Zone 8 but fruit best in Zones 9–10. Give the plants full sun. They tolerate a wide range of well-drained soil types.

HEIGHT AND SPREAD: Height 10–20 feet (3–6 m); spread 6–8 feet (1.8–2.4 m).

GROWING GUIDELINES: Set out container-grown plants anytime, or plant bareroot stock from spring to fall. Space plants 18 feet (5.4 m) apart. Cross-pollination sometimes increases yields, so grow at least two plants if you have room.

PRUNING: Train the plant as a multiple-stemmed bush or single-stemmed tree. Prune mature plants lightly each winter—just enough to stimulate some new growth and thin out excess fruit. Also remove suckers unless they are needed to replace a damaged trunk.

PROPAGATION: Seed germinates readily. Propagate cultivars by hardwood cuttings.

PEST AND DISEASE CONTROL: Generally no significant problems.

HARVESTING AND STORAGE: Clip fruits from the plant as soon as they are fully colored. Fruits refrigerated at high humidity store well for months.

COMMENTS: Dwarf cultivars are good in pots in colder climates. Besides eating pomegranates fresh, use the juice for jelly, in punch, and—mixed with equal parts of sugar—to make grenadine syrup.

*Opuntia* spp.                    Cactaceae

# PRICKLY PEAR

*Prickly pear fruits are about the size of an egg with red (or sometimes yellow or green) skin. The edible pulp is usually red, with many small, edible seeds and a mild flavor.*

BEST CLIMATE AND SITE: Zones 5–10, depending on the species. Prickly pear needs full sun and very well-drained soil.

HEIGHT AND SPREAD: Height 1–15 feet (30–450 cm); spread 3–15 feet (90–450 cm).

GROWING GUIDELINES: Plant any time the ground isn't frozen, spacing plants 3–15 feet (90–450 cm) apart (depending on their mature size).

PRUNING: No pruning is necessary.

PROPAGATION: Sow seed and keep it in the dark until sprouts appear. You can also use the fleshy pads to start new plants. Cut a pad from the mother plant, then let it dry for a few days before setting it upright with the bottom part in well-drained soil. Water sparingly until roots form and growth begins.

PEST AND DISEASE CONTROL: Generally no significant problems.

HARVESTING AND STORAGE: Wear thick leather gloves to harvest the flat, green pad, then remove the spines (and the tiny hair-like needles at the base of the spines) by rubbing them off with a rough cloth or peeling them off with a vegetable peeler. Also wear gloves when harvesting the fruits, which are ripe when fully colored. Rub off the needles and peel away the skin before eating.

COMMENTS: The fleshy green pads are also edible. Slice them and cook them as you would string beans. Eat the fruits raw.

*Cydonia oblonga*                    Rosaceae

# QUINCE

*Quinces produce yellow fruit that is covered with downy hairs. The skin and spicy, white or yellowish flesh are edible, but the flesh is too astringent to eat raw.*

BEST CLIMATE AND SITE: Zones 5–9. Plant in full sun with well-drained and moderately fertile soil.

HEIGHT AND SPREAD: Height 15–20 feet (4.5–6 m); spread 15–20 feet (4.5–6 m).

GROWING GUIDELINES: Plant container-grown stock any time the ground isn't frozen, or set out bareroot plants in spring or fall, while they are dormant. Space plants 15–20 feet (4.5–6 m) apart. Quinces are self-fertile, so you only need one plant.

PRUNING: Train as a small tree or large shrub. Each winter, prune off enough wood to keep the plant open to sunlight and air and to remove any diseased or misplaced branches.

PROPAGATION: Graft cultivars onto quince rootstocks, propagated by layering or from seed.

PEST AND DISEASE CONTROL: In summer, watch for blackened leaves and curled-over stems, which are symptoms of fire blight. For prevention and control suggestions, see "Fighting Fire Blight" on page 73.

HARVESTING AND STORAGE: Pick fruits when they are aromatic and fully colored. Handle ripe fruit gently. Store for 2–3 months at temperatures near freezing with high humidity.

COMMENTS: Quince fruit is edible when raw, but it adds pizzazz to an apple pie or a batch of apple sauce. Quince also makes a fine jelly.

| *Chaenomeles* spp. | Rosaceae | *Hovenia dulcis* | Rhamnaceae |

# QUINCE, FLOWERING

# RAISIN TREE

*Flowering quince fruits are yellowish green. Even when ripe, they are rock hard and astringent, but they make good jellies and jams after being cooked and sweetened.*

BEST CLIMATE AND SITE: Zones 5–8. Give flowering quince full sun and slightly acid soil. It tolerates dry soil.

HEIGHT AND SPREAD: Height 3–10 feet (90–300 cm); spread 3–10 feet (90–300 cm).

GROWING GUIDELINES: Plant container-grown shrubs any time the ground isn't frozen, or set out bareroot plants in spring or fall, while they are dormant. Space plants 3–10 feet (90–300 cm) apart. Flowering quince is self-fruitful, so you only need one plant to get fruit.

PRUNING: Prune in winter, periodically cutting away the oldest stems at ground level to make room for young stems. For drastic renovation, just lop the whole plant almost to the ground. Flowering quince can also withstand being sheared as a hedge, although you'll lose some of the flowers and fruit.

PROPAGATION: Seed germinates readily following 2–3 months of cool, moist conditions. Propagate cultivars by softwood cuttings, layering, or division.

PEST AND DISEASE CONTROL: Minimize leaf spot problems by planting in full sunlight in a breezy location and pruning for good air circulation.

HARVESTING AND STORAGE: Fruits ripen late in the season, changing color slightly. Harvest ripe fruits and store them at high humidity and temperatures just above freezing.

COMMENTS: Both the flesh and skin are edible.

*The tasty part of raisin tree is actually the gnarled, swollen fruit stalk, not the dark, dry fruits. The flavor, sweet with a hint of astringency, has been likened to pear or candied walnut.*

BEST CLIMATE AND SITE: Zones 5–8. Raisin tree is native to shady, moist glens but probably fruits best in full sunlight. It tolerates a wide range of soil conditions.

HEIGHT AND SPREAD: Height to 30 feet (9 m); spread to 20 feet (6 m).

GROWING GUIDELINES: Plant container-grown stock any time the ground isn't frozen, or set out bareroot plants in spring or fall, while they are dormant. Space plants at least 20 feet (6 m) apart. Plants are self-fruitful, so you only need one tree.

PRUNING: Train the young tree to a sturdy framework of branches. Beyond training, no pruning is needed other than what takes place during harvest.

PROPAGATION: If you first nick the hard seed coat with a file, seed should germinate within a week to a couple of months. With good moisture, fertility, and a long growing season, plants can produce their first fruits within 3 years; in less-than-ideal conditions, they may take 7–10 years.

PEST AND DISEASE CONTROL: Generally no significant problems.

HARVESTING AND STORAGE: Taste fruit stems to determine if they are sweet enough to harvest. To harvest from large trees, first lop off portions of branches so you can pick from ground level. Store the swollen fruit stems in a plastic bag in the refrigerator.

| *Rosa rugosa* | Rosaceae | *Elaeagnus angustifolia* | Elaeagnaceae |

# ROSE HIPS

# RUSSIAN OLIVE

*Rugosa rose flowers are followed by showy orange fruit (called hips) about 1 inch (2.5 cm) across. The ripe flesh is mushy, with a delicate sweetness. Both the skin and flesh are edible.*

*Russian olive fruit consists of a single, hard seed within a mealy, sweet pulp that becomes powdery as the fruit dries. Both the flesh and skin are edible.*

BEST CLIMATE AND SITE: Zones 2–7. Plant in full sun and any soil except one that is waterlogged.

HEIGHT AND SPREAD: Height 2–8 feet (60–240 cm); spread 3–6 feet (90–180 cm).

GROWING GUIDELINES: Plant container-grown roses any time the ground isn't frozen, or set out bareroot plants in spring or fall, while they are dormant. Space plants 3–6 feet (90–180 cm) apart. These roses creep by underground suckers, so plant them where they can spread freely, surround them with a barrier, or set them in a lawn where you can control the suckers with mowing.

PRUNING: In winter, prune back leggy or old and unproductive stems to the ground or to vigorous sideshoots. Also cut down the suckers if you do not want the bush to spread.

PROPAGATION: Divide the clump and replant pieces, or dig up suckers for replanting. You can also root hardwood or softwood cuttings or plant seed, which germinates after 3–4 months of being kept cool and moist.

PEST AND DISEASE CONTROL: Generally no significant problems.

HARVESTING AND STORAGE: Pick the hips as soon as they are fully colored. Store fresh fruit in a plastic bag in the refrigerator.

COMMENTS: Eat the hips fresh, dry them, or cook them into jam or fruit soup.

BEST CLIMATE AND SITE: Zones 3–7. Russian olive grows well in full sun and well-drained soil with a pH higher than 6.

HEIGHT AND SPREAD: Height to 20 feet (6 m); spread to 20 feet (6 m).

GROWING GUIDELINES: Plant container-grown trees any time the ground isn't frozen, or set out bareroot plants in spring or fall, while they are dormant. Space plants about 20 feet (6 m) apart (or closer if you want a hedge). You can get a harvest from just one tree, since the plants are self-fertile. Once established, Russian olive requires little or no care.

PRUNING: No regular pruning is necessary. This tree often develops a double trunk.

PROPAGATION: Russian olive is easy to propagate by seed sown outdoors, although it may take 2 years to sprout. To speed germination, nick the seed with a file and keep it cool and moist for 2–3 months before sowing.

PEST AND DISEASE CONTROL: Generally no significant problems.

HARVESTING AND STORAGE: There is no need to rush the harvest because ripe fruits hang on into winter unless eaten by wildlife. As the fruit hangs, it becomes drier inside, eventually turning almost powdery and sweet. Such fruits store well for months under refrigeration. Eat the fruit fresh, dried, stewed in milk, or boiled with sugar.

*Gaultheria shallon*                    Ericaceae    *Casimiroa edulis*                        Rutaceae

# SALAL

# SAPOTE, WHITE

*The sweet-tart fruits of salal resemble blueberries in both appearance and flavor. The whole fruit is edible. These bushy plants are related to blueberries and thrive in similar conditions.*

BEST CLIMATE AND SITE: Zones 6–9. Give salal full sun or partial shade and very acid (pH 4–5), well-drained soil.

HEIGHT AND SPREAD: Height 2–6 feet (60–180 cm); spread 2–6 feet (60–180 cm).

GROWING GUIDELINES: Before planting, work acid peat moss into the soil to maintain soil acidity, add organic matter, and improve drainage. Set out container-grown plants anytime, spacing them 3–6 feet (90–180 cm) apart. Salal enjoys cool soil, so spread organic mulch beneath plants.

PRUNING: Prune only as needed to shape the plant. Plants spread by underground runners, so cut back stems where they grow out of bounds.

PROPAGATION: Dig suckers and replant them, keeping them partially shaded and moist until new roots grow.

PEST AND DISEASE CONTROL: Generally no significant problems.

HARVESTING AND STORAGE: Harvest the berries when they are fully colored. For long-term storage, freeze or dry berries, or cook them into preserves.

COMMENTS: The handsome evergreen foliage is used by florists under the name "lemonleaf."

*The round or oval fruit of white sapote is covered with a thin, pale green or golden yellow skin. The buttery flesh is white or yellow and has a sweet and slightly resinous flavor.*

BEST CLIMATE AND SITE: Zone 10. White sapote needs full sun and well-drained soil.

HEIGHT AND SPREAD: Height 15–50 feet (4.5–15 m); spread 15–50 feet (4.5–15 m).

GROWING GUIDELINES: Set out container-grown plants anytime, spacing them 15–50 feet (4.5–15 m) apart. Many, but not all, cultivars are self-fruitful. Do not plant where the fallen fruit will be a nuisance. Trees require little care.

PRUNING: Shorten stems on young trees to promote branching. Prune mature trees to keep them from growing too large.

PROPAGATION: Propagate cultivars by grafting onto seedling rootstocks.

PEST AND DISEASE CONTROL: Generally no significant problems.

HARVESTING AND STORAGE: Watch for color change, which is subtle on green-skinned cultivars, as a signal to clip fruits from the tree with a piece of stem attached. Let harvested fruit ripen at room temperature.

COMMENTS: Only the flesh is edible, not the seeds or skin. (The seeds are poisonous.)

*Coccoloba uvifera*  Polygonaceae

# SEA GRAPE

*Sea grape fruits are reddish purple to almost white, with a mild sweet-tart flavor. They hang from the bushy plant in long clusters. Each berry has a single seed; the whole fruit is edible.*

BEST CLIMATE AND SITE: Zone 10. Give plants full sun or light shade and rich, sandy soil. Sea grape grows well along tropical ocean beaches.

HEIGHT AND SPREAD: Height 15–20 feet (4.5–6 m); spread 5–10 feet (1.5–3 m).

GROWING GUIDELINES: Set out container-grown plants anytime, spacing them 5–10 feet (1.5–3 m) apart. Grow sea grape as a multistemmed shrub, or train it to whatever form suits your fancy. A row of sea grape makes a decorative screen.

PRUNING: No regular pruning is needed.

PROPAGATION: Seed germinates easily. Cuttings of ripened wood root readily in sand. You also can propagate sea grape by layering.

PEST AND DISEASE CONTROL: Generally no significant problems.

HARVESTING AND STORAGE: Harvest the fruits when they are fully colored.

COMMENTS: Use the fruits to make jelly, syrup, sauces, and even wine—just like real grapes. The flowers are inconspicuous but fragrant.

*Amelanchier* spp.  Rosaceae

# SERVICEBERRY

*The fruit of serviceberry resembles a blueberry in size and often in color, although on some plants the fruit is red or even white. The edible berries are sweet, with a hint of almond flavor.*

BEST CLIMATE AND SITE: Zones 3–8. Serviceberries grow well in full sun or partial shade and tolerate a wide range of well-drained soil types.

HEIGHT AND SPREAD: Height 6–40 feet (1.8–12 m); spread 4–20 feet (1.2–6 m).

GROWING GUIDELINES: Plant container-grown shrubs or trees any time the ground isn't frozen, or set out bareroot plants in spring or fall, while they are dormant. Plants are generally self-fruitful, so you can get a harvest from just one plant. For a hedge, space bushy types 3 feet (90 cm) apart.

PRUNING: Tree species need little or no pruning. With bushy serviceberries, cut 4-year-old stems to ground level each winter to make way for new shoots.

PROPAGATION: Seed propagation is a good method because seedlings closely resemble their parents. Do not allow seeds to dry out, and keep them cool and moist for 3–4 months before bringing to warm growing temperatures. Bushy species also can be propagated by digging up suckers.

PEST AND DISEASE CONTROL: Birds enjoy the fruit, so cover plants with netting or share the bounty.

HARVESTING AND STORAGE: Harvest the fruit when the color darkens (except for some white-fruited cultivars) and when they taste sweet. The harvest period lasts for only a few days, so pick as much as you can and freeze or make jam with whatever you don't use fresh.

*Fragaria vesca*                    Rosaceae

# STRAWBERRY, ALPINE

*Alpine strawberries produce pointed fruits on low, clump-forming plants. The ripe fruits are usually red, although some white cultivars exist. The whole fruit is edible.*

BEST CLIMATE AND SITE: Zones 3–10. Plant in full sun or partial shade, with well-drained, humus-rich soil.

HEIGHT AND SPREAD: Height to 6 inches (15 cm); spread to 6–12 inches (15–30 cm).

GROWING GUIDELINES: Set out container-grown plants any time the ground isn't frozen, or plant bareroot stock in spring or fall, while the plants are dormant. Set plants 6–12 inches (15–30 cm) apart, planting so that the ground level is just below the lowest leaves on the crown. Alpine strawberries are self-fruitful, so you can get a harvest from just one plant. Plants fruit well even in small pots.

PRUNING: None.

PROPAGATION: To divide old plants, dig them up and cut off young crown pieces (with attached roots) from the outside of the clump. Throw away the old center part and replant the divisions immediately. To grow alpine strawberries from seed, scatter the fine seed on the surface of potting soil in a container. Transplant the seedlings when they are large enough to handle.

PEST AND DISEASE CONTROL: Keep birds at bay with netting, or grow white-fruited cultivars, which birds leave alone.

HARVESTING AND STORAGE: Harvest the fruits when they are soft and aromatic. Eat them fresh; they do not store well.

*Rubus phoenicolasius*             Rosaceae

# WINEBERRY

*Ripe wineberries are shiny and bright red and have a rich, tart flavor. The fruit within the leafy covering is wholly edible. Canes bear fruit in their second season.*

BEST CLIMATE AND SITE: Zones 5–8. Wineberries grow in full sun or partial shade; give them well-drained soil rich in humus.

HEIGHT AND SPREAD: Height to 6 feet (1.8 m); spread to 3 feet (90 cm) or more.

GROWING GUIDELINES: Plant container-grown stock any time the ground isn't frozen, or set out bareroot plants in spring or fall, while they are dormant. Space plants 3 feet (90 cm) apart, with a one- or two-wire trellis or a post next to each plant for support. To get plants off to a vigorous, healthy start, cut all canes to the ground right after planting.

PRUNING: Right after harvest or before growth begins the following season, cut down all the canes that produced fruit. Then thin out the remaining canes to leave the six sturdiest ones for each plant; tie those to the support wires.

PROPAGATION: Bend the tip of a cane to the ground and peg it down; it will form roots. Once the new shoot is well rooted, cut it from the mother plant and transplant it.

PEST AND DISEASE CONTROL: Generally no significant problems.

HARVESTING AND STORAGE: Pick the berries when they are bright red. Store at temperatures just above freezing and high humidity.

COMMENTS: The fruit is somewhat tart but still good fresh; use it as you would raspberries.

# USDA PLANT HARDINESS ZONE MAP

The map that follows shows the United States and Canada divided into 10 zones. Each zone is based on a 10°F (5.6°C) difference in average annual minimum temperature. Some areas are considered too high in elevation for plant cultivation and so are not assigned to any zone. There are also island zones that are warmer or cooler than surrounding areas because of differences in elevation; they have been given a zone different from the surrounding areas. Many large urban areas are in a warmer zone than the surrounding land.

Plants grow best within an optimum range of temperatures. The range may be wide for some species and narrow for others. Plants also differ in their ability to survive frost and in their sun or shade requirements.

The zone ratings indicate conditions where designated plants will grow well and not merely survive. Refer to the map to find out which zone you are in. In the plant-by-plant guide, you'll find recommendations for the plants that grow best in your zone.

Many plants may survive in zones warmer or colder than their recommended zone range. Remember that other factors, including wind, soil type, soil moisture and drainage capability, humidity, snow, and winter sunshine, may have a great effect on growth.

## Average annual minimum temperature (°F/°C)

| Zone | | Temperature | Zone | | Temperature |
|------|--|-------------|------|--|-------------|
| Zone 1 | | Below -50°F/-45°C | Zone 6 | | 0° to -10°F/-18° to -23°C |
| Zone 2 | | -40° to -50°F/-40° to -45°C | Zone 7 | | 10° to 0°F/-12° to -18°C |
| Zone 3 | | -30° to -40°F/-34° to -40°C | Zone 8 | | 20° to 10°F/-7° to -12°C |
| Zone 4 | | -20° to -30°F/-29° to -34°C | Zone 9 | | 30° to 20°F/-1° to -7°C |
| Zone 5 | | -10° to -20°F/-23° to -29°C | Zone 10 | | 40° to 30°F/4° to -1°C |

# INDEX

*The numbers in bold indicate main entries, and the numbers in italic indicate illustrations.*

Acid soil, 31
Acorns, 143, *143*
*Actinidia arguta,* 111
*Actinidia deliciosa,* 111
*Actinidia kolomikta,* 111
Akebia, **126**, *126*
Alkaline soils, 31
Almonds, **118**, *118*
  choosing, 34–35
  for flowers, 14
  grafting, 64
  for small gardens, 21
Alpine strawberry, **153**, *153*
*Amelanchier. See* Serviceberry
American beech, 128
American chestnuts, 119
American elder, 135
American filbert hedges, 19
American gooseberries, 106
American grapes, 107
American hazels, 120
American persimmon, 145
*Ananas comosus. See* Pineapple
Animal pests, 76–77
*Annona cherimola. See* Cherimoya
Anthracnose
  on blackberries, 102
  on grapes, 110
  on mango, 140
  on raspberries, 113
  spraying, 75
  on walnuts, 123
Aphids, *68,* 72
  on apricots, 86
  traps, 69
Apple, crab. *See* Crab apple
Apple maggots, *68,* 84
  traps, *68,* 69, 72
Apples, **80–85**, *80–85*
  choosing, 34–35
  for containers, 16, 22
  for flowers, 14
  harvesting, 36, 37, *37*
  for mixed-fruit gardens, 36
  for orchards, 24
  pests, *76,* 76
  planting, *45*
  pollination, 33
  ripeness, 63
  single-stemmed, *20*
  for small gardens, 21
  space required, 17
  storing, 63
  for trellised hedges, 19
Apple scab, 74
Apricots, **86**, *86*
  choosing, 34–35
  for containers, 22
  for hedges, 15, 19
  for mixed-fruit gardens, 36
  pollination, 33
  soil, *32*
Arbors, *15,* 16, 18
  for grapes, *109*
*Arctostaphylos uva-ursi. See* Bearberry
*Asimina triloba. See* Pawpaw
*Averrhoa carambola. See* Carambola
Avocado, **126**, *126*
Avocado root rot, 126

*Bacillus thuringiensis,* 73
Bacterial leaf spot, 99
Bagging to deter pests, 76
Bait, 72
Balloons to deter pests, 77, *77*

Banana, **127**, *127*
Barberry, **127**, *127*
Barberry, common, 127
Bareroot plants
  buying, 40
  height, 47
  planting, 45, *45, 46*
  storing, 44, *44*
  trimming, 47
Bark, shredded, *50,* 51–52
Bark nuggets, 51
Barrels, 22, *22*
Barrier plants, 15, *15*
Beaked hazels, 120
Bearberry, **128**, *128*
Beds, raised, 43, *43*
Beech, **128**, *128*
  for shade, 14
Beech bark canker disease, 128
Belgian fence, 61, *84*
Beneficial insects, 69
Beneficial microorganisms, 73
*Berberis. See* Barberry
*Berberis aristata,* 127
*Berberis asiatica,* 127
*Berberis vulgaris,* 127
Biological controls, 73
Birds
  and alpine strawberries, 153
  and blueberries, 105
  and cherries, *88,* 89
  and figs, 92
  and grapes, 110
  and raspberries, *113*
  and serviceberries, 152
  and strawberries, *76,* 115
Blackberries, **102**, *102*
  as barrier plants, 15
  for boundaries, *19*
  choosing, 34–35
  climbing, 18
  dividing, 65
  ease of maintenance, 16
  for hedges, 19
  layering, 65
  for mixed-fruit gardens, 36
  for orchards, 24
  for small gardens, 21
  trellising, 112
  trimming, 47
Black currants, 106
  harvesting, 37
Black knot
  on cherries, 89
  on plums, 99
Black rot, *75,* 110, *110*
Black sooty mold, 97
Black walnuts, 17, 123
Blight. *See* Fire blight
Bloodmeal, 55
Blueberries, **103–5**, *103–5*
  for borders, 15
  choosing, 34–35
  for containers, 22
  ease of maintenance, 16
  harvesting, 37
  for hedges, 15, 19
  layering, 65
  for mixed-fruit gardens, 36
  ripeness, 63
  for small gardens, 21
  soil, *31*
  space required, 17
  trimming, 47
Blueberry elder, 135
Blueberry maggots, 105
Bonemeal, *54,* 55
Bordeaux mix, 75
Borers
  in currants and gooseberries, 106
  in peaches and nectarines, 95
  in raspberries, 113

Botanical pesticides, 74
Botrytis blight (gray mold)
  on grapes, 108, 110, *110*
  spraying, 75, *75*
  on strawberries, 115
  thinning as prevention, *71*
Boysenberry, **129**, *129*
  layering, 65
Brambles. *See* Blackberries; Raspberries
Branches, removing, *59,* 60
Brown rot
  on cherries, 89, *89*
  on peaches and nectarines, 95
  spraying, 75
BT, 73
Buffalo berry, **129**, *129*
Bushes, **100–115**, *101–15*
Butternut, **130**, *130*
Butternut dieback disease, 130
Buying plants, 40–41
Bypass shears, 58, *58*

Cages, 77, *77, 88*
Calamondin, 90, **130**, *130*
Cane blight, 113
Cankers. *See also* Fire blight
  on beech, 128
  on peaches and nectarines, 95
Cape gooseberry, **131**, *131*
Carambola, **131**, *131*
Care, 49–65
  almonds, 118
  apples, 81
  apricots, 86
  blackberries, 102
  blueberries, 104
  cherries, 88
  chestnuts, 119
  citrus, 91
  currants and gooseberries, 106
  figs, 92
  grapes, 108
  hazelnuts, 120
  hickories, 121
  kiwi, 111
  peaches and nectarines, 94
  pears, 96
  pecans, 122
  plums, 98–99
  raspberries, 112–13
  strawberries, 114
  walnuts, 123
*Carissa grandiflora. See* Natal plum
Carob, **132**, *132*
*Carya laciniosa,* 121
*Carya ovata,* 121
*Casimiroa edulis. See* Sapote, white
*Castanea dentata,* 119
*Castanea mollissima,* 119
Cats, 111
Cedar-apple rust, 85
*Ceratonia siliqua. See* Carob
*Chaenomeles. See* Quince, flowering
Cherimoya, **132**, *132*
Cherries, **87–89**, *87–89*
  choosing, 34–35
  climate, *28*
  for containers, 22
  habits, 17
  for hedges, 19
  for mixed-fruit gardens, 36
  pollination, 33, *33*
  ripeness, 63
  for small gardens, *20,* 21
  space required, 17
  storing, 63
Cherry, Cornelian, **133**, *133*
Cherry, Nanking, **133**, *133*
  for hedges, 19
  for small gardens, *20,* 21

Cherry fruit flies, 89
  traps, 68, 69
Cherry leaf spot, 89, *89*
Chestnut blight disease, 119
Chestnuts, 117, **119**, *119*
  choosing, 34–35
  for mixed-fruit gardens, 36
  storing, 63
Chestnut weevil, 119
Chinese chestnuts, 119, *119*
  choosing, 34–35
Choosing plants, **33–35**
  almonds, 118
  apples, 80–81, 83
  apricots, 86
  blackberries, 102
  blueberries, 104
  cherries, 87
  chestnuts, 119
  citrus, 90
  currants and gooseberries, 106
  figs, 92
  grapes, 108
  hazelnuts, 120
  hickories, 121
  kiwi, 111
  peaches and nectarines, 93
  pears, 96
  pecans, 122
  raspberries, 112
  strawberries, 114
  walnuts, 123
*Citrofortunella mitis. See* Calamondin
Citrus, *17,* **90–91**, *90–91*
  choosing, 34–35
  for containers, 16, 22
  for flowers, 15
  for hedges, 19
  for mixed-fruit gardens, 36
  planting, *45*
  pollination, 33
  ripeness, 63
  for small gardens, 21
*Citrus aurantium,* 139
Clay pots, 22
Clay soil, 30
Clearing the site, 42
Climate, 28–29
  almonds, 118
  apples, 80, 83
  apricots, 86
  blackberries, 102
  blueberries, 103
  cherries, 87
  chestnuts, 119
  citrus, 90
  currants and gooseberries, 106
  figs, 92
  grapes, 107
  hazelnuts, 120
  hickories, 121
  kiwis, 111
  peaches and nectarines, 93
  pears, 96
  pecans, 122
  plums, 98
  raspberries, 112
  strawberries, 114
  walnuts, 123
*Coccoloba uvifera. See* Sea grape
Codling moth, *69,* 85
  on apples, 84–85
  traps, 69, 72
  on walnuts, 123
Cold storage, 63
Colored sticky traps, 68
Compost, 29, 52, *54,* 55
Compost tea, *46,* 55, *55*

Container grown plants, 40, 46, *46*
Containers, 16, *21,* **22–23,** *22–23*
  for citrus, 90, 91
  planting, *46*
Copper, 75
Cornelian cherry, **133,** *133*
*Cornus mas. See* Cherry, Cornelian
*Corylus americana,* 119
*Corylus avellana,* 119
*Corylus colurna,* 119
*Corylus cornuta,* 119
Cottonseed meal, 55
Cover crops, 43, 50
Crab apple, **134,** *134*
  soil, *30*
Cranberry, **134,** *134*
  for mixed-fruit gardens, 36
Cranberry, highbush, **135,** *135*
Cross-pollination, 33
Crown gall, 71, 113
Currants, *15,* 106
  ease of maintenance, 16
  harvesting, 37
  for hedges, 15, 19
  for small gardens, 21
  soil, *30*
Currant worm, 138
Cuttings, 65
*Cydonia oblonga. See* Quince

**D**eciding what to grow, **33–35**
Deer, 76, 77, *77,* 132
Digging, 42
*Diospyros. See* Persimmon
*Diospyros kaki,* 145
*Diospyros lotus,* 145
*Diospyros virginiana,* 145
Diseases, 66–75, *67–75*
  almonds, 118
  apples, 80, 84–85, *85*
  apricots, 86
  blackberries, 102
  blueberries, 105
  cherries, 89, *89*
  chestnuts, 119
  currants and gooseberries, 106
  grapes, 109–10, *110*
  hickories, 121
  minor problems, **70–73,** *70–73*
  peaches and nectarines, 95
  plums, 99
  preventing, **68–69**
  purchasing, 41
  raspberries, 112, 113
  serious problems, **74–75,** *74–75*
  strawberries, 114, 115
Dividing, 65
Downy midlew, 110, *110*
Drainage, 32
  plums, 98
Drip irrigation, *56,* 56–57
Dwarf fruit trees, *15*
  apples, 22, 81, *84*
  cherries, 88
  citrus, 16, 19, 90
  for containers, 16, 22, 23
  for espalier, 18, 61
  grafted, 20–21
  for hedges, 19
  peaches, *23*
  for trellised hedges, 19

**E**astern filbert blight, 120
*Elaeagnus angustifolia. See* Russian olive
Elderberry, **135,** *135*
  for hedges, 15, 19
  for mixed-fruit gardens, 36
  for small gardens, 21
Electric fences, 77

English walnuts, 123
Epsom salts/magnesium sulfate, 55
*Eriobotryta japonica. See* Loquat
Espalier, 16, 18, *19,* **61,** *61*
  peaches and nectarines, 93–95, *95*
  pears, 48
European beech, 128
European dessert gooseberries, 106
European elder, 135
European hazels (European filberts), 120
  choosing, 34–35
  for hedges, 15
European plums
  climate, *29,* 98
  soil, *31*
  for trellised hedges, 19
Eutypa dieback, 86

**F**abric mulches, 52
*Fagus. See* Beech
*Fagus grandifolia,* 128
*Fagus sylvatica,* 128
Fall planting, 44
Fan espalier, 61, *61*
Feijoa, **136,** *136*
Fences, 16, **18,** *18*
  against pests, 77, *77*
  of apples, 84, *84*
Fertilizing, **54–55**
  apples, 81
  cherries, 88
  containers, 23
  kiwi, 111
  peaches and nectarines, 94
Figs, *62,* **92,** *92*
  choosing, 34–35
  hedges, 19
  for small gardens, 21
Filazels, 120
*Filberts. See* Hazelnuts
Filbertworms, 120
Fire blight, 71, 73, *73*
  on apples, 80, 83, 85
  on loquats, 140
  on pears, 97
  on quinces, 148
  spraying, 75
Fish fertilizer, 55
Flea beetle traps, 68
Flower borders, 15
Flowering quince, **149,** *149*
Flowering trees, 14–15
*Fortunella. See* Kumquat
Foundation plantings, 15
Fox grapes, 107
*Fragaria vesca. See* Strawberry, alpine
Frost, *30,* 32
  apples, 80
  apricots, 86
  cherries, 87, 88
  citrus, 90, 91
  hazelnuts, 120
  pears, 96
  plums, 98
Fruit rot, 113, *113*
Fungal leaf spots, 115
Fungicides, 75
Fuzzy kiwi, *28,* 111

**G**aultheria shallon. See Salal
*Gaylussacia. See* Huckleberry
*Gaylussacia baccata,* 137
*Gaylussacia dumosa,* 137
*Gaylussacia frondosa,* 137
Genetic dwarf trees, 21
Gooseberries, **106,** *106*
  choosing, 34–35
  diseases, *71*

ease of maintenance, 16
  harvesting, *62*
  for hedges, 19
  for mixed-fruit gardens, 36
  ripeness, 63
  shade, *29*
  for small gardens, 21
Gooseberry, cape. *See* Cape gooseberry
Grafted plants
  dwarf trees, 20
  planting, 47
Grafting, 64, *64,* 65
Grape berry moth caterpillars, 110
Grapefruit, 90–91
  harvesting, 37, 63
Grapes, **107–10,** *107–10*
  for arbors and trellises, 16, *17*
  choosing, 34–35
  climbing, 18
  diseases, 75
  layering, 65
  for mixed-fruit gardens, 36
  pests, 76, *76*
  ripeness, 63
  for trellises, 18
  trimming, 47
Gray mold. *See* Botrytis blight
Green fruit worm traps, 69
Greenhouses, 91
Greensand, 55
Guarantees, 40
Guava, **136,** *136*
Gypsy moth traps, 69

**H**abits, 17
Handpicking pests, *70,* 70–71
Hand pruners, 58
Hardiness zone map, 28, **154–55**
Hardwood cuttings, 65
Hardy kiwi, 111
  for mixed-fruit gardens, 36
Harvest ladder, 89, *89*
Harvests, 36–37, **62,** *62*
  almonds, 118
  apples, 84
  apricots, 86
  blackberries, 102
  blueberries, 105
  cherries, 89
  chestnuts, 119
  citrus, 91
  currants and gooseberries, 106
  figs, 92
  grapes, 109
  hazelnuts, 120
  hickories, 121
  kiwi, 111
  peaches and nectarines, 95
  pears, 97, *97*
  pecans, 122
  plums, 99
  raspberries, 113
  strawberries, 115
  walnuts, 123
Hazelberts, 120
Hazelnuts (filberts), **120,** *120*
  choosing, 34–35
  for hedges, 15, 19
  layering, 65
  for mixed-fruit gardens, 36
Heading cuts, 60
Heartnut, **137,** *137*
Hedgegrow trellis, 112
Hedges, 15, *15,* **19**
  trellised, 19
Height, planting, 47
Hickories, 117, **121,** *121*
  habits, 17
  for shade, 14

Highbush blueberry, 103, 104, *104*
  for hedges, 15
Highbush cranberry, **135,** *135*
Hill system for strawberries, 115
Hilltops, 32
Horticultural oils, 74
Hoses, 56, *57*
*Hovenia dulcis. See* Raisin tree
Huckleberry, **137,** *137*

**I**nsecticidal soaps, 74
Insects
  beneficial, 69
  pests. *See* Pests
Irrigation. *See* Watering

**J**apanese plums, *29,* 98
Jostaberry, **138,** *138*
*Juglans ailantifolia* var. *cordiformis. See* Heartnut
*Juglans cinerea. See* Butternut
*Juglans nigra,* 123
*Juglans regia,* 123
Jujube, **138,** *138*

**K**elp extract, 55, *55*
Kiwis, 111, *111*
  for arbors and trellises, 16
  choosing, 34–35
  climate, *28*
  climbing, 18
  for mixed-fruit gardens, 36
  for trellises, 18
Kniffen training of grapes, 109, *109*
Kumquat, 90, **139,** *139*
  for small gardens, *20*

**L**ady beetles, 69
Landscape fabrics, 52
Landscaping, **13–25**
Layering, **65,** *65*
Leaf blights, spraying, 75
Leafhopper traps, 69, 72
Leaf spot, spraying, 75
Leaves, shredded, as mulch, 52
Lemons, 90–91
Limes, 90–91
Lime-sulfur, 75
Lingonberry, **139,** *139*
Liquid fertilizers, 54, 55
Loams, 31
Loppers, 58, *58*
Loquat, **140,** *140*
Lowbush blueberry, 103, *104*
  borders, 15
  layering, 65
Low-lying areas, 32

**M**agnesium, 55
Mail-order nurseries, 41
Maintenance, 16
*Malus. See* Crab apple
Manchurian bush apricot hedges, 15, 19
*Mangifera indica. See* Mango
Mango, **140,** *140*
Map, 25, *25*
Matted row system for strawberries, 115
Maypop, **141,** *141*
Mealybugs
  on calamondin, 130
  on kumquat, 139
Medlar, **141,** *141*
*Mespilus germanica. See* Medlar
Mildew
  on apples, 80, 85
  spraying, 75

Mites
  on apricots, 86
  on calamondin, 130
  on citrus, 91
  on kumquat, 139
  spraying, 75
Mixed-fruit garden, 36
Monitoring traps for pests, 68–69
*Morus. See* Mulberry
Mulberry, **142,** *142*
  habits, 17
Mulching, **50–53,** *50–53*
  almonds, 118
  apples, 81
  apricots, 86
  cherries, 88
  currants and gooseberries, 106
  grapes, 108
  hickories, 121
  kiwi, 111
  pears, 96
  pecans, 122
  pests, 68
  plums, 99
  strawberries, 114
Mummy berry disease, 105
*Musa. See* Banana
Muscadine grapes, 107
  layering, 65

Nanking cherry. *See* Cherry,
  Nanking
Natal plum, **142,** *142*
Navel orangeworm, 118
Nectarines, **93–95,** *93–95*
  harvesting, *37, 62*
  pollination, 33
  for small gardens, 21
Nepal barberry, 127
Netting animal pests, 76
Nitrogen, 54, 55
Northwest American hazels, 119
Nutrient deficiencies, *71*
Nuts, 63, *116–23,* **117–23**

Oak, **143,** *143*
  for shade, 14
Oils, horticultural, 74
*Olea europaea. See* Olive
Olive, **143,** *143*
Olive knot disease, 143
*Opuntia. See* Prickly pear
Orange rust, 113, *113*
Oranges, *17,* 90–91
  harvesting, 36
Orchards, **24–25,** *24–25*
Organic fertilizers, 54–55, *55*
Organic matter, 29
Oriental fruit moths
  on peaches and nectarines, 95
  traps, 69, 72
Oriental persimmon, 145
Overhead sprinklers, 56

Palmette verrier, 61, *61*
Paper bags against pests, 76
Parasitic wasps, 69
*Passiflora. See* Passionfruit
*Passiflora incarnata. See* Maypop
Passionfruit, **144,** *144*
Pawpaw, **144,** *144*
Peaches, **93–95,** *93–95*
  choosing, 34–35
  for containers, 16, 22, *23*
  for flowers, 15
  harvesting, *36, 37, 62*
  for mixed-fruit gardens, 36
  for orchards, 24
  pests, 76, *76*
  pollination, 33
  for small gardens, 21
  storing, 63
  for trellised hedges, 19

Peach leaf curl, spraying, 75
Peach tree borers, 95
  traps, 69
Pear psyllas, 97, *97*
  traps, 69
Pears, **96–97,** *96–97*
  choosing, 34–35
  for containers, 22
  for espalier, *48*
  for orchards, 24
  pollination, 33
  ripeness, 63
  for small gardens, 21
  space required, 17
  storing, 63
  for trellised hedges, 19
Pecans, 117, **122,** *122*
  choosing, 34–35
  grafting, 64
  for mixed-fruit gardens, 36
  pollination, 33
Pecan weevils, 122
Perlite, 65
Pergolas, 18
  for grapes, *109*
*Persea americana. See* Avocado
Persimmon, **145,** *145*
  harvesting, 63
  for mixed-fruit gardens, 36
Pesticides, 69, 74
Pests, **66–77,** *67–77*
  almonds, 118
  animals, 76–77
  apples, 84–85, *85*
  apricots, 86
  blueberries, 105
  cherries, 89
  chestnuts, 119
  citrus, 91
  currants and gooseberries, 106
  figs, 92
  grapes, 110
  hickories, 121
  kiwis, 111
  minor problems, **70–73,** *70–73*
  peaches and nectarines, 95
  pears, 97
  plums, 99
  preventing, **68–69,** *68–69*
  purchasing, 41
  raspberries, 113, *113*
  serious problems, **74–75,** *74–75*
Pheromone lures, 69, 72
Phosphorus, 54, *54*
pH value of soil, 31
  in containers, 23
*Physalis pruinosa. See* Cape
  gooseberry
Pine, **145,** *145*
  for shade, 14
Pineapple, **146,** *146*
Pine needles, 52
*Pinus. See* Pine
Pistachio, **146,** *146*
*Pistacia atlantica,* 146
*Pistacia integerrima,* 146
*Pistacia terebinthus,* 146
*Pistacia vera. See* Pistachio
Planning, 14, **27–37**
  orchard, 25
Plant hardiness zone map, 28,
  **154–55**
Planting, **44–47,** *44–47*
  almonds, 118
  apples, 81
  apricots, 86
  blackberries, 102
  blueberries, 104
  cherries, 88
  chestnuts, 119
  citrus, 91
  currants and gooseberries, 106
  delays, 44

figs, 92
grapes, 108
hazelnuts, 120
hickories, 121
kiwi, 111
peaches and nectarines, 94
pears, 96
pecans, 122
plums, 98–99
raspberries, 112–13
strawberries, 114
walnuts, 123
Plastic mulches, 52
Plastic pots, 22
Plumcot, **147,** *147*
Plum curculio
  on apples, 85
  on plums, 99
Plums, **98–99,** *98–99*
  choosing, 34–35
  climate, *29*
  for containers, 22
  for flowers, 15
  for mixed-fruit gardens, 36
  for orchards, 24
  pollination, 33
  for small gardens, 21, *21*
  soil, *31*
  storing, 63
  for trellised hedges, 19
Pole pruners, 58–59
Pollination, 17, 33
  almonds, 118, *118*
  apples, 80–81
  blackberries, 102
  blueberries, 104
  cherries, 88
  chestnuts, 119
  figs, 92
  hazelnuts, 120
  pears, 96
  pecans, 122
  plums, 98
Pomegranate, **147,** *147*
*Poncirus trifoliata,* 139
Potassium, 54
Pots. *See* Containers
Powdery mildew, *71*
  on currants and gooseberries,
    106
  on grapes, 110
  on raspberries, 113
  spraying, 75
Praying mantises, 69
Prickly pear, *124,* **148,** *148*
Propagation, **64–65,** *64–65*
  almonds, 118
  apples, 81
  blackberries, 102
  blueberries, 104
  currants and gooseberries, 106
  figs, 92
  grapes, 108
  kiwi, 111
  peaches and nectarines, 94
  pears, 96
  pecans, 122
  raspberries, 113
  strawberries, 114
Pruning, **58–61,** *58–61*
  almonds, 118
  apples, 82
  apricots, 86
  blackberries, 102
  blueberries, 105, *105*
  cherries, 89
  chestnuts, 119
  citrus, 91, *91*
  currants and gooseberries, 106
  for disease control, *71,* 71–72
  figs, 92
  grapes, *108,* 108–9
  hazelnuts, 120

hedges, 19
hickories, 121
kiwi, 111
peaches and nectarines, 94
pears, 96, 97
pecans, 122, *122*
plums, 99
raspberries, 113
strawberries, 115
walnuts, 123
Pruning saws, 58, *58, 59*
Pruning shears, 58, *58*
*Prunus. See* Plumcot
*Prunus americana,* 98
*Prunus tomentosa. See* Cherry,
  Nanking
*Psidium. See* Guava
*Psidium guajava,* 136
*Psidium littorale,* 136
*Punica granatum. See*
  Pomegranate

Quercus. *See* Oak
*Quercus alba,* 143
Quince, **148,** *148*
Quince, flowering, **149,** *149*

Rabbiteye blueberry, 103,
  104, *104*
  harvesting, 37
Rabbits, 76, 77, 132
Raised beds, 43, *43*
Raisin barberry, 127
Raisin tree, **149,** *149*
Raspberries, **112–13**
  as barrier plants, *15*
  for boundaries, 19
  choosing, 34–35
  dividing, 65
  ease of maintenance, 16
  harvesting, *36, 37, 62*
  for hedges, 19
  layering, 65
  for mixed-fruit gardens, 36
  for orchards, 24
  for small gardens, 21
  trimming, 47, *47*
Red-banded leaf roller traps,
  69
Red currants, 106
Red stele, 115
Repellents, pest, 77
*Ribes hirtellum,* 106
*Ribes nidigrolaria. See*
  Jostaberry
*Ribes nigrum,* 106
*Ribes uva-crispa,* 106
Ripeness, 63
Rock powders, 55
Rodents, 76, 77
Root rot, 115
Rootstocks
  for apples, 83
  for oranges, 90
  for plums, 98
*Rosa rugosa. See* Rose hips
Rose hips, **150,** *150*
*Rubus. See* Boysenberry
*Rubus phoenicolasius. See*
  Wineberry
Russian olive, **150,** *150*
Rust
  on apples, 80, 85
  pruning for, *71*
  spraying, 75

Salal, **151,** *151*
*Sambucus. See* Elderberry
*Sambucus caerulea,* 135
*Sambucus canadensis,* 135
*Sambucus ebulus,* 135
*Sambucus nigra,* 135
Sandy soil, 30

Sapote, white, **151,** *151*
Sawdust, 52
Saws, 58, *58, 59*
Scab
  on apples, 80, 85
  on pecans, 122
  spraying, 75
Scale insects
  on apricots, 86
  on calamondin, 130
  on carob, 132
  on citrus, 91
  on kumquat, 139
  on mulberry, 142
Screens, 18, *19*
Sea grape, **152,** *152*
Seed, 64
Serviceberry, **152,** *152*
Shade
  citrus requirements, 90
  surveying, 29–30
  trees for, 14
Shagbark hickories, 117, 121
Shellbark hickories, 117, 121
*Shepherdia argentea. See*
  Buffalo berry
Shredded bark, *50,* 51–52
Shrubs, 15
Site, **28–32**
  almonds, 118
  apples, 80
  apricots, 86
  blackberries, 102
  blueberries, 103
  cherries, 87
  chestnuts, 119
  choosing, 17, 37
  citrus, 90
  currants and gooseberries, 106
  figs, 92
  grapes, 107
  hazelnuts, 120
  hickories, 121
  kiwis, 111
  for orchards, 24
  peaches and nectarines, 93
  pears, 96
  pecans, 122
  plums, 98
  preparation, **42–43,** *42–43*
  raspberries, 112
  strawberries, 114
  walnuts, 123
Size of plants, 16
Sloping sites, 32, *32*
Slugs, *68*
  traps, 72, *72*
Small gardens, **20,** *20*

Snails, *68*
  traps, *72*
Soaker hoses, *56,* 57
Soaps, insecticidal, 74
Softwood cuttings, 65
Soil, 30–32
  almonds, 118
  apples, 80
  apricots, 86
  blueberries, 103, 104, *104*
  for containers, 23
  and cover crops, 43
  drainage, 32
  and mulch, 50
  organic matter, 29
  pears, 96
  pH, 31
  plums, 98
  preparation, 42
  raspberries, 112
  strawberries, 114
  texture, 30–31
Sour cherries, 87–89
  choosing, 34–35
  for flowers, 14
  pollination, 33
  for small gardens, 21
Sour orange, 139
Space required, 17
Spacings in orchards, 24
Spraying
  fungicides, 75
  pesticides, 74
Spring
  planting, 44
  pruning, 59
Sprinklers, 56
Spur-bearing apples, 81, *81*
Squirrels, 76, *77,* 120
Storing, **62–63,** *63*
Straw, 52, *52*
Strawberries, **114–15,** *114–15*
  for borders, 15
  choosing, 34–35
  for containers, 16, 22, *23*
  dividing, 65
  ease of maintenance, 16
  harvesting, 37, *37*
  layering, 65
  for mixed-fruit gardens, 36
  for orchards, 24
  pests, 76
  planting, 47
  pollination, 33
  site, *32*
  soil, *31*
  trimming, 47
Strawberry, alpine, **153,** *153*
Strawberry guava, 136, *136*
Sulfate, 55
Sulfur, *74,* 75, *75*

Summer
  cherries, 87
  pruning, 59–60
Sun, 29–30
  almonds, 118
  apples, 80
  apricots, 86
  blackberries, 102
  citrus, 90
  plums, 98
  strawberries, 114
Sweet cherries, 87–89
  choosing, 34–35
  for mixed-fruit gardens, 36
  pollination, 33, *33*
  for small gardens, *20*
  space required, 17

**T**arnished plant bugs
  on strawberries, 115
  traps, 68
"Tedder's trap," 85, 122
Thinning cuts, 60, *60*
Thinning pears, 97
Thrips, 91
Tools for pruning, 58
Trace minerals, 54
Training
  almonds, 118
  apples, 82
  apricots, 86
  blackberries, 102
  blueberries, 105
  cherries, 89
  chestnuts, 119
  citrus, 91
  currants and gooseberries, 106
  figs, 92
  grapes, 108–9
  hazelnuts, 120
  hickories, 121
  kiwi, 111
  peaches and nectarines, 94
  pears, 96
  pecans, 122
  plums, 99
  raspberries, 113
  strawberries, 115
  walnuts, 123
Transitional garden, 14
Traps, *68,* 68–69, *72, 72,* 76, 85
Trazels, 120
Trellised hedge, 19
Trellises, *15,* 16, 18, *25*
  for apples, 81
  for blackberries, *102,* 112
  for grapes, *109*
  for raspberries, 112
Trickle irrigation, 56, *56–57*
Trifoliate orange, 139
Trimming, 47
Tropical guava, 136

Trunk wraps, 72
T-trellis, 112
Turkish filberts, 120

**U**SDA Plant Hardiness Zone
  Map, 28, **154–55**

*Vaccinium angustifolium,* 103
*Vaccinium ashei,* 103
*Vaccinium corymbosum,* 103
*Vaccinium macrocarpon. See*
  Cranberry
*Vaccinium vitis-ideae. See*
  Lingonberry
Valleys, 32
Vermiculite, 65
Verticillium fungi, 146
Verticillium wilt, 115
*Viburnum trilobum. See* Cranberry, highbush
Vines, **100–115,** *101–15*
  planting, 47
  trellises for, 18
Vinifera grapes, 107
Virus-indexed plants, 41
*Vitis labrusca,* 107
*Vitis rotundifolia,* 107
*Vitis vinifera,* 107

**W**alls, 16, *16,* 18, *18*
Walnut bunch disease, 137
Walnuts, 117, **123,** *123*
  grafting, 64
  for mixed-fruit gardens, 36
  planting, *44*
  pollination, 33
  for shade, 14
Watering, 47, **56–57,** *56–57*
  almonds, 118
  pecans, 122
Water supply, 16
Weeding, 47
Weevils, 122
White currants, 106
Whiteflies
  on calamondin, 130
  on citrus, 91
  on kumquat, 139
  traps, 69, 72
White oak, 143
White pine blister rust, 106
White sapote. *See* Sapote, white
Wineberry, **153,** *153*
  for hedges, 19
Winter
  pruning, 59
  temperature, 28
Wire trellises, 18
Woolly beech scale insect, 128

*Ziziphus jujuba. See* Jujube